ROCKING AMERICA

ROCKING *America*

An Insider's Story

BY RICK SKLAR

How the All-Hit Radio
Stations Took Over

St. Martin's Press New York

 For information, address St. Martin's Press, 175 Fifth Avenue, New York, N.Y. 10010.

Library of Congress Cataloging in Publication Data

Sklar, Rick.
Rocking America.

Includes index.
1. Radio and music. 2. Radio broadcasting. 3. Radio broadcasters. 4. Rock music. I. Title.
ML68.S55 1984 384.54'43'0973 83-26850
ISBN 0-312-68797-4

First Edition

10 9 8 7 6 5 4 3 2 1

Rocking America could not have been completed without my wife, Sydelle, whose perceptive and sensitive suggestions, rewriting, and editing gave form and perspective to years of notes, clippings, and reminiscences. Her loving encouragement kept the idea of this book alive and gave me the inspiration and determination to write it.

CONTENTS

ACKNOWLEDGMENTS

I am grateful to the many people who relived with me those moments when they were a part of the story. They include Harold "Hap" Anderson, Murri Barber, Ralph Beaudin, Jeff Berman, Sid Bernstein, Julian Breen, Stan Z. Burns, Joe Cook, Bob Crewe, Dan Crewe, Ray Dariano, Paul Ehrlich, H.G. "Jock" Fearnhead, Calvin Fox, John A. Gambling, Rupert Hitzig, Dan Ingram, Steve Labunski, Jack Lacy, Chuck Leonard, Ron Lundy, Ed McMullen, Herb Mendelsohn, Ruth Meyer, Bruce Morrow, Brad Phillips, Steve Riddleberger, Herb Rosen, Ruben Rodriguez, Tom Rounds, Kal Rudman, State Senator Bob Ryan (Nev.), Allen Shaw, Walter A. Schwartz, Bob Smith, Bill Stewart, Mickey Wallach, Jim West, Bruce Wendell, George H. Williams, and Larry Wynn. I am also indebted to Tom O'Brien for additional information on the phantom General Charles de Gaulle. My thanks to Henry Kavett, who spurred this project along, and to Mortimer Matz for his keen memory and his photographs. And a special thanks to Jonathan and Mary Lyn Wolfert for the use of their collection of WABC memorabilia, and to my literary agent, Arthur Pine.

The songs that run across the bottom of each page represent a sampling of the top songs for each year, as determined by the ranking systems at the stations where I worked. For more complete lists, and a fuller explanation of the ranking system, please see the Appendix, "The Songs That Got the Ratings."

PREFACE

When radio people talk about ratings, the benchmark they use is WABC, New York. For an incredible decade roughly paralleling the Beatle era, WABC was the highest-rated radio station in America, achieving audience sizes never before reached and never since surpassed. Weekly audiences of five to six million listeners were common. WABC's programming worked as nothing that preceded it or followed has worked. For almost a dozen years, WABC's share, or percentage, of the total radio audience in the New York metropolitan area was measured in double digits. The Saturday night "Cousin Brucie Dance Party" alone reached 25 percent of all listeners regularly—an astonishing feat when you consider that today's top market radio programmers often scramble to bring their share of the audience from 5 percent up to 5.5, fighting for each tenth of a point.

I came to WABC before it climbed to market dominance and built it into the highest-rated radio station in the Western hemisphere, holding it in first place against all competitors during an unprecedented ten-year onslaught that saw company after company bring one program director after another into the largest and most lucrative radio battleground in the country to try to unseat us.

During those years, hundreds of other program directors and radio station managers made the pilgrimage to the Big Apple, where they listened to WABC, taped its music programming, and then returned to clone local versions of it back home. As a result, the sound spread. WABC became the most widely imitated radio station in the nation. Listeners from Atlanta to Los Angeles, Miami to Seattle, Dallas to Chicago, and everywhere in between began to hear a new kind of radio. In Tulsa and Detroit, in Boise and Kansas City, and in Denver and Boston, Americans found themselves listening to popular music in a different way.

The new sound featured far fewer songs. Instead of hundreds of "hits," a few dozen records were played over and over again until they became so popular that both young people *and* their parents

1953 • "Song from *Moulin Rouge*" / *Percy Faith* • "Vaya con

knew them. Everybody who grew up at that time, regardless of their color, their sex, or their wealth—whether they watched the sun come up over a wheatfield, a mountain, or a skyline of skyscrapers—can hum those songs to this day. They also remember the incessant jingles that tied the songs together while drumming the station's call letters into the listener's head. If a station was a close copy of WABC, its disc jockeys' voices were enhanced by an echo chamber, and at least one jock, usually the evening teen-appeal air personality, had a delivery that was so rapid-fire the words tumbled on top of one another. WABC became so well known that at night when the skywave spread its signal across half the nation, radio groupies would pull it in, listen, tape it, and send copies of the tapes to their friends. Eventually broadcasters from England, France, Spain, Mexico, Canada, Australia, South Africa, Brazil, and Japan visited WABC and began duplicating its sound overseas.

Those were fascinating times for American radio and fabulous years for the lucky few who shared the experience at WABC. The sense of exultation when those gigantic quarterly ratings came in was overwhelming. It was like crossing the finish line of a marathon. You go a mile into the air and don't come down for two weeks. It was an incredible high, and it came four times a year.

When I left WABC to move up in the American Broadcasting Company, it was the way I wanted to leave, with the station still on top. It stayed there for another year. The WABC story is a record that stands alone, unbroken, in a field where success is elusive to most and usually brief for the few who make it.

In the years that followed the WABC era, the idea of playing all mass-appeal hit songs on one radio station (the essence of true Top Forty) became anathema. With the growth of FM, the number of stations in America had doubled, and still more stations were being licensed. In each city, what had been a grove of transmitter towers became a small forest. As competition grew, individual stations' audiences became smaller, and many broadcasters began to offer more specialized programming and commercials aimed at specific groups of listeners who used the same products and services. Some stations appealed to upscale adults, while others went after blue-collar workers, Hispanics, urban teens, or other audiences.

But as the mid-eighties approached, most of the music-radio listeners had accumulated on the FM dial and were no longer dis-

Dios" / *Les Paul and Mary Ford* • "Doggie in the Window" / *Patti*

persed over AM and FM, again providing a mass-audience potential. A few believers tried once more playing the top hits over and over, and were gratified to find a new generation of listeners responding to Top Forty with the enthusiasm of a child discovering ice cream. The format is again producing dominant radio stations. The extent of its success will depend on programmers who understand it and advertisers who appreciate its multiple demographic potential. Understanding begins at the beginning. The WABC story began at a station called WINS.

I learned radio programming as an apprentice copywriter and producer at WINS, the first New York station to program rock & roll music, sharing my office there with big beat's first champion, disc jockey Alan Freed. I eventually took over the programming of the station, after some of the staff and talent fled under a cloud of indictments during the payola investigations that brought the fifties to an end.

In tracing my personal remembrances of the rise of rock & roll radio in New York—the people, the stories, the stations, and particularly the drama of WABC—I have tried to offer glimpses of the inner workings of the radio business from some unusually revealing perspectives. Viewed from within, the most powerful stations seem like fragile giants—intricately structured money machines capable of pumping millions of dollars in after-tax profit into a company year after year, but also capable, with the slightest mishandling, of suddenly drowning their owners in red ink. The radio networks themselves have also been economic roller coasters whose riders—executives and performers alike—have been alternately dizzied and exhilarated by the ups and downs, sometimes hanging on desperately through a succession of unexpected dips before soaring to success.

More often than not, the villains are people and politics. In a business where the product is as ethereal as the air itself and the audiences volatile and hard to measure, posturing can sometimes outmaneuver performance, and people who give the appearance of knowing what they're about can coast for a time before they crash on the realities of the ratings. The people in the business are the most fascinating part of the whole radio industry. The power of the media has always magnified the best and worst qualities of its practitioners.

The stakes are also defined by the dollars. Today over five billion dollars of advertisers' money flows into radio stations and networks each year. The New York billing alone represents almost a quarter-billion of that amount. This puts a value of $2½ million dollars on every share point that a program director can raise a station's ratings for a year. That is the kind of leverage programmers dream of. Under those circumstances, the power of a transmitter can inspire creativity bordering on genius.

In the days since I entered radio in the late fifties, the number of stations has almost tripled. There are now nearly ten thousand. The ranks of networks and syndicators supplying news and special programming have risen from a handful to many dozens. FM joined AM as a mass medium and has now surpassed it in numbers of listeners. Monaural broadcasting has been enhanced by stereo. Digital transmission has arrived: We can now break a radio signal into static-free bits of computer information and reassemble it as pure sound. The technology that will enable us to deliver more and higher-quality programming is exploding. Network lines have been replaced by satellites in the sky.

Looking back, these changes are less amazing to me than radio's first metamorphosis and how I became a part of it. Popular-music programming was the last goal I might have set for myself when, as a child in the late thirties and forties, I first became entranced with radio. Radio dominated entertainment then in much the way that television does today. All the big "names"—the comics, the actors, the commentators, and the singers—were on radio. Sitting in the studio audience of a big show was the dream of every kid who lived in or visited New York or Hollywood. We would wait for months for the tickets to arrive so we could attend a live network broadcast. We felt intense anticipation sitting in those studios, for we knew that the program was being broadcast to the entire country as it was created in front of us. There was no such thing as tape recording, and so no way to pre-time or edit material. The programs went live for all America to hear. The entire Fred Allen show, with orchestra, singers, skits, and commercials, was performed twice, with two different studio audiences, so it could reach both coasts at prime times.

In those moments of immediacy, a world was created in each listener's mind that was far different from the one unfolding in front of us in the studio. There, sound effects men, actors holding scripts as they stood in front of microphones, a live orchestra, announcers and other performers, working usually in front of a cyclorama that displayed the name and likeness of the sponsor's product, created the sounds that painted the picture in the listener's "theater of the mind." In a soundproof glass booth off to one side, a director controlled the show with hand signals. Different gestures told the performers when to speed up or slow down so the show would end "on the nose." The engineers sat next to the director. I could imagine myself in one of those booths someday, directing a show. In a second glass booth on the other side of the stage sat the sponsor and the sponsor's guests. Clocks dominated the walls. The moment that the STAND BY sign lit up was surpassed in excitement only by the actual second that the ON THE AIR light flashed on.

Sitting in those studios, we radio freaks of that era knew that it was more than glamour that made radio so wonderful and special. We were keenly aware that radio reaches people through only one of their senses—hearing. It was this singularity that gave radio the unique ability to entertain, inform, sell, and motivate. Sound, imaginatively used, stimulated the listener to create in his or her mind a picture of the ideal face, the ideal scene, and the ideal product. Each listener saw the scene and the people and the show exactly as the listener wanted to see it. Every listener "saw" a different show, but each show was perfect.

Radio was what television is today, and more. It delivered the Wild West at home courtesy of sound effects, actors' voices, and music, tied together by the words of a writer trained to "visualize sound," and spoken by a narrator. That "West" was exactly as we imagined it should look. We saw our idealized Lone Ranger's horse, Silver, and the outlaws' steeds in flight. The canyons stretched before us. The action took place against perfect sunsets more vivid than any TV screen can deliver. The Green Hornet's car, Black Beauty (the names always had colors in them), brought to life by the resonance of announcer Hal Neal's descriptive phrases from WXYZ Detroit, was as real to me as the squad cars I watched in later years on "The Streets of San Francisco" and "Hill Street Blues" televison series.

For many of us, radio was the only place to make a career. We were hooked on sound, and there was no turning back—despite the urging of professors who warned us that the future was television.

As the fifties began, however, the great radio networks of America *were* collapsing under the impact of the new visual medium. Radio stations were starting to be viewed as the albatrosses of broadcasting. In the year I graduated from college, 1954, broadcasting companies were unloading stations and selling out, desperate to beat a retreat from the dying medium. Radio entrepreneurs, scrambling and groping through the wreckage of big-time radio, fought with ingenuity and intuition to remain solvent. They improvised instinctively in order to survive. Imagine the dilemma of the first person who proposed playing records instead of broadcasting live bands over the radio. Records? Who will listen to records played over the radio? People play records on phonographs. They'll think we're putting one over on them if we play records on the radio. But as early as 1948 the first bands were being laid off. And when it became obvious that records would have to be played, broadcasters everywhere followed the example of WNEW, New York, where a disc jockey, Martin Block, had been holding forth with a stack of platters instead of a baton since 1935 on a show called "The Make-Believe Ballroom."

In every respect, radio would have to be reborn. Radio people had to rethink their business and their careers right down to the most basic concepts. The industry would be kept alive by determined programmers, talented disc jockeys, and the music itself.

Clooney • "Sh-Boom" / *The Crew-Cuts* • "Oh, My Papa" / *Eddie*

ROCKING AMERICA

CHAPTER 1

The Magic of the Music

In 1968, the pop music business was riding the crest of the greatest creative wave in its history. The Beatles had their all-time top seller, ''Hey Jude''; Simon and Garfunkel's ''Mrs. Robinson'' was a huge hit. It was a time when America had a national music—songs shared and enjoyed by young and old. With hits like Paul Mauriat's ''Love Is Blue,'' Herb Alpert's ''This Guy's in Love with You,'' Otis Redding's ''(Sittin' on) The Dock of the Bay,'' and Jeannie C. Riley's ''Harper Valley P.T.A.,'' 1968 was not a year in which I, as program director of America's most successful radio station, had to take chances on untried artists or innovative arrangements to get ratings.

Our first April WABC weekly music meeting began like many others. Disc jockeys Ron Lundy and Dan Ingram, a production assistant, our music librarian, my secretary, and I gathered in my office on the eighth floor of the ABC corporate headquarters building in New York City. Offices at ABC were apportioned by size and furnishings—according to one's rank in the hierarchy—and designated A, B, C, D, and D-without-windows. I had a white B, a square office fifteen feet on a side, with three picture windows overlooking the Avenue of the Americas. The only larger office on the floor belonged to the station's general manager. B-office occupants were entitled to one company-issued plant, poster-level artwork on the walls, and their choice of either a couch facing the desk or a credenza behind the desk. (I had managed to get both by ordering a couch and then requesting special and costly construction for playback and taping equipment cabinets. Predictably, the real-estate department turned that down, substituting the cred-

Fisher • ''Three Coins in the Fountain'' / *The Four Aces* • "Secret

enza instead.) One wall was covered with awards and photos of rock stars.

As the first order of business, we scanned the music trade magazines, looking at their singles charts for records that we could add to the playlist, which was changed every Tuesday. We looked for growth patterns that matched certain standards of consistency I had set up. We read reviews of new material by major artists and selected records to audition.

I put the first record on the turntable behind my desk and lowered the tone arm. The meeting was underway. It moved along with a discipline that I had cultivated over the years. Song after song was voted down or put on hold for another week. Finally two records by top artists were picked. Then a few older records were moved to the "new gold" category, where for another six weeks they would continue to be played, but less often; the teens were tiring of them, but they still did a great job attracting adult listeners for our advertisers. As long as we didn't play the "new golds" too often, most teens would tolerate the sound. It was a good tradeoff.

As the last item on the agenda, the unique or so-called novelty records were played. These were usually good for a few laughs and almost never made the playlists. By now, my office was filled with cigarette smoke, and I opened the door. I also lowered the volume so we wouldn't disturb the rest of the WABC staff working in offices and at desks along the hall outside.

One entry was from ABC Dunhill Records, a division of our own company. It was a test record—what record companies call an acetate dub. ABC had pressed only a handful of these because they weren't certain whether to release the song as a single or let it just remain as a part of the album. They were hoping radio stations would show some interest in the song.

Relations between ABC Radio and ABC Records were not always the most cordial in the business. The executives at ABC Records thought that the WABC Radio management went out of its way *not* to play new ABC product in order not to appear to favor our own company's label. Once I was even blamed by the record company for being a major cause of its low profits. They claimed that if Rick Sklar didn't go on a record, then other stations wouldn't add it either, and they couldn't start it climbing up the charts. In reality, our music meetings were "label blind." We

Love" / *Doris Day* • "Young at Heart" / *Frank Sinatra* • "This Ole

never noted the name of the record company until after the record was selected. It was the sound—and our research—that influenced our decisions.

So it was that on this particular day we had an ABC dub under consideration. I glanced at the handwritten label. The reason why ABC had been afraid to start pressing the discs in quantity was obvious. At a time when most records ran two and a half or three minutes at the most, this daring effort (produced by songwriter Jimmy Webb, and sung not by a career vocalist but by British actor Richard Harris) ran seven minutes and twenty seconds. True, there had been a precedent the previous summer when Bobbie Gentry's "Ode to Billy Joe" nudged the four-minute mark, and "Mrs. Robinson" had slipped over the three-minute taboo earlier in the year. But short records helped radio stations create the illusion that they were playing more music. You could play three records in the time it took to broadcast this one.

I put "MacArthur Park" on the turntable, cued it up, and hit the start button. We sat back and listened. This record was not only long, it was different. The song, about a romance set in a park in Los Angeles went in part:

MacArthur Park is melting in the dark,
All the sweet, green icing flowing down.
Someone left the cake out in the rain,
I don't think that I can make it
'Cause it took so long to bake it,
and I'll never have the recipe again.

The lyrics were full of poetic imagery. The composition was broken into contrasting movements like a miniature symphony. A second melody line was introduced for a lengthy instrumental portion of the record. As it played, a silence fell over the meeting. Because the door was open, secretaries passing by stopped, slipped into the room, and sat down on the floor, entranced. By the end of the song, there were half a dozen extra people at the music meeting. No one wanted to leave. They wanted to hear it again. I played the record once more. Some of the young women began to sing along with it. The music had reached some special place in all

House" / *Rosemary Clooney* • "Cross Over the Bridge" / *Patti*

of them. I decided to add "MacArthur Park" to the WABC playlist.

After the meeting ended, my telephone lines were jammed with the usual deluge of calls from record companies and music publishers eager for the results of our deliberations. When I told ABC's local promotion director Mickey Wallach the news, he panicked.

"Don't put it on," he pleaded. "We have no pressings. There are no copies in the stores. Give us two weeks."

As part of WABC's music policy we polled record stores each week to find out if the public liked the songs we were playing well enough to buy them. If the songs sold well, we would keep playing them. Mickey Wallach feared that I would play "MacArthur Park," get no sales reports, and yank the record.

"It's absolutely a great song," I told Wallach. "We want to be first. This one will appeal to everybody."

He asked that we at least give them a week to get the record out to the stores on a rush basis, and I agreed.

The following Tuesday, "MacArthur Park" was played on WABC. Within five weeks, by mid-May, it had sold over a half-million copies and was headed for the top of the charts. Virtually every Top Forty station in the country had added it.

After that music meeting ended and everyone had left my office, I sat for a long time, thinking about the music selection process and all the other systems and concepts that I had so carefully devised to create this largest of all radio audiences—these six million consumers whose musical tastes we reflected and in turn shaped and multiplied into both a national and world sound. The process stood out all the more vividly on those rare occasions, like today, when the artistic appeal of a new recording was so strong that it rose above the numerical qualifications and the sales graphs to make it on creativity alone.

I remembered the first time I'd taken a chance on a record. It had happened in 1957, over ten years earlier, when I was working at WINS with Bruce Morrow. The studio phone rang in the middle of the program. There were some visitors from Canada in the lobby, they had a record, and they wanted to come up to the studio.

A well-spoken man introduced his nephew, a young man who had written and recorded a song. The kid was very shy, so Uncle

John sent him for coffee and told us how great the song was and how much they wanted it to be played on WINS first. Bruce and I listened to the record. It was terrific. By the time the kid returned with our coffee, the song was on the WINS turntable and was being heard by hundreds of thousands of people.

Listeners began phoning the station, asking for replays. The song caught on quickly and became number one on our playlist. The audience response was the same across the country as stations picked up on the record and played it. It became one of the year's biggest hits. The song was ''Diana'' and the singer was Paul Anka.

Playing the right songs was a key ingredient in attracting listeners to radio stations, and the radio stations in turn were the launching pads for the stars and the million-selling gold records.

I thought of all the talented performers I had met over the years who had shared their yearnings, fears, aspirations, and success stories with me as their careers blossomed. I remembered an afternoon in the MGM production building in Culver City, California, sharing a chef's salad with Barbra Streisand as we reminisced about our childhoods in Brooklyn. That day she personally edited scenes from one of her forthcoming movies, taking herself in and out of scenes again and again until the juxtaposition seemed right. (Fame for Barbra meant never having to make the beds in the house again.) I remembered dancing with Carly Simon at a party celebrating a new Bee Gees' album while we worked out a plan for her to guest lecture my St. John's University classes as a way of overcoming her shyness and stage fright. Carly's hour-long talk on how to negotiate a record contract, plus questions and answers on life in a two-rock-star household, made for the most fascinating class of the semester. I thought of the unusual opportunities I had enjoyed producing recording sessions with Barry Manilow, Neil Sedaka, and other stars whose top hits I had rewritten every year for the United Way. Having them sing my lyrics had been absolutely thrilling. I recalled dinners where I traded wisecracks with Bette Midler; evenings with Burt Bacharach and Frankie Valli; sitting on my terrace overlooking the Hudson River with John Lennon and Yoko Ono, singing American folksongs with John as I played the guitar; my children cooking a spaghetti send-off dinner at home for Tony Orlando when he got his TV series; inspiring the students in my college courses by inviting guest lecturers including

Janis Ian, Larry Gatlin, Marvin Hamlisch, and the deeply missed Harry Chapin who gave firsthand accounts of careers in the world of music.

Yes, the business was a kick! How lucky I was to have had the opportunity to take WABC and make it into the giant that it was. I also thought about how much of WABC had evolved out of those earlier experiences I had at WINS. Basic training for me really began at WINS, where I worked with some of the most unusual and colorful people ever to walk into a radio station.

CHAPTER 2

From the Boonies to the Big Time

Sound has always been an important part of my life. During my early childhood years in Brooklyn's Brighton Beach, I learned how to tune in a radio before I learned how to read. Radio was the medium that brought the world to children who grew up in the thirties. A seemingly limitless universe poured out of that loudspeaker grille on the big cabinet standing in the corner of our living room. By the age of four, I could turn the knob that controlled its amazing dial, and it took me swinging on vines through jungles for fifteen minutes and then charging across the plains with the cavalry for the next quarter hour. Every night at six, Uncle Don played the piano, told stories, and even read my name when I became an "earnest saver" at his sponsor's bank. By the time I tried to read, I found that I was *hearing* each word on the page. To this day as I read books, magazines, and even memos, I hear the words and sentences aloud.

Even after I began reading, my afternoons and evenings were planned around the program schedules of the Red Network's WEAF and the Blue Network's WJZ. To pull in broadcasts, we helped our dad string aerial wires thirty feet across the flat rooftops of the six-story apartment buildings where we lived. Antenna poles made a forest of the skyline, and thousands of lead wires snaked down the sides of the buildings to bring the magic world of sound effects, music, and actors into our homes. They brought us justice as meted out by "Mr. District Attorney," "Dick Tracy," and "Gangbusters." Leading actors of the stage and screen re-created

Williams • "Ballad of Davy Crockett" / *Bill Hayes* • "Ain't That a

the greatest movies at night on "The Lux Radio Theatre." Radio also brought us the voice of God in the form of President Franklin D. Roosevelt and his fireside chats. He had been president as far back as we could remember, all our lives. When his resonant tones rang out, we were reassured that times would get better.

Another voice spoke to us Sunday nights at nine. "Good evening, Mr. and Mrs. North and South America and all the ships at sea. Let's go to press. Flash." Walter Winchell would deliver the news, the news behind the news, and startling news we didn't know was happening in a staccato and authoritative style that gave each phrase an aura of authenticity. On Sunday nights, all nonradio activities stopped for me at seven o'clock when my hero, Jack Benny, went on the radio. Back then, I was sure that if I didn't grow up to be the next Jack Benny, I would at least direct the show and help create that incredible world in which Benny's automobile wheezed and sputtered and died every few feet. The voice at Benny's train station would someday announce, "Train leaving on track nine for Anaheim, Azusa, and Cucamonga," through my filter microphones.

In high school, I was president of the Erasmus Hall Radio Workshop, creating dramas and comedy shows in our campus studio. We student radio actors and directors regarded our medium as a popular art form. It never crossed our minds that radio would someday undergo a total change. The thought that it would eventually become a medium whose primary programming consisted of phonograph records was beyond our comprehension. Perhaps it occurred to the smartest kid in the school, Clive Davis, later the president of Arista, the student honor society whose office was down the hall. Could Davis have envisioned himself as the head of a record label even then? He was probably too busy finding out which college had the best pre-law program.

I went to college at New York University and spent afternoons hanging out downtown at the studios of the city-owned WNYC. Its civil servant copywriters were only too happy to let aspiring students do volunteer work behind the scenes. There were always a few of us banging away on the typewriters. For young writers, it was a thrilling experience to hear your words broadcast over the radio and know they were also being heard by thousands of other people and possibly affecting the lives of some of those listeners. One writer, Ed Albee, told me he could trace his family back to the founders of the great vaudeville circuits, and was really interested in writing for the theater. I next heard about him when he was on Broadway with *Who's Afraid of Virginia Woolf*.

Tradition says you should start your radio career at a small station, where you trade your lack of experience for their lack of money to pay you a decent salary. While you're there, you try every radio skill until you find out what it is you do best. Then you leave and do your best elsewhere.

After college I followed the pattern, but I was to go from the boondocks to the big time in one jump. My first year in radio was at WPAC, Patchogue, New York, on Long Island's South Shore. I turned on the transmitter, wrote copy, announced news, spun records, and ran to the bank on Fridays to cash my paycheck before the station ran out of funds, which usually happened by eleven A.M.

To supplement my $55-a-week salary, I wrote at night for a book syndication factory cranking out *Tom Swift and His Giant Robot* under the pseudonym Victor Appleton II, filling the boys' adventure novel with minor characters based on people who worked at the radio station. An attempt to save on rent by living at Mrs. Barton's boarding house for announcers backfired because the landlady, a gray-haired widow in her seventies whose mild manner belied her secret bottle of gin and her abilities as a card shark, ran Wednesday night poker parties where she and her next door neighbor, Mrs. Kelly, regularly cleaned out the WPAC announcers.

While at the station, I got married and then I needed to earn even more money. I couldn't wait to get out of WPAC. One day I noticed a blind want ad in *The New York Times* that simply read "copy/contact—Radio." I answered it and was surprised to get a call from station WINS in New York City.

WINS was located in one of the many older brick office buildings that make the side streets of so much of Manhattan appear canyon-walled. Its only distinguishing feature was a block-through lobby that ran from Forty-third to Forty-fourth Street. Its only claim to fame: the upper floors were home to *The New Yorker* magazine's editorial offices.

I never saw the WINS studios that day. I was directed to a large, noisy second-floor office filled with cubicles and occupied by tired looking salesmen and old furniture. There I was greeted by a short, balding man whose thick, horn-rimmed glasses rested on an eagle's beak of a nose. He wore a suit with wide padded shoulders, and as soon as he spoke, it struck me that, with his gruff, heavy New York accent and his sharp appearance, he would have fit right into the cast of Damon Runyon's musical, *Guys and Dolls,* then in its fifth year at the Forty-sixth Street Theater two blocks away.

He told me he was Perry Plager, night sales manager, and asked if I could write commercials. I handed him samples of copy I had written in Patchogue. He looked at them for about twenty seconds, smiled, put a fatherly arm around my shoulders, and asked me to fill out a withholding-tax form. I could start work the next day.

I couldn't believe that I had gotten a job at a New York radio station that easily. (What I didn't know was that Plager—called Perry the Pirate by his sales force—while technically an employee, was, for all intents and purposes, a time broker who ran his own operation, split the take on the all-night show with the station's owner, and had very little else to do with WINS.)

Another fact that I had no way of knowing was that I had arrived at WINS at a propitious moment. In 1954, the management of the Crosley Broadcasting Company had become convinced that radio was dead. They sold their 50,000-watt New York property for $450,000 to a Seattle entrepreneur named J. Elroy McCaw, who had barely been able to scrape together the down payment.

McCaw would sell WINS seven years later for ten million dollars, at that time the largest sum of money that had ever been paid for a radio station, but in 1955 WINS was losing money. McCaw had no cash flow to keep his newly acquired station operating. He had bought a block-long layout of studios and offices in one of New York's highest rent areas, where his neighbors included the Harvard Club, the Princeton Club, the New York Yacht Club, and the New York Bar Association, all off Fifth Avenue.

McCaw desperately began slashing his costs. He locked out the studio orchestra. He ordered the light bulbs changed to sixty watts. To save paper costs, he switched the United Press Teletype machines from costly multicopy carbon paper rolls to the free single-roll paper that came with the service, and he issued a directive to single-space the program logs. Elroy McCaw was the perfect person to have bought WINS under such circumstances. If, through natural selection, a new humanoid species were to evolve that could instinctively survive without any money of its own, Elroy McCaw would have been the progenitor.

Elroy believed that there was virtually no reason to have to pay for any goods or services in this world. If one applied just a little effort, some other person, some corporate entity, or some branch of government would give you whatever you wanted. I have seen Elroy talk people into driving him to the airport in their cars, then give them a circuitous route to avoid the tollbooths. He rarely used his own phone and would resurrect an old pair of crutches to make his entry into union negotiations. Three different people told me virtually identical stories concerning dinner experiences with Elroy McCaw. Two were wealthy women who had accepted invitations from him to dine at exclusive New York restaurants. When the check was presented, McCaw had been unable to find his wallet or credit cards, and the women ended up paying the bills. After similar situations occurred involving radio station owners, several of them conspired and invited Elroy to dinner. Following a sumptuous, extravagant meal, they excused themselves one by one to visit the men's room. None of them returned to the table, leaving McCaw to pay the entire check.

McCaw's economies eventually created an evening of havoc over the air. When he bought WINS, he had to take over a commitment to broadcast play-by-play professional basketball and hockey games. Many of the games were played out of town, but the cost of high-quality long-distance transmission lines, which the telephone company rented to the radio station and over which the programs were delivered to New York, were beyond his budget. Elroy called his chief engineer, Paul von Kunitz.

To Elroy McCaw, who had been an OSS agent during World War II, the solution was child's play. He knew that the reason for the poor sound quality was the cheap carbon microphone in the telephone handset. By replacing the handset on a regular telephone with a quality microphone, earphones, and an amplifier, he could turn that phone into a miniature radio studio console and feed high-fidelity play-by-play sportscasts through the regular telephone lines. McCaw could transmit the out-of-town basketball and hockey games for the price of an ordinary long-distance phone call. McCaw had von Kunitz build several of the modified telephone units.

On the other end of the line, McCaw ordered regular telephone jacks instead of broadcast lines installed in broadcast booths at sporting arenas across the country. Sportscasters Jim Gordon or Les Keiter would fly into a city carrying the von Kunitz device in a camera bag slung over one shoulder. The night of the sporting event, they would simply plug it in, dial New York, and go on the air.

The phone company eventually found out what was going on and began watching the circuits for unusually long station-to-station phone calls during WINS sportscasts. One Thursday night, Anheuser-Busch was sponsoring the Knicks game from Philadelphia. Les Keiter dialed New York.

"It's game time, and the New York Knicks are on the air," came the prerecorded announcement from the New York studios. The musical theme song, "Where There's Life, There's Bud," began to play. The announcer continued, "Anheuser-Busch, the brewers of Budweiser beer—bringing you Knicks basketball at home and away, Ranger hockey at home and away—presents the New York Knickerbockers. Tonight from Convention Hall in Philadelphia, here's Les Keiter." Keiter came on, but had a bad connection. He couldn't hear the cues from New York on the headset of von Kunitz's device. He wasn't sure he was on the air. Then he was sure he *wasn't* on the air and hung up. The producer at the station hastily filled with music. They eventually got the coverage going, but again ran into trouble at halftime. In the second half of the game, with the score tied at 44-all, telephone company detectives discovered the broadcast. Armed with the knowledge that McCaw had violated their regulations by attaching non-phone company equipment to their lines, they permitted telephone operators to break in on the broadcast and begin disrupting it. Listeners heard operators trying to communicate with Keiter. "I beg your pardon, sir. Is this Judson 2-7012?" Keiter refused to acknowledge the operators and continued broadcasting. They broke the circuit on him several times and finally cut him off altogether. Back at the studios, station announcer Lew Fisher introduced a "transcribed interlude." Keiter redialed the station and went back on the air. Again the operators broke in, badgered him, and then cut him off. Again the station played music, "Twenty-four Miles Across the Sea, Santa Catalina Is Waitin' for Me." The audience heard ''Santa Catalina'' and Les Keiter alternate two more times before WINS engineers gave up and terminated the broadcast.

McCaw took AT&T to court. He admitted attaching unauthorized equipment to the phone lines, but showed the judge how much money radio stations could save by using such devices. The judge was impressed and ordered the phone company to build similar equipment that could legally be attached to phone company lines, and rent it to radio stations at a reasonable charge.

During my first months at WINS, I knew McCaw only as a shadowy figure who slipped in and out of offices at the most unexpected times. He had not yet acknowledged that he knew of my existence. I was busily learning how to operate in a sales ''boiler room'' and I quickly found out that my writing ambitions would have to take a back seat to my ability to ''get the check.''

(the theme from *Picnic*)" / *Morris Stoloff* • "Love Me Tender" /

CHAPTER 3

One Hundred Records, Fifty Kilowatts, and Alan Freed

There was room for one hundred and eight commercials between midnight and dawn on WINS's "Original Milkman's Matinee with Stan Shaw," and Elroy McCaw wanted a sponsor for every minute. No matter that almost nobody was listening to the all-night disc jockey show. A team of telephone pitchmen calling car dealers, restaurant owners, and other retailers—from "Your Yankee Ballgame Station"—explained how the previous sponsor of the commercial that followed the Yankee games had retired to Florida. If they were qualified and acted quickly, they could get that valuable air time free. Free? Yes, if enough people passed their establishment each day to make it worth our while to put a Stan Shaw clock in their window, they would get the commercials free, paying only a service charge. The service charge was always collected before the commercials started on the air. McCaw cleaned up on service charges. And it was my job to collect the checks.

The entire operation, from the opening pitch to the depositing of the advertiser's check in McCaw's bank account, took place in a few hours. After the telephone call from a salesman whetted the prospective sponsor's appetite, the pitch would end with the words, "I'm not sure this spot is still available, I'm sorry." The salesman would hang up on the prospect.

Perry Plager would call back ten minutes later for the close and ask the prospective sponsor questions about how many people would see the clock. By then the prospect would be pleading for the free air time. He would be told that our copywriter would be out to see him in an hour, write the copy, and would have with him a simple one-paragraph agreement form calling for one hundred spot announcements. The client was to give me the signed contract and a check for the service charge. The reason for cash in advance was simple—because the air time was free, we couldn't afford billing and bookkeeping charges later.

By the time I got to the car dealership, pizzeria, or bowling alley, there was a fifty-fifty chance the prospect had changed his mind. I was spending as much time "saving the deal" as I was writing copy. A few days later there were usually some fireworks. The excited new sponsor would tune in after the Yankee game to hear his "free" announcement. After the first night the commercial would be on ten minutes later. After a few weeks it would slip to 4:00 A.M., having made way for dozens of other "lucky new advertisers." By then the sponsor had usually read the fine print in the contract and realized that nowhere did it say *how long* after the Yankee game the spot would air.

This was not how I had imagined big-time radio to be—writing commercials and collecting cash from hapless sponsors. It was frustrating work, but after a few weeks one of the salesmen landed St. Mark's Turkish Baths, an advertiser we might really be able to help. Their pitch was simple: If you were listening to the radio at that ungodly hour, it was because you were restless and couldn't sleep; you were tossing and turning. What you needed was a night at the Turkish baths. A few hours in the steam room, a rubdown, and a massage, and you would sleep like a baby.

"For your health's sake," I wrote, "go now to Saint Mark's Turkish Baths." The owners of the baths loved the show. It was actually bringing in customers. But even they couldn't win.

One night, Stan Shaw had just finished saying, "For your health's sake, go now to Saint Mark's Turkish Baths," when a newsman ran down the hall with a bulletin, burst into the studio, and announced, "Jimmy Trombetta has just been gunned down while seated in a steam cabinet at Saint Mark's Turkish Baths, apparently the victim of a gangland slaying . . ."

We lost the account. It went the way of Pop's Pizzeria (closed by the health department), Vicki Welles's Burlesque House, and all the others.

I have vivid memories of the Burlesque account. In those days, striptease shows were illegal in New York, so every pimple-faced high-school boy in town went across the river to Union City, New Jersey, to see Rose La Rose, Vicki Welles, and other big-name burlesque queens at Minsky's Theater.

Most strippers never make it from performer to owner, but Vicki Welles had dreams of glory. When a Union City theater became vacant, she rented it and started her own show. Perry Plager called her on opening day, and I was in front of her theater box office an hour later with a contract, only to be told that Miss Welles was performing, and I would have to sit through the show before I could see her. That show was my first experience with on-the-job fringe benefits.

After the performance, I went backstage where Welles, now in a kimono, was seated at a desk signing checks drawn on account at the bank next door. I had to wait in line behind the scenery company, the lighting man, and the costume people there to collect payments. When I saw all those checks being made out I became worried and had ours certified before I returned with it to New York. It was lucky I did that, because the following week the newspapers carried stories of the theater being closed by the sheriff after a check made out to the scenery company—for almost the identical amount as the WINS check—bounced.

Working for the all-night show had only one advantage over the other jobs at WINS. We had the only air-conditioned office at the station. In 1954, office buildings were not necessarily air conditioned and McCaw would pay only to cool the studios. However, our big green Fedders air conditioner brought us a bonus. When WINS hired Alan Freed he demanded an air-conditioned office and was given space to share with us.

The hiring of Alan Freed marked the first turning point for the radio station. While feverishly slashing operating costs, Elroy had also been focusing on how he could begin to make some real money with his new radio station. To bring in big advertising bucks, he needed ratings.

McCaw knew that the most successful station in town was WNEW, whose manager, Bernice Judis, had pioneered the first disc jockey format (twenty-five minutes of music followed by five minutes of news). Elroy called in WINS manager Bob Leder and program director Bob Smith, and they discussed disc jockeys. Only two WINS shows had any ratings. Bob and Ray's costly morning comedy show, with skits and takeoffs on soap operas, had a band of fanatic devotees who loved features like "Mary Backstage, Noble Wife." On Sundays, Brad Phillips's "Battle of the Baritones" was good for a regular mention in Nick Kenny's radio column in the *Daily Mirror,* as he premiered promising new voices including Steve Lawrence and Tony Bennett. The remaining shifts were covered by the former announcing staff who only now were learning how to introduce records.

As McCaw and his managers talked about alternatives, one name began to dominate the conversation—Alan Freed. Freed had brought an exciting new dimension to radio and was tearing up the Cleveland airwaves with a new kind of music that had made WJW the biggest station in Ohio.

People in the business were beginning to take notice. Taped versions of Freed's show were being syndicated and had found their way as far east as WNJR, a small station in Newark, New Jersey. A few bits and pieces about Freed had appeared in the trade press. When I interviewed him for an article, I found out that Freed had grown up in the age of swing, playing trombone for the Salem, Ohio, High School Band. When Benny Goodman and his orchestra played a one-night stand in Youngstown, Freed and his buddies piled into a car, raced twenty-five miles, and then stood in line for hours at the downtown movie house to hear the music and dance in the aisles. Tempo was as important as melody to composers during those years. By the time Freed broke into big-time radio in Cleveland in 1951, the bands had long since lost the beat. American music was dominated by crooners like Tony Bennett and Perry Como, and the sound was soft and sticky. As the rhythm disappeared from the melodies, the young people stopped dancing.

Freed had gotten hold of a major radio station's turntables at an ideal moment. Nobody was dancing. He decided to introduce dance music to a new generation of Americans. He couldn't find any appropriate music in the station's record library, so he started exploring the shelves at Cleveland's biggest record store. As he listened to the songs, he realized that he was putting aside most of the records released by the major companies. What remained was a

Dorsey • "Banana Boat (Day-O)" / *Harry Belafonte* • "A White

collection of discs by artists he had never heard of. They had names like Sam "the Man" Taylor, LaVern Baker, and Della Reese. Their voices were rich and the music was different. It featured tenor saxes squealing under the pressured playing of Red Prysock and Big Al Sears. Ivory Joe Hunter played mournful blues. Familiar 16- or 32-bar melodies were missing. This music had a 12-bar tempo that throbbed with a heavy, pulsating afterbeat.

The music that Freed had found was rhythm and blues, an outgrowth of the swing and jump blues being performed by black artists in small nightclubs. It had started in the forties and had been nurtured by artists like Louis Jordan, Big Joe Turner and Dinah Washington. Standing in the record shop, Freed made a sudden decision. He scooped up several handfuls of the records, returned to the studio, and placed the first one on the turntable. That night a predominantly white listening audience heard rock & roll music for the first time. Record after record blasted over WJW's transmitter as the Buckeye State was pounded with fifty thousand watts of the big beat. Freed himself was caught up in the exciting rhythm and began beating out the time on a telephone book. The result was instant and electrifying. Hundreds of listeners bombarded the station with phone calls. They loved what they were hearing. Many others hated it, but the ratings soared. From that night on, the entire show consisted of those records.

Before long, Freed had a second source of income. He was organizing dance concerts in and around Cleveland featuring the artists whose records he played. They were only too happy to come and perform. The concerts culminated in the Cleveland Coronation Ball—which drew twenty-five thousand teenagers to the ten-thousand-seat Cleveland Arena—an evening that set the pattern for the coming era of rock.

As shock waves from Cleveland spread across the nation, Freed began syndicating the radio show. He restaged the Cleveland concert at Newark's Sussex Armory. A standing-room-only crowd bounced to the beat of the Clovers, Nolan Lewis, Muddy Waters, and the Harptones. Six thousand were turned away.

Elroy McCaw was convinced. He would let his managers spend some real money. They offered Freed $75,000 to come to New York. In the fall of 1954, Alan Freed brought himself, his wife, Jackie, and four children, ages one to ten, to the Big Apple. Along with Freed came hundreds of 45-rpm singles that he piled helter-

Sport Coat (and a Pink Carnation)" / *Marty Robbins* • "Come Go

skelter in an old five-shelf supply cabinet in our office. That chaotic, uncatalogued collection would become the most influential record library in commercial radio, imitated by stations everywhere. It would change the sound of popular music in America and the world for generations.

Freed went on WINS in September of 1954 calling himself Moondog, the same name he had used in Cleveland. "The Moondog Show" hit the New York nighttime radio dial like a sledgehammer, knocking dents in the ratings of competing DJ's programs. He was quickly embroiled in a lawsuit when a blind composer named Louis "Moondog" Hardin claimed prior title to the name. The composer, an eccentric, was a familiar Manhattan sight. Clad in a helmet and Viking garb, he would stand motionless, leaning on his staff at key midtown intersections.

Freed and PD (program director) Bob Smith decided to retitle the show, naming it in a way that would describe the music. The new program, "Alan Freed's Rock & Roll Party," marked mass media's first major use of the phrase "rock & roll" (which Freed had coined and at one time even attempted to copyright).

Freed himself picked the music for every show and soon became a familiar adjunct to our boiler room. His slender figure (so unlike the pudgier depiction of him in the film *American Hot Wax* made in 1978, thirteen years after his death) seemed electrically charged. Even Freed's wavy hair looked as if it was crackling with voltage. Freed would snap open the lock on the battered green doors of the supply cabinet, flip rapidly through the piles of records, selecting discs and handing them to his young black producer, Johnny Brantley. Brantley would find matching request letters from listeners and arrange the letters and the records in racks. There were no categories such as fast or slow records, no alternating of male and female singers with groups, and no pacing of the show based on song popularity—all dogma to many program directors of latter-day pop radio stations. Freed had four hours to fill with music, and he put the show together according to his personal likes and dislikes. Repeat plays were based on understandings and arrangements he had reached with the individual record companies, music publishers, managers, and performers. Freed's name even appeared as co-composer on some of the records. Those deals would plague Freed in later years when "payola" became an ugly word. (It was coined to describe transactions in which disc jockeys, mu-

With Me" / *The Del-Vikings* • "Wake Up, Little Susie" / *The Everly*

sic directors, and programmers received cash, gifts, or services for playing a record. One easy way to do this was to give a DJ co-writer credit on a song, making him eligible for royalty payments based on record sales.) At that moment, though, Alan Freed was a hero to these tiny companies and struggling artists. The songs were very short. Some records would be repeated hourly. Freed would go into the studio with a hundred platters and the highest energy level in radio. Freed-style shows also began to appear in half a dozen other cities, the nearest being the "Symphony Sid Show" in Boston. Los Angeles, San Francisco, and Atlanta audiences were among the first exposed to rock & roll parties by local jocks.

With Freed's ratings offensive underway at night, Elroy McCaw turned his attention to the rest of the day. As the cost cutting extended to all levels of expenses and compensation, station manager Bob Leder jumped ship and turned up a week later at rival station WOR. Program Director Smith soon followed. McCaw left it up to a new manager, Jock Fearnhead, to continue the economies and reprogram the station while he, Elroy, looked for low-rent studios for the station and a free place for himself to live in New York.

Commercials for the Hotel Wyndham solved Elroy's living problems for a time, and Fearnhead dropped "The Bob and Ray Show," using old-time sportscaster Bill Stern to host "Contact," a new concept in morning radio. The show needed a producer, so I was liberated from the boiler room and became producer of "Contact."

The show's gimmick involved interspersing interviews among the records as Bill Stern made "contact" with newsmakers across the country. Where "The Milkman's Matinee" had been frustrating, "Contact" was a nightmare. Stern would come in with a list of celebrities, politicians, oddballs, and even a talking gorilla for me to phone and put on the air. Many of his guests lived in California. It may have been 7 A.M. in New York, but it was the middle of the night in Hollywood. Stern had private numbers that I dialed to wake up senators and movie stars, and they would sometimes hang up. When they did, Stern would explode. Several times he ripped out the phone and once hurled it right through a studio wall.

I began to dread the sound of Stern coming down the hall in the morning. That uneven clomp of his wooden leg resounded down the corridors as he stomped along, followed by his lovely Scan-

Brothers • "You Send Me" / *Sam Cooke* • "Diana" / *Paul Anka* •

dinavian gal Friday, Inga. Thank heaven for Inga. She would nod and smile and was the cheerful, stabilizing influence that kept the show from capsizing.

I couldn't imagine Stern getting ratings, and I didn't see much hope for the new chit-chat for housewives that followed where Maggie McNellis held forth interviewing the Grace Kellys and Sloan Simpsons (wife of New York Mayor Bill O'Dwyer) of this world.

Luckily for McCaw, the Freed program kept getting hotter. Alan began to produce stage shows featuring the groups whose records he played. His first New York dance concert ran for two nights at the St. Nicholas Arena on Sixty-sixth Street and Columbus Avenue, and was attended by sixteen thousand fans. He followed this with the 1955 Easter Jubilee at the Brooklyn Paramount that shattered the all-time attendance record there and grossed $107,000 in ten days—a lot of money in 1955. Freed got every act he asked for. They were grateful to him not only for the songs he played but for the songs Freed refused to play. Listeners never heard "covers" on WINS.

As rock & roll music caught on, the big record companies began "covering" the black artist's hits. If a rhythm & blues hit started moving up the charts and it was on a small label and featured one of the names Freed was promoting, the major labels would move in quickly, copy the arrangement note for note, and release it by one of their—usually white—superstars. A buyer walking into a record store would hear what sounded exactly like Lillian Briggs singing "I Want You to Be My Baby," buy the record, and find it was now Mercury label release 70635 by Georgia Gibbs. Fats Domino's "Ain't That a Shame" was followed by five copy versions and stalled at number seventeen on the pop charts while a cover version by Pat Boone hit number one on the pop charts. LaVern Baker was also victimized. She had done the original "Tweedle Dee." These "covers" cost the artists who produced the originals tens of thousands of dollars in lost income for each song that was copied. Extreme cases would result in losses in six figures. Other records that were "covered" included "Melody of Love" by Billy Vaughn (covered by the Four Aces), "Hearts of Stone" by the Charms (covered by the Fontane Sisters), "Ko Ko Mo" by Gene and Eunice (which was first covered by the Crew-Cuts and then by Perry Como), and the famous "Earth Angel" by the Penguins. "Maybellene" by Chuck Berry was one song that beat out the covers. WINS and Freed played only the original versions.

As the stage shows kept doing better and better, record companies began supplying acts and sharing receipts, while Freed expanded to low-budget feature films starring those same acts. If he had to miss a broadcast to be present when a scene was being shot, he had staff announcer Paul Sherman do the show for him. Freed called Sherman "The Crown Prince of Rock & Roll." As for himself, Alan was "The King."

Freed's first film, *Rock Around the Clock* (1956), starred Bill Haley and his Comets, the first rock & roll act to make the top of the charts. A second movie was called *Rock, Rock, Rock* (1957). His off-air activities hit a high point on Washington's Birthday in 1956 when he opened simultaneously on the stage and screen at the New York Paramount where his third feature film, *Don't Knock the Rock*, shared the bill with his all-time great "discoveries" on stage, including the Platters, Frankie Lymon and the Teenagers, Ruth Brown, the Cleftones, the Cadillacs, Bobby Charles, Maureen Cannon, the Duponts, Nappy Brown, and Robin Robinson.

The crowds started lining up for the first morning show at midnight, and when the box office opened, the traffic leading into Times Square was halted as thousands blocked Forty-second and Forty-third Streets in twin rivers of fans that surged toward the Paramount's distinctive marquee. Scores of mounted police and foot patrolmen attempted to hold back the crowds. In the ensuing crush, store-front windows caved in, and the box office window was shattered. The theater filled quickly, leaving thousands outside. During the first show the balcony began to vibrate from the foot stomping, and a frightened building inspector ordered a partial evacuation. By midnight the opening record for the New York Paramount had been broken. The six stage shows and seven screen shows had been seen by a total of 15,220 people.

Freed moved to a white-carpeted waterfront mansion in Stamford, Connecticut. It was a long commute, and Alan hated to drive. He had been in a car crash before arriving in New York and was reminded of it every time he saw his flattened nose in the mirror. He had the station build him a studio in the guest house of his sixteen-room home and arranged for a record company to pay for broadcast lines and an engineer. But he didn't go home every night. There were acts to catch. Some nights I would go with Alan to midnight shows at the clubs. He was frenetic during the shows and gulped shots of Scotch one after another. I remember him leaning forward from our ringside table and sliding shot glasses filled to the brim across the stage floor as the Treniers, a twin-brother R&B duo, finished their act and joined him in a toast.

When Alan stayed in town he sometimes came into the station in the morning. On one visit he spotted Inga, still working on Bill Stern's show. After that he did fewer shows from Connecticut. A relationship began that was to culminate a few years later in his divorce from Jackie and marriage to Inga.

But at that moment Alan was wondering how much higher he could kick the ratings, I was wondering how much more of Bill Stern I could stomach, and Elroy's worry was cutting his rent.

CHAPTER 4

Assault on the Marketplace

Elroy McCaw scavenged relentlessly through the less fashionable neighborhoods of 1956 Manhattan looking for a low-rent location for his radio station. On Columbus Circle he discovered his bargain. Nobody wanted the upper floor of the old two-story building that fronted the circle and extended up Broadway and Central Park West to Sixty-first Street. (The Gulf + Western building occupies part of that site today.)

The address was 7 Central Park West. Its downstairs clientele included assorted used-car showrooms, burger joints, and about a billion cockroaches. On the roof a four-story Coca-Cola weather sign featured a giant arched temperature gauge framing a neon country scene that could be drenched with rain or sun, a garish backdrop for the statue of Christopher Columbus below.

Elroy reasoned that if he signed a cut-rate lease and made the rear of the building into small offices, he could sublet them for more than his rent and have a free home for WINS in midtown Manhattan. Nobody could beat that deal.

We moved. There were no studios in the new location, but by our knocking a few holes in the walls and putting in windows, some of the rooms began to resemble studios even though they weren't soundproof. McCaw also spent fifteen dollars to have the letters WINS hand-lettered in white on a 21-by-15-inch piece of black cardboard that he helped tack above the double doors leading into the new headquarters of his Gotham Broadcasting Company.

His own office, below the Coca-Cola sign, had picture windows facing Columbus Circle, Central Park, and Broadway.

People entering the building were engulfed in a sort of Disney-and-doom fantasy architecture that set the tone for the atmosphere of the radio station. Massive early gothic stone vaultings lit by sconces gave the lobby a medieval feeling. The arches also framed a staircase leading to a catacomblike basement that had once connected to the train platforms of two of the largest subway stations in the city. The janitor claimed that William Randolph Hearst had built the structure as a train depot, hoping to compete with Grand Central Station. He also showed off its most interesting and curious feature, which was hidden from both the street and most visitors. A triangular interior courtyard was the setting for an exquisite two-story gothic chapel complete with miniature flying buttresses, gargoyles, and stained glass windows. The initials *M* and *D* were engraved in large escutcheons on the walls.

"Marion Davies," he told us, adding, "She was Hearst's mistress, you know. Needed her own church. Couldn't pray in public. So he built her this one." Millions of people passed within fifty feet of the chapel every day of their lives and never knew it was there.

Elroy saw the chapel as a way to do the Wyndham Hotel out of free commercials. He put a kitchen in the back, a bed in the nave, and a second floor above. He now had a rent-free midtown apartment for himself. Upstairs he built an office.

By the time we moved into 7 Central Park West, the boiler room operation had shut down and Perry the Pirate had retired. Alan Freed got his own office, I got my own office, and to make things even better, I ended the year by being appointed promotions director. McCaw hired a young Amherst graduate, Tom Rounds, to do my old job as Bill Stern's producer. I began writing press releases and placing items about WINS in the newspaper columns.

Although we began 1957 with our ratings climbing at night, the rest of the daytime programming was still in trouble. In other parts of the country some radio stations were doing better. McCaw came in one day with a magazine containing an article about a group of stations in the Midwest that were getting big ratings by playing only the same forty records over and over again. Accompanying graphs demonstrated impressive rating gains. The article quoted

Todd Storz, the owner of the chain, telling the now-legendary story about sitting at a bar with his station manager, Bill Stewart, observing how patrons played the same forty records over and over again on the jukebox and how, at closing time, the waitresses who had already heard these songs all day long spent their tip money playing them once more. Storz and Stewart came to the conclusion that a radio station format based on only forty records might work and might just be sensational. They tried the idea first at KOWH, Omaha, and then at stations in Minneapolis, Kansas City, and New Orleans. While some DJ's protested and even resigned, the public began to respond.

McCaw wanted to get the same results but without spending any money. He went looking for somebody from the Storz organization who would come to New York and work cheap. Mel Leeds, a former assistant record librarian at WNEW, had gone from New York to Kansas City to work as a program assistant at Storz station WHB. Leeds, a diminutive and wiry man who carried a pistol, acted impulsively, and had a show-biz flair, did not hit it off well with the more conservative Storz organization. He was soon asked to leave.

Mel Leeds returned to New York an expert in the Todd Storz Top Forty format and was hired by WINS for $175 a week. Leeds moved into an office where he sat for days listening over and over again to a one-hour tape of WHB. Between plays he interviewed the different people who worked for the station and evaluated them. He called me in, and I listened to the tape with him. I was impressed. The Kansas City station sounded different. It had rudimentary jingles, early attempts at contests, and some special promotional features that involved the audience writing or phoning the station. I was even more excited by the music. I sensed a potential if the songs were rotated more by categories.

From my earlier talks with Alan Freed I knew that his "Rock & Roll Party" program was not at all structured for maximum ratings. Imagine how much higher the ratings could be if we could control the air exposure of each piece of music, basing its repeat plays on the current popularity of the song.

At that moment in 1957, thousands of other radio stations across America were turning to records and disc jockeys for salvation. With no previous models to guide them, these first efforts had resulted in a formless sea of music, blandly presented, and without any sense of excitement. In only a few cities, where a handful of innovators owned stations, did radio begin to grab listeners by the ear and get their attention with a music-and-news format. In Dallas, broadcaster Gordon McLendon adapted his own version of the Storz format for KLIF. Minneapolis listeners actually had two stations to pick from when competitor Gerald Bartell went against Todd Storz station WDGY with Top Forty on WOKY. Tapes of those stations sounded similar to the WHB tape.

Leeds asked what I thought of the WHB jingles. I said I thought they were okay, but that WINS should have original stuff. He asked me if I could write jingles. I had never done so but felt sure I could. I said yes. I also said yes when he asked if I could create original contests. "Start writing," he said.

I began with a slogan and it became the basis for the first jingles:

For music, news, time, and the weather
keep your dial where the tens come together—
ten-ten WINS New York.

From there I went to variations:

For the news and the music where the records spin
where the tens come together it's W-I-N-S WINS . . . WINS!

Mel Leeds loved the slogans and I was made assistant program director. He then went on a housecleaning spree. Ten thousand albums were stored in cabinets lining the walls of the record library. They had been cross-indexed and catalogued over a period of years. The results of this effort filled two gigantic waist-high Rolodex wheels. Leeds tossed the wheels into the trash bin and shipped the albums to storage.

Next came the disc jockey staffing. Former Storz DJ Irv Smith, who broadcast under the name "A Smith Named Irv," was brought in to be the morning man. (Smith had been in more car crashes than Alan Freed. He had creases on both cheeks, souvenirs of a day when he drove a car through a barn and out the other side.) DJ Jack Lacy was assigned a double shift, nine to noon and four to seven, and staff announcer Stan Z. Burns (later known for the slogan "From high noon to three, this is the orbit to be, for

Stan Z.'') filled the midday slot. The basic WINS DJ lineup was complete. Now I began to produce the new intros, contests, features, promotions, and jingles. Eventually all the pieces were in place, and we were ready for a run at the New York ratings.

The new WINS hit the air in September of 1957 with sharp jingles, screaming contests and promotions, and Top Forty music. The city had never heard anything like it. The jocks had personalities. A Smith Named Irv was funny, Jack Lacy had a dry sense of humor, and Alan Freed was all power and energy. The only show that didn't play only forty records was Freed's. Mel Leeds knew better than to mess with Freed or his music. Alan had too big a name and too much power with the record companies, the publishers, and the acts.

I produced every second of WINS features for excitement and ratings, even the newscasts. News was introduced with ear-splitting sensationalist effects. ''Sounds make the news!'' shouted an announcer in a recorded news opening. This pronouncement was followed by a horrifying sound. A different sound was played each hour. One newscast would be introduced by a woman screaming, another by a fire engine siren, and still another by the sound of machine guns.

Attention-getting features were dropped in between the records. One that Mel brought with him, called ''Sound Off,'' gave listeners a chance to write in, sound off about their gripes, and hear the complaints read over the air. We began to promote, ''Bucks for Breaks"—a dollar for every station break slogan written by a listener that we used on the air. We offered twenty-five dollars for every baby born at 10:10 A.M. or 10:10 P.M. Women actually timed their Caesarean operations to collect. Tying it all together was the incessant, repetitive music pounding away with station call letters and jingles all over the place.

By October, WINS was in first place in New York audience share between 7 A.M. and 11 P.M. It had all been done over the air. There had not been one penny spent in advertising, because McCaw had never authorized an advertising budget. As 1957 drew to a close, I began to wonder how high was up.

Nineteen fifty-eight began with all sorts of innovations to build our audience. The WINS time-and-temperature chime was introduced. It was a simple device, but it served a number of purposes. When it rang at the conclusion of a record, it gave the station a

Knife" / *Bobby Darin* • "Personality" / *Lloyd Price* • "Put Your

distinctive sound, so people knew they were tuned to WINS. It also alerted the audience to get ready to set their watches and to listen for the weather forecast. Later, one of the most important jingle concepts was introduced. Although called "the subliminal," it was hardly that. The famous "10-10 WINS New York" jingle was tagged to every record, reniforcing the station's call letters in the minds of listeners who would later be polled by rating companies.

A continuous-loop tape was installed to create a slight delay, or echo, of the station's sound. It gave a concert-hall effect to the music and to the announcers' voices. For the first time, WINS used newspaper ads, first as teasers, and then to introduce the effect, which we called Soundarama. For two hours before Soundarama began, the engineers pulled the station's power down, switching to a ten-kilowatt auxiliary transmitter so the signal sounded weak. Then, at the appointed time, the tape loop was started and the station went back to its original fifty thousand watts. The contrast was startling. (Soundarama was my first experience in attempting to control the reverberation of a station's signal. I would enhance it and the time chime in later years at WABC.)

We instituted police honor awards, a town crier who read community events, and a contest to find a bell for the town crier ("walk in off the street with a bell and we'll ring your chimes at our microphones"). We added a "Pick Hit of the Week"—our choice of the best new record releases that week—and we announced a night patrol, a mobile unit in which newsman Tom O'Brien and Mel Leeds cruised the streets all night monitoring police calls and responding to the most sensational breaking stories.

We held a "wives day," when the disc jockey's wives substituted for them on the air, and it made a mini-star out of Agnes Lacy. When the Russians sent a dog into space, we sent a pooped pooch to Florida on a vacation, allowing him to bring along "two owners of his choice" as WINS Goes to the Dogs week was celebrated. When the boat show opened at the New York Coliseum across the street from WINS, we had listeners write in and tell us why they were "Up the Creek without a Paddle." The best letter got its author a paddle and the canoe to go along with it. We had a "performing people contest" with dogs as the judges. The dog owner whose cartwheel or other trick got the dogs barking the loudest, won.

To give away a day at the races, we turned the tables and had a horse pick the people—who offered him apples, oats, and other goodies in the hope of being chosen. I still remember pushing that pony into the freight elevator and bringing him up to the station's "Jack Lacy Show" to make his selection over the air. During a water shortage we gave away twelve thousand gallons of water and the swimming pool to put it in. (The winners lived in an apartment, so we gave them lifetime passes to the giant saltwater pool at Palisades Amusement Park.) At Christmas we ran a tie exchange in which listeners would swap their atrocious gift ties with one another. In a one-month promotion for the watchmakers of Switzerland, we awarded a Swiss watch every night to the listener whose own watch kept the worst time of all the old watches we received each morning.

For a contrast to all the music we played, we hired actor Sidney Gross—who spoke with an English accent—and had him read horror stories at midnight on Friday nights to the accompaniment of organ music, sound effects, and shrieks. And when things really got dull, we dressed a time salesman up in an old King Kong–style gorilla suit and sent him to the roof to scale the Coca-Cola sign.

I couldn't believe we were moving so fast. We got competition. I knew that sooner or later it would happen, but the first salvo came from an unlikely direction—Nathan Straus's radio station, WMCA. A family-owned offshoot of the Straus–DuParquet hotel supply company, WMCA served as both a commercial business and a political platform for Nathan Straus and his son Peter. Family ties linked the Straus dynasty (which included cousin Jack's Macy's department store) to the Sulzbergers, who published *The New York Times*, and to New York's former governor, Herbert Lehman. WMCA was known for broadcasting radio editorials at a time when nobody else in radio would dream of taking a stand on public issues. The station offered one of the earliest talk shows, with host Barry Gray, and frequently ran lengthy documentaries in prime times during the day and evening, despite the risk to the ratings.

But in 1958, former Storz broadcasting executive Steve Labunski (later president of NBC Radio and executive director of the International Radio and Television Society) suddenly surfaced as manager of WMCA. Labunski had been in sales at WHB and had then managed the Todd Storz rating battles at WDGY in Minneapolis. Not only was Labunski at the New York station, but Storz's Top Forty expert, Ruth Meyer, had joined him there as program director. WMCA began to rock.

A second competitor quickly joined the fray. Loew's Theatres Broadcasting Corporation owned MGM. It had been a part of the Metro-Goldwyn-Mayer distribution empire that the government had forced the giant film corporation to spin off. WMGM started to play the hits. Unlike WMCA, WMGM had no large public service program obligations of the type that turn off listeners, so we instantly identified them as a serious threat. The New York ratings war was heating up.

CHAPTER 5

Vive de Gaulle

WINS's ascent in the ratings sparked a rivalry that resulted in what to this day remains one of the greatest stings ever pulled off in radio. All the ingredients were present: a group of undisciplined young Turks at WINS feeling their first power, a single, absentee owner three thousand miles away and not always in control, and across town that "other" station—WMGM.

WMGM was in many ways the opposite of WINS. WMGM's sleek studios in a modern Park Avenue glass office tower were a vivid contrast to the improvised and hardly soundproof rooms in the truncated medieval structure on Columbus Circle where WINS rock & roll music originated. WMGM also played rock music, but it had low ratings. Still, the station brought some dollars into the budding empire of Bob and Larry Tisch. They had placed WMGM under the stewardship of Art Tolchin. Tolchin, a towering, gray-haired and handsome Rex Harrison type, romanced the dollars out of the time-buying community with his charm. His executive office at WMGM was a virtual separate wing of the station and could be sealed off from the studios and other offices by a rolling double-thick soundproof door. Inside, the complex was like a small apartment, complete with bath and shower, a mirrored wall whose panels folded out to reveal a long, well-stocked bar, and drapes that closed instantly should party activities reach a point at which prying eyes from Lever House across Fifty-fourth Street were not welcome.

Equipped with theater tickets, a large expense account, this unique office, and New York's exclusive East Side restaurant district just outside the door, Tolchin was guaranteed a modicum of support from the then almost entirely female corps of aging, bored radio time buyers looking for a night of excitement.

Art Tolchin yearned for big ratings. Time buyers could not justify large schedules of spot announcements on low-rated stations that had a rock & roll image. Tolchin figured that, until the ratings rose, something could be done about the image. The best chance, he decided, was in the area of news and public affairs.

The WMGM news department consisted of a group of former soap opera announcers and fairly unsophisticated writers and reporters who had been dubbed the WMGM Minute Men. The name implied, of course, that they got to fast-breaking news stories quickly and had lots of scoops. In fact, they operated out of a mobile unit that could easily have been mistaken at fifty yards for a Good Humor ice cream truck, and their efforts were no match for the heavily staffed and experienced news crews of the network-owned radio stations or big independents.

It was against this backdrop that the WMGM news department labored, searching for a really big scoop that could change WMGM's image. Building on a first success, they could perhaps do some genuine investigative reporting, perhaps win some awards. With prestige like that, WMGM's advertising rate could be raised, and the minute men's salaries would go up along with the new profits. So they watched the Teletype machines regularly for a hot story that held the promise of a scoop for WMGM and could be the first step in making their name on Madison Avenue.

The big story breaking that sunny Wednesday morning of May 28, 1958, had a Paris dateline. France was in turmoil; the government was collapsing. For days, rumors had been sweeping the capital that Charles de Gaulle, World War II hero and the liberator of Paris, would seize power and take over the reins of the republic. Heavy crowds of left-wingers led by former Premier Pierre Mendès-France surged into the Place de la Bastille chanting "Fascism shall not pass." Their roars drowned out the rush hour traffic. A sudden transport strike shut down the subways, buses, and suburban trains. Anti–De Gaulle mobs surged down the Champs-Élysées toward government buildings surrounded by massed ranks of police. Inside the National Assembly, President René Coty was conferring with the leaders of the center parties.

The news editors at WMGM decided to try for a big scoop.

They would go right to the source. They would call Paris and ask General de Gaulle if he was indeed about to seize power. Not only would they make the call, but they would do it live, on the air.

Having decided on a strategy that most seasoned reporters would regard as extremely naïve, they moved one step closer toward disaster and actually broadcast over the radio what they were planning to do. Disc jockey Jerry Marshall was in the middle of his program when he announced, "The number-four best-selling disc in the area coming up . . . right after a little visit to the newsroom, right here on 'Jerry Marshall's Record Room.' It's ten-thirty A.M. on the WMGM clock. Bill Edmunds with the news highlights."

Edmunds led into the newscast with the story: "French President Coty is conferring with political leaders after receiving the resignation of Premier Pflimlin. A new government may be created today with General de Gaulle at the helm, and WMGM has a call in, long distance, overseas to General de Gaulle to bring you a direct interview with the general, and as soon as that call is completed, we'll put that call and the interview right on the air. So stay tuned for firsthand information from France."

Edmunds continued with news about the latest twenty-inch satellite that the U.S. Navy had launched from Cape Canaveral, but listeners all over the city had heard the opening story and were staying tuned to hear General de Gaulle.

The newscast was also being monitored by competitors. Across town, the WINS newsroom staff was incredulous. They knew there was no way WMGM could deliver de Gaulle. Even William Randolph Hearst, Jr., who had been trying for three days to get a scoop for his papers, had been unable to get through. WINS news director, Tom O'Brien (who in later years rose to be vice president of Radio News for ABC and then head of Mutual News), realized that WMGM's listeners were in for a big disappointment. So was their news staff. How could they possibly expect de Gaulle to call them? But wait. Perhaps there was a way. Imagine the possibilities that the situation presented. O'Brien began to think.

Two hours later, the phone rang at the WMGM switchboard. A foreign sounding female voice, speaking over the sound of transatlantic static, said that the call that WMGM had placed to Paris was ready. The WMGM news crew rushed into action. Two tape recorders were turned on, and the switchboard lines were fed into the news control room. Public affairs director Ted Schneider took command. In a few seconds Art Tolchin had been called. He rushed to the newsroom from his executive suite. Long minutes passed, punctuated by buzzes and beeps and silence. The wait was agonizing.

Finally, an operator's voice said, "Just a moment please, de Gaulle will be right here. All right. One minute, please."

Schneider put down the phone and ran to make certain the tape machines were rolling.

The operator spoke again. "Hello, New York? New York? Hello, New York?"

Finally Schneider returned to the phone. "Yes, this is New York."

"The general's aide wishes to know if you would like to speak in English."

"Yes, in English please."

"All right. Just one moment, please."

"Right."

"Hello?"

"Yeah?"

"We're ready when you are."

"All right, put him on."

"All right. Go ahead, Paris."

Background static characteristic of overseas calls filled the line. Schneider cued newsman Bill Edmunds, who took the phone and said, "General de Gaulle?"

A voice with a French accent said, "Alloh?"

"Hello General de Gaulle—"

"Yes?"

"This is WMGM's Minute Man, Bill Edmunds, in New York City."

"Yes?"

"And I would like to know, General de Gaulle, if you would make a statement for the American people."

"In New York City?"

"In New York City, yes."

"I certainly will. Err . . . ah . . . what is this statement for . . . a newspaper?"

"No, for the radio . . . for our radio station."

"Err, what radio station?"

"We're broadcasting. Yes."

"I see. Am I on the radio now?"

"No. You're not on the radio now. We're making a tape and we're going to use it throughout the day and on our newscasts."

"All right." The French voice paused and seemed to reflect. Then it continued. "I would not like to be recorded because I have not granted any of the French press any of that information."

Edmunds was disappointed. "I see," he said.

"One thing I will do, however," said the voice at the other end. "I will broadcast but I do not want it repeated because, err, the various French news agencies have been after me and I have not granted them that per-mi-shown."

Edmunds seemed perplexed. "Well, will you hold on . . . a . . . just a second, and then we'll put you right directly on the air. Can you do that?"

"All right, yes. But make it very fast. I have to go to the National Assembly."

"All right. We . . . we're ready in just a second. Uh . . . What we will do . . . we were going to tape this interview but inasmuch as you can't give, uh, give this release, you know, on tape, why we'll switch it right on the air and we'll do it right now."

Edmunds frantically signaled the engineers to continue taping but to simultaneously switch the feed on the air. They indicated it would take a few minutes.

Edmunds started to vamp. "It's exactly eighteen minutes before eleven here in New York City, and we have a vast news audience here in New York City, and we cover news from all over the world so just as soon . . . just a second . . . as soon as they give me the go-ahead, I would like for you to make a statement for the American people concerning the crisis in France right now."

"Certainly," replied the voice, sounding calm despite the delay.

"So I'll tell . . . I'll tell you," Edmunds was nervous. "I'll start all over just as soon as they give me a go-ahead."

"All right, all right," the voice reassured Edmunds.

The WMGM engineers finally switched the hookup. They explained to disc jockey Jerry Marshall what was happening, and Marshall, surprised and excited, called for the microphone.

"Ladies and gentlemen," Marshall began, "we have just contacted General Charles de Gaulle in France, and we are about to put him on the air just as the broadcast is being made by special telephone . . . Here is General Charles de Gaulle."

The Everly Brothers • "Everybody's Somebody's Fool" / *Connie*

The engineers switched the feed to the news studio, and Edmunds went on the air with the live phone call.

“This is Bill Edmunds in New York City,” he began, “And I have on the phone with me General Charles de Gaulle in France. General de Gaulle, I would like to have you make a statement for the American people, for our listening audience here in New York City, and all the territory that we cover, about the crisis in France. Would you care to make a statement at this time?”

“I certainly would, Mr. Edmunds,” said the accommodating voice on the other end of the phone. “There is one thing that I want to make clear. When I assume power . . . if Monsieur Pflimin permits me to assume power, I will not take it by any dictatorial means. I am too much of an old soldier not to realize that the people of France have gone through enough trouble, and I will give them a good government which they should have had ever since the war.”

Listeners all over the New York area stopped what they were doing and listened. This was a most unusual broadcast, particularly coming from rock & roll WMGM radio.

Edmunds, elated, continued the interview. “Well, do you think that you will assume leadership of France within the next few days . . . or how soon do you think this will happen, General de Gaulle?”

“Well,” said the voice on the other end of the phone, “it is really too soon to tell. Err, monsieur, can you tell me who I am speaking to?”

“My name is Bill Edmunds.” said Edmunds, a bit perplexed, “and I'm one of the Minute Men here at WMGM.”

“Oh, MGM zee motion picture company?” The accent was thickening.

“Yes,” said Edmunds. “Well, we have a radio station here in New York City, a fifty-thousand-watt station, and we cover all of the metropolitan area and all over, uh, the eastern part of the United States.”

“I see,” said the voice, reassured. “Well, of course, everybody knows that the best radio station in New York”—the French accent suddenly disappeared—“is WINS . . . . Vive la France!”

There was a click as the phone on the other end was hurriedly hung up. Edmunds stared at his phone, flabbergasted.

“Hello,” he shouted. No answer. “Our . . . our wire seems to

Francis • “Itsy Bitsy Teenie Weenie Yellow Polkadot Bikini” /

have . . . uh . . . seems to have gone dead.'' Pausing in disbelief after every word, he said, ''And . . . we . . . were . . . just speaking . . . with . . . General Charles de Gaulle. And now . . . back to Jerry Marshall.''

The engineer threw a switch, changing studios, and Marshall's microphone went back on the air just as he shouted an incredulous ''What!'' Tolchin turned without saying a word to anybody and left the control room. Jerry Marshall grabbed for the next record.

Tolchin hurried down the hall to his office and called Jock Fearnhead, manager of WINS, and threatened to come over to WINS and flatten Fearnhead, who seemed totally bewildered by Tolchin's call.

Within moments, the WINS switchboard was flooded with calls from listeners asking if we knew what General de Gaulle had said about us on WMGM. By mid-afternoon, the story was front-page news on the newsstands, with the *New York World-Telegram* saying it all: WHO HAD DE GAULLE TO CALL WMGM, accompanied by a picture of a crowd of paratroopers and Gaullists on Corsica singing the ''Marseillaise'' in support of a Committee of Public Safety, which had seized rule of the island.

The story was all over the country, in *Time* and *Newsweek*, and WMGM asked for an FCC investigation. But the FCC never followed through. Tolchin, however, received a cable from Paris the next day. It read:

I WAS CUT OFF. WHAT HAPPENED?—CHARLES DE GAULLE

Tom O'Brien's fiancée, Hazel—a British Overseas Airways stewardess—had arrived in France.

The de Gaulle incident summed up a contagious ''soldier of fortune'' attitude of fun-loving adventurism that surfaced every now and then among the young newsmen who were trying to learn broadcast journalism at the rock & roll music stations. Several times I observed WINS news crews in action. I once went along as they surveyed the location of an unauthorized demonstration.

''The protesters are going to come down this street,'' one of the newsmen remarked to his crew. ''The cops will probably intercept them just about there. We'll do an actuality tape and then we'll have to feed the tape back to our newsroom somewhere along the next two blocks of the march.''

The newsman then staked out telephone booths along the street for several blocks, putting Bell System OUT OF ORDER signs on the phones and unscrewing the mouthpieces from the handsets, pocketing the carbon microphones, and replacing the mouthpieces. In one move he had temporarily disabled the phones and exposed the metal contacts in the handsets, to which he would later attach the clip-on leads of his tape recorder when feeding the news reports back to the station.

He also showed me how easy it was to penetrate a security cordon, even getting within touching distance of a head of state. The secret was to begin talking into a microphone as if you were on the air and then walk toward the king or prime minister, while still talking. There were few security guards in those days who would stop what appeared to be a broadcast in progress.

One day I was with a news crew that had been assigned to cover Fidel Castro on a day of speech making and rallies in New York. For three hours Castro had been exhorting followers from a podium on the mall bandshell in Central Park. It was a hot afternoon. The longer Castro spoke, the hotter the sun became. Finally, at about 4:30 P.M., he finished speaking. The news crews packed their gear and were ready to head from the sweat and dust of the park to the nearest bar when radio personality Barry Farber invited several of them to a party in his penthouse atop a high rise overlooking the Hudson River at Seventy-ninth Street. Farber, who speaks sixteen languages, also invited many members of the United Nations community. Grateful and tired, they adjourned to the Farber penthouse.

It was one of those great New York parties where the people, the timing, and the surrounding events combined to create a special ambiance. The air was filled with animated discussions in many languages, analyzing the developments of the day and then moving on to who was sleeping with whom in the international set.

Suddenly a news announcer looked at his watch. He was supposed to be at Manhattan Center, an auditorium on Thirty-fourth Street, at 8:00 P.M. for another Castro speech. But the party was too good to abandon. He decided to wing it from the penthouse on Seventy-ninth Street.

At the appointed time the announcer called his station's newsroom from Farber's living room and asked to be put on the air. "Just one minute of your time," he asked the partygoers. "When I wave my hand, start cheering and applauding as loud as you can."

The announcer got his cue. "An enthusiastic crowd at Manhattan Center," he began, "is awaiting the arrival of Fidel Castro." He paused. "And here comes the bearded Cuban leader now. He's entering the hall, and the people have spotted him." The announcer waved at the room, and the entire party broke into cheers. "Viva Castro, Viva Castro!" they screamed.

"What a welcome!" The announcer described the procession down the aisle and up to the podium, and then added, "and so Fidel Castro has arrived to another triumphant reception in New York. More later. Now back to our studios."

The announcer returned to his drinking. Across town, Manhattan Center was dark and quiet. A bomb threat had caused the cancellation of the rally. Fidel Castro never left the Waldorf-Astoria that night—except on one New York city radio station.

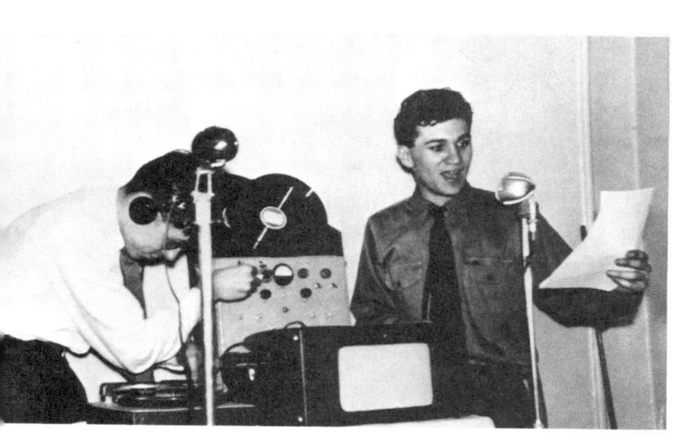

Brooklyn, New York, 1947. Rick Sklar, president of the Erasmus Hall High School Radio Workshop, reading lines from a radio play while engineer Alan Bernhardt cues up a sound effects record. *(Rick Sklar, private collection)*

Left: Introducing a record at my first radio station, WPAC in Patchogue, New York, 1954. *(Rick Sklar, private collection)*

Below: WINS Disc jockey Jack Lacy holding the "cheap bargain watch" that kept the worst time of all watches received from listeners that day. The sender won a costly imported watch from the Watchmakers of Switzerland, who sponsored the contest. *(Mortimer Matz)*

Left: Lee Keiter, WINS sportscaster, recreating a baseball game with sound effects. The actual game was occurring two thousand miles away. This technique saved us the cost of expensive broadcast lines, as well as airline and hotel bills. *(Mortimer Matz)*

Disc jockey Murray the K interviewing Johnny Mathis in 1958 when the vocalist brought one of his early recordings to WINS. *(Mortimer Matz)*

Left: WINS sales manager Chuck Le Mieux holds up fake ancient Egyptian stone whose hoax hieroglyphics read ''Everybody's Mummy Listens to 1010 WINS.'' The station's general manager, Harold ''Hap'' Anderson, looks on. *(Mortimer Matz)*

New York World-Telegram and The Sun

IN TWO SECTIONS — SECTION ONE

Final — Complete Stocks, Bonds—Bid and Asked Prices

Local Forecast: Clear tonight, mostly fair tomorrow. Weather Forecast on Page 25.

VOL. 125—NO. 227— NEW YORK, WEDNESDAY, MAY 28, 1958 TEN CENTS

COTY CALLS DE GAULLE

Hostile Crowds Marching in Paris

4 Teens Given Stiff Terms in Farmer Killing

By THOMAS MACCABE, World-Telegram Staff Writer.

General Sessions Judge Irwin D. Davidson today sentenced four teen-agers to prison for their part in the slaying of polio-crippled Michael Farmer last July 30 in Highbridge Park.

Sentences of 20 years to life were given Louis Alvarez, 17, of 1484 Amsterdam Ave., and Charles (Big Man) Horton, 18, of 740 Riverside Dr., both convicted of second degree murder.

Leroy (The Magician) Birch, 19, of 333 W. 151st St., who was convicted of second degree manslaughter, received a seven and a half to 15-year sentence, while Leoncio De Leon, 17, of 569 W. 150th St., also found guilty of second degree manslaughter, got a five to 15-year term.

2-Month Trial.

A jury convicted the four youths April 15 after a trial lasting more than two months. Three other defendants were acquitted.

The seven were accused of murdering young Farmer, 15, of 573 W. 175th St., when they took him for a member of a rival gang. The Farmer boy, son of a city fireman, was fatally beaten and stabbed.

'Sense of Frustration'

Judge Davidson told a half-filled court today:

"I approach this task with a sense of frustration because I am forced to say that the trial in and of itself has neither

Continued on Page Two.

Auto Union Asks U.S. Mediation

By JIM KLOCKENKEMPER, United Press International.

DETROIT, May 28.—The United Auto Workers today asked the Federal Mediation and Conciliation Service to step in to end deadlocked, final-hour bargaining with General Motors, but the company said it is opposed to mediation.

GM's refusal of mediation was expected to block the federal agency from entering the talks.

UAW Vice President Leonard Woodcock said mediation is needed because General Motors has stood pat on a two-year contract extension offer and refused to bargain on the union demands.

Mr. Woodcock disclosed the union today offered to drop either its demand for a 22 per cent increase in pensions or cost of living protection in pensions.

But Louis Seaton, GM vice president, said in rejecting mediation that the union's modifications of demands have been small. He indicated the union will have to come down a lot more before GM is willing to give ground.

Last week the union trimmed its bargaining goals to 11 headed by better unemployment benefits, pensions and job security.

Mr. Woodcock said he saw no hope for a settlement before the contract covering 325,000 GM workers expires at midnight tomorrow. He asked that the contract be extended on a day-to-day or week-to-week basis while negotiations continue.

Latest News

United Press International.

WASHINGTON, May 28.—The House today passed a bill to admit Alaska to the Union as the 49th State. The bill now goes to the Senate, where it is given a good chance of passage. (Earlier details on page 2.)

— Slow Down and Live —

Windfall Notices Seek Debt Data

By H. W. CONNORS, World-Telegram Staff Writer.

Within the past few weeks hundreds of persons in the metropolitan area have been delighted to receive what they thought was notice of a windfall due them from the gov- … velope impressively self-addressed to "Treasurer's Office, Headquarters Building, Washington 6, D. C."

And attached is an even more impressive form with a king-size American eagle printed at the top. …

Led by French paratroopers, exuberant crowd of Gaullists in Corsica sings the "Marseillaise" in support of Committee of Public Safety which has seized rule of the island. United Press International Photo.

. . . his theme is the glory and messianic mission of France . . . he drips contempt for America and hatred for Britain. . . . His chief supporters are militarists and imperialists. Democrats are now being blackmailed by threat of civil war. . . . In recent weeks he has continued his secret meetings with Soviet agents. . . . France cannot stand alone; so long as he maintains his hostility to America and Britain he needs a Soviet deal. . . .

—From an editorial, "DeGaulle Has a Record," on Page 20.

Who Had DeGall To Call WMGM?

The switchboards at radio stations WMGM and WINS were as hot as the French crisis today—and Gen. Charles de Gaulle was at least partially responsible.

WMGM had been laboring through the early morning hours trying to reach Gen. de Gaulle by phone for a statement. Success seemed near at 10:30 a.m. when a telephone jangled in the WMGM newsroom and an operator announced the general was ready to talk.

Break in Rock 'n' Roll.

Announcer Bill Edmunds dashed into the studio where Jerry Marshall's Record Room was rocking and rolling along, grabbed the open mike and told his listeners the next voice they heard would be Gen. de Gaulle's with a message for the American people.

The conversation that listener's heard went somethink like this:

EDMUNDS: This is WMGM, general. Do you have a statement to make?

VOICE: Are you a newspaper?

EDMUNDS: No, a radio station in New York City.

VOICE: I see. I will say that I am prepared to take over the government by peaceful means as an old soldier of France. Who did you say you were again?

EDMUNDS: WMGM radio in New York, general.

VOICE: But my station in New York is WINS. Vive la France! (Click).

Spokesman Called It Hoax.

Furious, WMGM promptly called the New York Telephone Co. and was told no overseas call had been completed for the station today.

"Hoax!" a WMGM spokesman cried. "And we intend to have the Federal Communications Commission get to the bottom of it."

Asked for comment, Art Tolchin, vice president and general manager at WINS, declared: "Don't know a thing about it."

Meanwhile, the switchboards of both stations are sizzling.

General on Way, 100,000 Protest

By JOSEPH W. GRIGG, United Press International.

PARIS, May 28.—President Rene Coty today summoned Gen. Charles de Gaulle to Paris—possibly to take over leadership of France.

Informed sources said President Coty had won agreement from the Catholic Popular Republicans and Independents) for Gen. de Gaulle to become premier. Together, the two parties control 175 votes in the 595-member National Assembly. A formal announcement of the new premier-designate was scheduled for 10 p.m. (5 p.m. New York time).

The general headed at once for Paris from his home at Colombey-les-Deux-Eglises, 150 miles away.

His apparent moment of destiny arrived just as an estimated 100,000 leftists and moderates marched across Paris protesting his rise toward power.

Police took elaborate precautions at Colombey to keep newsmen from trailing Gen. de Gaulle. Roads were blocked for 15 minutes.

For the first time, an escort car from France's Surete Generale, accompanied him.

At that moment tens of thousands of anti-de Gaulle demonstrators surged into the Place de la Bastille where the French Revolution of 1789 erupted. Former Premier Pierre-Mendes-France, head of the Radical (moderate) party, was among them.

"Fascism shall not pass," the crowd chanted in a rolling crescendo that drowned out rush-hour traffic "Long live the republic."

A lightning strike shut down Paris subways, buses and suburban trains, coinciding with the demonstrations and hitting the capital at its rush hour.

Powerful police reinforcements massed again around government buildings, the National Assembly, the Champs Elysees and particularly in the east end ready to act in case of disturbances. The Place de la Bastille, where the greatest demonstrations took place, is in eastern Paris.

Coty Sees Leaders.

President Coty was acting with all possible haste.

Earlier in the afternoon he conferred for two hours with leaders of three of France's middle-line parties. They were Socialist leader Guy Mollet, Independent leader Antoine Pinay and Catholic Popular Republican leader Pierre Henri Teitgen.

Informed sources said the call to Gen. De Gaulle was

Continued on Page Three.

Vanguard Soars 2000 Miles, Falls

By CHARLES TAYLOR, United Press International.

CAPE CANAVERAL, May 28.—The Navy reported early today the full-scale satellite launched last night with the Vanguard rocket shot 2000 miles into space but at an off-angle which caused it to plunge back to earth and burn.

It was the second consecutive failure of the Vanguard to blast a fully instrumented 20-inch satellite into orbit, the satellite President Eisenhower talked about in 1955 when he first announced this country's space program for the International Geophysical Year.

The Vanguard was fired at 11:44 p.m. New York time. It pierced a puff of clouds and in about two minutes was no longer visible.

At first it appeared the launching was successful and that the satellite would join in space the 6.4-inch Vanguard test moon put into orbit March 17, the two Explorers and gigantic Sputnik III which weighs 1½ tons.

Radio Corp. of America at Riverhead, L. I., reported it picked up a signal at 11:50

Continued on Page 14.

Safe Driving Is a Hit

United Press International.

CHESTERFIELD, England, May 28.—Drivers of two police cars staging a road safety demonstration before 8000 persons were unhurt yesterday when their autos crashed headon.

— Slow Down and Live —

Pickled Pink

United Press International.

CHICAGO, May 28.—Thom Koutsoukos, 27, who had his name changed to Johnny Pickleseed, has covered Indiana and Illinois on a pickle planting spree. "I've always had an ambition to be a deliverer of dills," he explained.

— Slow Down and Live —

The Weather

Safety Air Lanes Ordered by CAB

Stock Prices Drift In Light Trading

Results at Belmont Park

Steamroller Fails To Hurt Boy

Track Day for Orphans

Today's Index

For This Week Only SWEEPUZZLE Will Be Published TOMORROW Instead of Friday

A live broadcast over radio station WMGM, in which General Charles de Gaulle was heard to promote rival station WINS, made the front page.

Below: A free day at Aqueduct Race Track went to lucky listeners in "The Horse Picks the People" contest. Left to right: Jack Lacy, Nellie the Nag, and Rick Sklar. *(Mortimer Matz)*

Right: Al "Jazzbo" Collins, WINS air personality, at a contest in which listeners tuned in to learn where disc jockeys were handing out silver dollars. *(Mortimer Matz)*

Below: The WINS "Out-of-Gas Economy Run," which offered prizes to listeners who guessed how far each disc jockey could drive before running out of fuel. The race never officially started, because the announcers' union, The American Federation of Television and Radio Artists, refused to let its members race. Some of the DJs competed anyway. The WINS building at 7 Central Park West is in the background. *(Mortimer Matz)*

Right: Murray the K gives out free anti-freeze during a WINS promotion. *(Mortimer Matz)*

Below: The Murray the K subway promotion. Murray promised to live in the newly refurbished West Side IRT subway system until somebody found the silver subway token he had used. Here Murray gives away free records and broadcasts his show. *(Mortimer Matz)*

Murray the K gets donuts and coffee in the subway. *(Mortimer Matz)*

A staged shot of Murray in the subway. *(Mortimer Matz)*

Above: When New York City Parks Commissioner Robert Moses banned Joseph Papp's free Shakespeare in Central Park, I sent Murray the K into the park to do Hamlet. *(Mortimer Matz)*

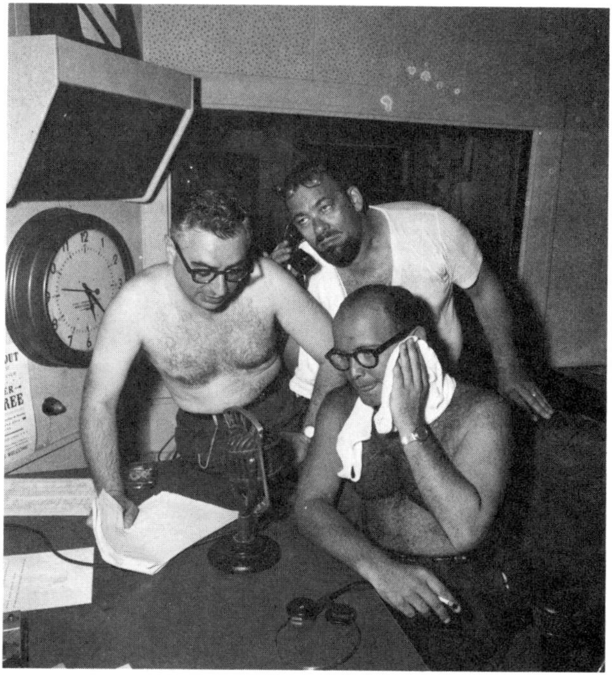

Right: WINS disc jockeys (left to right) Jack Lacy, Al ''Jazzbo'' Collins, and Stan Z. Burns, broadcasting from sweltering studios during New York City's 1959 power blackout. *(Mortimer Matz)*

DAILY NEWS

NEW YORK'S PICTURE NEWSPAPER®

5¢

Vol. 41. No. 283 Copr. 1960 News Syndicate Co. Inc. New York 17, N.Y., Friday, May 20, 1960* WEATHER: Mostly fair and mild.

ARREST FREED, 7 IN DJ PAYOLA

Queen Mother to Remarry?

Stories on Page 3

(NEWS foto by Hal Mathewson)

Tuned Out by DA. Program director Mel Leeds and disk jockeys Peter Tripp and Alan Freed (l. to r.) stand alongside Detective Michael Canning as they're booked at Elizabeth St. station. They were among eight radio personnel arrested on charge of commercial bribery, growing out of payola probe. —Story on page 3

The front page of the New York *Daily News* headlined the arrest of Disc jockey Alan Freed (second from right) on charges of commercial bribery for illegally taking money to play records on the radio. Freed later pleaded guilty to some of the charges. WMGM Disc jockey Peter Tripp (second from left) went to trial and was convicted. Charges against former WINS program director Mel Leeds (left) were eventually dropped. *(Copyright 1960, New York News Inc. Reprinted by permission.)*

J. Elroy McCaw, owner of WINS in 1960. McCaw purchased the station for $450,000 in 1954 after scraping together a small down payment. Shortly after this picture was taken, McCaw sold WINS for ten million dollars, at that time the highest price ever paid for a radio station. *(Mortimer Matz)*

CHAPTER 6

Riding the Rocket with Murray the K

The de Gaulle incident was the icing on the cake. WINS's rocket shot up to its ratings apogee in the spring of 1958.

I was happy. I was at the typewriter ten hours a day, knocking out contests, jingles, and promotion ideas. I saw less and less of WINS Program Director Mel Leeds, who was now spending much of his time in his office behind closed doors. The scene outside resembled a doctor's waiting room, but instead of patients the chairs were filled with record pluggers representing the major labels and artists. The smaller labels were dispatched to the record library where record librarian Ronnie Granger, a young black ex-city patrolman whom Leeds had hired, handled the "extras." There was pandemonium every day in the corridors near Leeds's office. Four hundred new singles were being released each week now. It cost very little to record a session; bands were doing it in hallways. Then they'd press five hundred copies and take them to radio stations. Only one record in a hundred might make it to the airwaves, but if that one clicked it was the pot of gold at the end of the rainbow.

The months moved along. Leeds married Ginny Collins, former wife of DJ Al "Jazzbo" Collins and moved to a penthouse at 37 Riverside Drive, where garage attendants each morning would deliver his Lincoln Continental sedan or racy white two-seat Jaguar convertible.

McCaw began to worry. The ratings and the music were making the station too prominent. He didn't want to be first or second in the market; he told me he would rather be a solid fourth. He wanted WINS to quietly appreciate in value as a property. His mind was already on the capital gain he would make when he sold the license and had to give only one dollar in every five to the government.

Leeds was also thinking about finances. He called me into his office one morning and told me he was borrowing some money but didn't want his wife to know about it so he was having the checks made out to me. That said, he held out a check and asked me to endorse it back over to him. My heart suddenly began to beat quickly.

"Mel, I can't do that," I told him. "I know you're my boss and I've always followed your instructions, but I can't have my name used that way. Years from now if anybody ever asked about it, how could I explain?"

"I shouldn't have asked," Leeds said.

A few weeks later, Leeds applied for a pistol permit. The police tried to talk him out of it, but he persisted and soon went everywhere with a small pistol in his belt.

Elroy began fencing with Leeds. McCaw had a crony, Irving Rosenthal, who owned Palisades Amusement Park across the Hudson River in New Jersey. Small and silver-haired, impeccably dressed in his custom-made blue suits, always with a twinkle in his eye, Rosenthal was the Walt Disney of his day in the amusement park business. In many ways he was very much like Elroy. He had worked his way up from the Cyclone roller coaster at Coney Island to secure his tenacious hold atop the cliffs the hard way. He often told the story of how he had opened his glittering rainbow-colored fantasy park, on the edge of the Palisades, with its soaring, dream-like towers and giant coaster lit by a million lights during the Depression-ridden thirties. The New Jersey Public Service Gas and Electric Company had asked him for a $5,000 deposit before they would turn on the lights and the rides, assuring him they would pay him four percent interest on his funds. Irving didn't have the money. He picked up the phone and called their president.

"I understand you'll pay me four percent on my money," he said.

"That's right, Mr. Rosenthal," the utility president told him.

"I'm sending over thirty thousand dollars," Irving replied. There was a long pause.

"Forget it," the voice on the other end said. "Your credit is good. We don't need a deposit from you."

Irving opened the park.

Irving wheeled and dealed with every radio station in town. He got free commercials on WNEW in return for putting their call letters on balloons he sold at Palisades Amusement Park. WMGM got space on the running electric sign facing Manhattan for *their* time. WOR got three-sheet posters that Irving's men plastered on vacant fences. Irving got more valuable air time from WOR.

Still, Irving Rosenthal had a problem. Irving lured crowds away from Coney Island and Rye Playland by staging free rock & roll shows in his park. But Irving's emcee lacked the clout to get big-name acts. Rosenthal was using Murray Kaufman, the all-night DJ on WMCA. When Irving pressured Kaufman, the DJ explained his dilemma. None of the performers cared whether or not Murray gave their records a spin in the middle of the night on WMCA. What Murray really needed was a gig on WINS. If Murray had a show on WINS he could get all the big-name acts Irving needed. Irving Rosenthal agreed. He would speak to Elroy McCaw the next time Elroy called to borrow Irving's car. Elroy's rule of never paying for anything extended to chauffeurs and limousines. When in New York, Elroy regularly borrowed transportation from Irving Rosenthal.

On Wednesday, Elroy phoned Irving; he needed the car. Irving took the occasion to explain the little problem he and Murray were having and to ask if Elroy could help him out.

Elroy knew Irving was pulling in one of his IOUs. The previous year, when McCaw was having trouble getting Anheuser–Busch to sponsor the play-by-play broadcasts of the New York Ranger hockey games and Knicks basketball, he had appealed to Rosenthal, who was close to the brewery management. A few weeks later Budweiser beer simultaneously picked up the sponsorship of the sportscasts and became the exclusive beer sold at Palisades Amusement Park in a three-way deal. Now came the payback.

"No problem," Elroy said. As long as Murray would work for three hundred dollars a week, the job was his. Murray Kaufman could start on WINS Monday night, right after the Alan Freed program.

But Elroy neglected to tell Mel Leeds about the deal. Leeds would only be upset anyway, since as program director he was in charge of hiring talent. Elroy disliked unpleasantries.

On Thursday night, Mel Leeds was sitting home in his penthouse. He could see the sun setting across the Hudson and the lights of Palisades Amusement Park glowing. Searchlights atop the cliffs swept the sky. Irving Rosenthal was running a charity telethon. Murray Kaufman was the emcee, and tonight at least, the show boasted big-name acts because it was all for a good cause. Crowds were pouring in to see the free show and spend their money on the rides and concessions.

Leeds sat back in his recliner and snapped on the TV set for a rare, quiet evening of entertainment and relaxation. The first thing he saw was Murray Kaufman's face filling the screen. The first thing he heard was Murray Kaufman's voice. It was saying something incredible. Murray was telling the viewers to tune him in on his new all-night show starting Monday on WINS. Leeds went bonkers. He jumped out of his chair and reached for the phone to call Elroy McCaw. Then he thought the better of it and hung up. As the telethon proceeded, Murray continued to promote himself and his new WINS show. Leeds didn't sleep that night; he didn't know what to do. In the morning he was tempted to walk into McCaw's office and resign. But after I talked with him for about an hour, he calmed down and decided to stay. His job was too good to give up.

On Monday morning, an enthusiastic Murray showed up to do his show. He asked me to help him. We began working together, and I took a liking to him. He was always good for a funny story and, like me, was determined to succeed. Together we worked out a new name for his show and a new name for Murray. It became "Murray the K and the Swingin' Soiree." He wanted gimmicks, but most of all, he wanted a way to introduce the oldies.

We were standing in the studio talking about it when I spotted a carbon dioxide fire extinguisher on the wall. I thought of a rhyme, grabbed the extinguisher, pulled out the safety pin, and yelled, "Here's a blast from the past" as I squeezed the firing handle. We recorded the sound with Murray doing the line and "A Blast from the Past" was born. Over the years the line spread to stations all over the country. Even on Radio Saigon, as portrayed in the film *Apocalypse Now*, they were announcing "A Blast from the Past."

Murray invented "Meussuray," a new way for teens to double-talk. It was simple and silly and involved adding an "eus" after the first consonant or diphthong of a word, or before the word if it began with a vowel. In a few weeks all the kids were speaking Meussuray. Over the air he began doing nonsensical shouts that sounded like old Indian rain chants: "Ahbay, ahbay, ooh wah wah, ahbay, ahbay, ooh wah wah, koowee summa summa." Submarine-race watching was the late-fifties idiom for making out in a car parked by a beach. Murray hosted imaginary Saturday night submarine-race watching parties along Brooklyn's Plumb Beach.

Meanwhile, McCaw, the genius at not spending his own money, had instituted still another economy—baseball re-creations. Instead of broadcasting the Yankee games from out-of-town stadiums and flying sportscasters all over the country where he would have to feed them and put the up in hotels, he re-created the games from the WINS studios using a running account of the play-by-play sent in by telegraph. Baseball, unlike basketball and hockey, was a game that could be described easily this way.

To set the atmosphere in the studio, Elroy's sportscaster, Les Keiter, wore Bermuda shorts under a Hawaiian-print, open sports shirt, and had a baseball cap pulled low on his forehead. Hunched over the microphone, he would eat popcorn while he described the game.

On the other side of the studio window, an engineer mixed in sound from two turntables. One contained a background recording of a stadium crowd, and the other a record of an excited crowd. By varying the balance between the two discs, the engineer could create any effect from a low murmur to the bedlam that follows a grand slam. When a batter hit a ball, Keiter would tap a small hollow sounding box with a drumstick to simulate the crack of the bat.

One afternoon, the Western Union circuit went out somewhere between New York and Chicago in the middle of a Yankee away game. Keiter found himself cut off from the action. Although Yankee baseball continued under sunny skies at Comiskey Park, dark clouds appeared on the horizon and it began to rain on the version of the game being broadcast from New York. Keiter suspended play and a mythical ground crew rolled out the tarpaulin and covered the infield for thirty minutes until the telegraph line began working again and play resumed. The audience never caught on.

The baseball season was barely underway before Elroy had other concerns. Alan Freed, now married to Inga, was rarely at WINS. When he wasn't broadcasting from Connecticut, he was on the

K-Doe • "There's a Moon Out Tonight" / *The Capris* • "Daddy's

road doing concerts. While WINS was presenting Freed's show with Paul Sherman sitting in, Freed was making headlines ruining an expensive vicuna coat, which ripped when he sat down in a football stadium the first time he wore it. Freed laughed off the incident.

Freed's concerts, however, were becoming less of a laughing matter. The audiences were getting harder to control and they clashed repeatedly with police, whom Freed accused of provoking the violence.

Every headline about a Freed concert caused McCaw to worry more. The publicity was bad, it was centering on a WINS disc jockey, and WINS's license was now worth millions of dollars.

Rumors began to circulate about the use of drugs by teenagers in the Freed audiences. Drug use by teens in the fifties was rare. In addition, the audiences were interracial, another fifties rarity. Parents were up in arms. Matters came to a head on May third when a Boston concert ended in a riot.

When Freed returned from Boston, McCaw wanted no more of him. His contract was just ending and Elroy decided not to renew. Freed met all day with McCaw and tried to convince Elroy to keep him. Freed pleaded. He had a sold out concert in Newark that weekend. The acts would perform only if Freed could play their records. Without a radio station there would be no concert. Elroy was unmoved. Freed called the arena and tentatively canceled the concert while he bargained with McCaw.

Freed was still in McCaw's office when a concert promoter burst in the rear door to the station (next to the record library), gun in hand, looking for Freed. My pregnant wife, Sydelle, and Inga Freed, who were standing at the Coke machine, took one look and dashed into the record library, locking the door and barricading themselves inside.

The executive offices were also locked from the inside. The promoter left the station frustrated, unable to find Freed who was still meeting in McCaw's office. By 9 PM, when the meeting ended, Freed was still alive, but he was finished at WINS. That night Paul Sherman, the "Crown Prince of Rock & Roll," replaced Alan Freed at the microphones.

With Sherman and Murray the K on the air at night, McCaw and Leeds hoped to make it through the summer while looking for a permanent replacement for Freed. But the arrival of summer

Home" / *Shep and the Limelights* • "A Hundred Pounds of Clay" /

marked the expiration day of the union staff announcers' contract. McCaw sallied forth to do battle. Now that WINS was making money, the staff announcers wanted in on the big bucks. On July 1, 1958, the American Federation of Television and Radio Artists (AFTRA) struck WINS. A picket line of announcers driving open convertibles with picket signs mounted on the back seats circled the block continually. By the third day, they were picketing in the morning and driving to the beaches to go swimming in the afternoon. McCaw's answer to the strike was to first call the air force and then tell Leeds to find some new jocks. (McCaw maintained a commission in the Air Force Reserve, and he sometimes used air force flights to get back and forth between New York and Seattle for free. He was in no hurry to negotiate with AFTRA.)

Leeds brought in some unknown DJs, including a young Brooklynite who had recently graduated from New York University and was now Bermuda's first rock jock, the fast-talking Bruce Morrow. Bruce had always been interested in radio and had started a radio station for New York University during his years on the Washington Square campus. When Bruce Morrow came on the air for the first time, at a salary of $80 a week, the striking announcers thought McCaw had lost his mind, putting such a sound on the air. The rapid-fire patter, punctuated periodically by a warbling "eeeyaaaaeeeyaaaeeeyaaa" that seemed to come from deep in his throat, was beyond their comprehension. The kids thought otherwise. Delirious with disbelief, they mobbed the studio. They had found their idol. Bruce, who had been brought up in Brooklyn and had gone to Madison High, spoke the language of the baby-boom teen generation.

The weather finally cooled down. It got too cold to go swimming, so the announcers came back to work. Rather than give them a big raise, Elroy wrote their individual names into the contract for life. He would let the next owner of WINS worry about fulfilling *that* obligation. One of the other settlement terms agreed to by the union was that Bruce Morrow would be permitted to stay on at WINS.

After the strike ended, WINS was beset by one calamity after another. Good ideas brought unexpected results. We ran announcements stating that each week we would pay $10.10 for the best news tip phoned in by a listener. I was walking through the newsroom one day when the news tip phone rang. I picked it up.

"Is this WINS?" It was the voice of a young man. I assured him it was. "I have a scoop for you. Are you the station that has commercials every ten minutes for the Polo Grounds Rodeo?"

"That's right," I told him. Our sales department had signed a huge contract with a big smiling cowboy who called himself Oklahoma Tex. Since the rodeo had arrived in town, the temperature had risen to the upper nineties with no breeze. The rodeo had been playing to groups of eight hundred and nine hundred people in the sweltering 50,000-seat stadium.

"Well," said the caller, "I live in an apartment overlooking the George Washington Bridge. It was so hot last night I couldn't sleep. About three in the morning I saw fifty head of cattle, a wagon train, thirty cowboys, and ten Indians heading west across the bridge. I think it was your rodeo."

I called the Polo Grounds. Then I checked the sales department. We were out more than $10.10. We had lost the biggest account of the month.

In the fall, Bruce Morrow was moved into Freed's slot. He got his on-the-air nickname one night when an elderly black woman preaching brotherly love visited the studio, told him all men were cousins, and called him "Cousin Brucie." Bruce built on the philosophy and began doing record hops at Palisades Park, where—clad in a leopard skin print tuxedo (fifties rock & roll chic)—he strove to create an atmosphere of wholesomeness and fun among the teens. Bruce drank only milk and orange juice and never smoked.

In Freed's former time slot, Bruce Morrow found himself besieged by rock acts and their managers. Every act that hit New York headed first for Bruce's WINS studios. One afternoon Ray Peterson drove up to WINS in a van with his protégé, Curtis Lee, and the Curtis Lee show. They ran upstairs to play their new record, "Pretty Little Angel Eyes," for Bruce. He liked it and put it on his show. They thanked everyone at the station and went back down to the van. It was empty. Their luggage, costumes, guitars, and amplifiers were gone. They had left the doors of the van unlocked in midtown Manhattan. All they had left was the song. But it was on WINS, it was a hit, so they could use the proceeds to buy new threads and new boxes. And they did.

* * *

"Mashed Potato Time" / *Dee Dee Sharpe* • "Duke of Earl" / *Gene*

To enhance the new image of the station, we ran a contest to find the world's youngest disc jockey and ended up hiring clean-cut, sixteen-year-old high school student, Mitch Lebe.

WINS's new image extended all the way into the news department. One of our sponsors, Northwest Orient Airlines, lent WINS a bicycle-drawn rickshaw called a pedicab. We taped signs that read WINS MOBILE UNIT ½ over the airline insignia, parked the rickshaw in the lobby, and planned to use it when we covered fun news events.

One day at lunchtime, some fun-loving salesmen decided to take the rickshaw for a joyride. One sat on the bike while the others drank martinis in the cab. As they drove out of the lobby, they failed to notice that the axle of the front bike wheel was held in place only by a clumsy yoke mechanism and that the wing nuts on the yoke were loose. The driver pedaled into Central Park, across the street from the radio station, staying on the pedestrian path. The path was a downhill; the rickshaw picked up speed. As it lurched forward, the driver began hunting for the brake controls. He found a lever on his left side and pulled it, but not hard enough. The pedicab hurtled forward. Just then the front wheel started to slip loose and the rickshaw went out of control. The salesman shouted for the people in their path to get out of the way. Most did. An elderly ex-boxer, in need of a shave and his clothes in tatters, stumbled directly in front of them. At that instant, the front wheel slipped out of the yoke and the rickshaw overturned. The salesman who had been pedaling threw himself at the old man in their path, knocking him aside. As the other salesman pulled themselves out from under the wreckage, the old man who had been knocked down started to get up, but another shabbily dressed geezer whispered something in his ear and the man dropped to the pavement, moaning and rolling about. One of the salesmen quickly pulled the WINS sign off the the pedicab, revealing the Northwest Orient Airlines insignia.

By this time I was aware of the commotion and, after observing the scene from my office window, I alerted station manager Jock Fearnhead, Mel Leeds, and other WINS officials. We raced downstairs. By now several hundred people were forming a circle around the overturned rickshaw, several policemen were on the scene, and the sound of an ambulance siren could be heard in the distance. As many of us as possible piled into the ambulance with

Chandler • "I Can't Stop Loving You" / *Ray Charles* • "Big Girls

the man and raced to Roosevelt Hospital, sirens wailing. When it backed up to the emergency room and the doors opened, the startled interns saw a scene out of a circus act. Sixteen people—the victim, his friend, station officials, police, and the radio salespeople—piled out of the back.

''What happened? one of the doctors asked.

''This man,'' the ambulance attendant replied, ''was run over by a rickshaw.''

After Thanksgiving, the atmosphere changed; the engineers union struck WINS and a car struck Elroy. On one of his trips home to his family in Seattle, Elroy McCaw's sedan was hit head-on by an auto driven by an army sergeant. Elroy sustained multiple leg fractures that took months to heal, and he was unable to negotiate. The engineers' union had planned the strike at the height of the basketball and hockey season to put added pressure on Elroy. With Elroy out of action, we gave mailroom boy Bruce Wendell a crash course in engineering and sent him around the country to hook up the sports remotes. Secretaries manned the simpler setups in the Central Park West studios. The broadcasts were flawless. McCaw decided to stay away from WINS even after he recovered, hoping the cold weather would drive the men back to work. The strike dragged on through Christmas and into 1959. Elroy started negotiating in January. One day, pickets, knowing Elroy had recovered from the accident but was using the crutches for sympathy, deliberately bumped into him as he crossed the picket line and sent the crutches flying. Elroy slipped on the icy sidewalk and fell. Then he got up and walked into the station without the crutches. His ruse was exposed, but he won anyway. The engineers came back to work with a token raise and mailroom boy Wendell, an Alan Freed fan who had walked in off the street at the age of eighteen begging to sweep the floors, was promoted to DJ-show producer.

No sooner had the strike ended than tragedy struck WINS. Morning man Irv Smith, who was supposed to be asleep in his suburban home by 9 P.M. so he could get up at 4:30 A.M. and drive into town for his show, was spending more and more nights in Greenwich Village living it up. One night after midnight, he was racing home to get a few hours of sleep when his Chrysler, which was going ninety miles per hour, hit a lamp post on the

Henry Hudson Parkway. They found his body slumped over the wheel and a highway patrolman called the station after seeing a WINS employee ID card in Irv's wallet.

Murray the K was thrown into the mornings while Leeds looked for Irv's replacement. To distract the audience, we began involving Murray in frantic station promotions. The West Side subway had just been upgraded, and I had a gimmick. Murray would be the first passenger on the new system and would drop a silver subway token into the turnstile, putting it in circulation. The token would be used again and again until some lucky passenger spotted it and turned it in. Until then Murray would have to live in the subway as "The Mole in the Hole." The finder would win a year's supply of tokens.

Bruce Morrow's father silver-plated some tokens for us in his kitchen canister factory, and I cut identifying grooves in them to guard against fraudulent copies. Then we announced over the air that Murray the K would broadcast his show from the Columbus Circle subway station hot dog stand. He would continue to do so until somebody turned in the token. In reality, subway detectives assigned to Murray smuggled him out of the subway each night and into the Mayflower Hotel upstairs, where Murray had a suite of rooms stocked with food, drink, and female companionship for all.

Bogus silver subway tokens, made mostly in high school chemistry labs, flooded the subway system. I knew they weren't the real thing because they didn't have the grooves cut in them. Mel Leeds was sure none was the real token because he had pocketed it when Murray entered the subway system the first time.

After eight days, Leeds, accompanied by a parade of photographers, posed as a token attendant at the West Twenty-eighth Street subway station and slipped the real silver token to the first photogenic blond who came along. She happened to be a psychoanalyst's receptionist who knew nothing about the token and had never listened to WINS. The station's public relations director had to explain it all to her before Murray the K was "released" to the sunshine and fresh air.

While the city cooperated with us and let us use the subway system for our promotion, they were giving a hard time to a young producer named Joe Papp whose troupe was giving free performances of Shakespeare in Central Park without permission. When

New York City Parks Commissioner Robert Moses banned Papp from the park, I sensed a publicity bonanza. I dressed Murray the K as Hamlet. Escorted by two part-time models in Elizabethan costumes and with his own eight-year-old son Keith dressed as a page, Murray strode into the park with a Pocket Books edition of the play in hand.

Murray performed Hamlet's soliloquy. We tipped off every paper in town and called the police and the parks department, hoping for a confrontation. The authorities looked the other way, but we made the centerfold in every paper in town. It was a spectacular shot. Murray was pointing his sword in the air and bellowing, "To be or not to be," as the press cameras went off.

The next week we sent Murray to Mitchell Field to do his show from an air force jet trainer at forty thousand feet. The flight broadcast sounded thrilling, but I later found out that Murray had taken one look at a jet fighter doing rolls in the air and decided to do the show from the ground with the engines roaring in the background.

The summer was drawing to an end and we gave the ratings one more shot in the arm. We announced we would give away a car to a morning listener who picked the key to it from a barrel at Roosevelt Raceway. The car dealer had put thousands of keys in the barrel, but had made sure that none of them fit. Leeds, however, had a key that worked, and he tossed it in with the others. When a track patron won the car, the dealer was furious, but had to give it away.

By then, Murray thought he was entrenched in the morning show, but Mel Leeds's attention was on developments at WNBC across town. NBC had canceled Al "Jazzbo" Collins. The child support that Mel's wife Ginny was getting for Bruce Collins, Jazzbo's son from his previous marriage to Ginny, stopped.

Leeds announced that he was putting Al Collins on the morning show. "I'm giving my husband-in-law a job," he told me.

Leeds had earlier put another relative on the payroll as a producer and had given Ginny's brother, Fred Parsons, the "golden time" Sunday night announcing shift (the only night shift where the AFTRA contract did not permit McCaw to pay a reduced rate differential).

Collins had a low-key, cool style on the air and normally played jazz. That didn't bother Leeds. Mel would handle his music scheduling.

Leeds also had to handle all the other music scheduling for a while because our music librarian, Ronnie Granger, decided to get married. The low-salaried Granger invited every record company executive, music publisher, and promotion man in the city to a wedding that strained the facilities of the Grand Ballroom of the Roosevelt Hotel. After the nuptials Granger and his bride drove off in a new Thunderbird and headed for a Paris honeymoon. (When Ronnie Granger returned from his honeymoon Elroy gave him a ten-dollar-a-week raise and transferred him to the news department. Granger quit WINS the next week.)

One of the quietest guests at the reception was Elroy McCaw. He was becoming more and more concerned about the possibility of payola threatening his right to own WINS. As McCaw knew only too well, the FCC could move to revoke the license of a station if it could prove severe wrongdoing or could show that the station was not operating in the public interest.

There were several incidents that caused apprehension. One night Murray called in sick at the last minute, and I had to scramble to get a substitute disc jockey. I finally located one of our part-timers, who raced to the station while I hastily assembled a stack of records.

A little over an hour after we went on the air, the control room phone rang. I picked it up. A gutteral voice asked, "Where's my record?"

"I beg your pardon?" I replied.

"Where's my record?" The caller was getting angry.

"I don't know what you mean," I said.

"My deal with Murray is that he plays my record at eight-fifteen. Where's my record?"

I looked at the clock. It was 8:24. "I don't know anything about your deal with Murray," I replied. "Who is this?" The phone went dead. After the show I checked back and found that every night at 8:15 for the previous six weeks Murray had featured the same record on his show.

As rumors of payola grew, and Elroy became more uneasy, he began ordering that records he didn't like be taken off the air. Then he would wait and see if anybody on the staff became unduly

Rose • "He's a Rebel" / *The Crystals* • "Palisades Park" / *Freddy*

upset. One record that he yanked was Johnny Horton's "The Battle of New Orleans," the song that became the number one record of the year. McCaw began making so many changes in the music lists that, musically speaking, we had one station when he was in town and virtually another format when he went home to Seattle.

One day Elroy banned some records, checked the plane schedules to the West Coast, and asked to be driven to the airport. That night, after the records had been put back on the air, McCaw showed up at the station and took them off again.

Manager Jock Fearnhead decided he'd had enough of McCaw's antics. He quietly bought a radio station in Honolulu, sending WINS's bright young producer, Tom Rounds, on ahead to run it. Fearnhead then left on an ocean liner via the Panama Canal.

McCaw grew more and more troubled. He learned that a major federal investigation of the broadcasting industry was brewing. Elroy's government contacts were extensive. He had maintained many of his OSS connections after the war and was quite possibly still engaged in government intelligence work during the time that he owned WINS. (McCaw associates tell of saying good-bye to him in New York, with plans to meet him in Chicago the next day, only to have McCaw call from Cairo and cancel the meeting.) Elroy McCaw quietly began assembling a private team of his own investigators to look more closely at the activities of his own employees. (McCaw was the unauthorized civilian whose inadvertent admission to a National Security Council meeting at the White House caused a furor in 1961. He was a member of the National Security Advisory Council, placed there, along with other key industry figures, by his old boss, Air Force General Hap Arnold. One day Elroy came to Washington for an advisory council meeting, unaware that it had been canceled. When he couldn't find the meeting, he called Arnold's office and, at the mention of the words Security . . . Council" was told by a confused secretary that the meeting had already started. She sent an air force staff car for him and called ahead to alert the White House that McCaw was coming. When McCaw arrived, he was rushed to the session. He was taken to a darkened room where President Kennedy and the Joint Chiefs of Staff were studying slides and maps of the Berlin Blockade. When the lights came up McCaw found himself sitting near Kennedy and joined the conversation, making what he considered an appropriate remark about the situation. Kennedy left the room

Cannon • "She Cried" / *Jay and the Americans* • "Breaking Up Is

for thirty minutes while members of the council began whispering discreetly to their aides, asking who McCaw was. By the time the meeting ended, it was obvious that the nation's top-level security procedures had been breached. Although McCaw produced his Air Force Reserve card and explained himself, he was detained until the council's actions had been carried out and his own status in the Air Force Reserve had been retroactively reactivated to sanction his presence. A fictionalized version of this incident later appeared in the novel *On Instructions of My Government* by ex-presidential press secretary Pierre Salinger.)

The government's investigations went public with a bang. Television's top-rated program, a quiz show called "The $64,000 Question," was exposed as a sham in which contestants had been rehearsed. We broadcast a parody of the exposé on WINS that I called "The Big Fix"—a gag feature where our own employees were contestants. All had been coached and already knew the answers, which were displayed ahead of time in the window of a local bank. We got some laughs, but only for a week. The next thing we knew, the government was turning its attention from television to radio, and was looking in particular for payola to disc jockeys and program directors.

When investigators for Oren Hatch's House Legislative Oversight subcommittee raised the question of payola, Elroy McCaw sat tight, hoping WINS would not be involved. Murray the K, however, fired off a telegram to the committee calling the charges "without foundation" and demanding that a public apology be made immediately. He signed the telegram as head of the National Council for Disc Jockeys for Public Service. When reporters asked Kaufman who the other council members were, he was unable to name anyone except WNEW DJ Art Ford, who he said was "inactive."

The atmosphere at WINS grew tense.

CHAPTER 7

Stakeout at Stampler's

It's now called The Conservatory, and in the late fifties when I worked at WINS it was known as Bob Olin's Restaurant. But for most of the years in between it was Stampler's Steak House, a watering hole and one-time radio hangout in a corner of the Mayflower Hotel on Central Park West just north of the WINS studios. I still think of it as Stampler's.

On December 18, 1959, at 3:05 P.M., Mel Leeds called me into his office.

"I have just had the most peculiar phone call," he said. "A man who called himself Mr. Jordan told me that my telephone at home was being tapped. He said he could make a call and prove it. He told me not to say anything other than the ABCs over the telephone. He also said he wanted to meet me and told me that I could identify him by a red shirt and some bridgework he was having done in his mouth."

Mel talked continually, explaining every detail of the telephone conversation.

"That's wild," I said. I sat down. "What are you going to do about it?"

"I've already called the police. I tried to get [Captain] Matarese at the Eighteenth Precinct, but he wasn't in. One of the detectives told me it was okay to meet with the man but only in some public place . . . you know, not any alleys."

I thought for a moment.

"Mel," I guessed, "this must be the guy who's doing the tapping. He probably wants to blackmail you. Is there anything you've been saying over the telephone that you wouldn't want anyone to know about?"

"Rick, absolutely not," Leeds replied. He then surmised that the caller was attempting a random canvass of New York radio executives in the hope of striking pay dirt over payola. Leeds then asked me if I would accompany him when he met the man.

"I've told him I would meet him in the lobby of this building at three-thirty." It was already 3:15.

"Don't you think my presence might frighten him away?" I asked.

"Maybe, but let's see how stupid he is. At the very least you might get a look at him." Leeds explained that he was also going to have his secretary, Florence Ludwig, replace the lobby switchboard operator and observe the situation unseen from her little cubbyhole.

"Who is this guy?" I asked.

"He says his name is Jordan and that he's staying at the Alvin Hotel, but I called the hotel and there is no such person registered."

I shrugged my shoulders.

When we were in place, only Leeds could be seen from the street doors. At 3:30 a heavyset man entered the lobby from the Central Park West side. He wore a solid red shirt open at the collar under his coat. I began playing Sherlock Holmes and took snapshots of him in my mind. His right front tooth was missing, as was the tip of his right ring finger. His ears were set unusually close to his head. His black hair was combed back and was turning at the temples, and his nose was flattened like a boxer's.

Leeds went up to meet Jordan and immediately waved me over and introduced me as his assistant. Jordan, a tough talker, suggested we go somewhere for a cup of coffee. He didn't want the coffee shop next door because it was crowded. We adjourned to Bob Olin's Restaurant, where we sat down in a booth.

"Let me tell you, Leeds," Jordan began, "your home phone's being tapped. I know who's doing it, and I'm in a position to stop it."

"Are *you* doing it?" I interrupted.

"Oh no," he said, "most of the taps in New York are being handled by a Mr. Weinert, and the people doing the taps are supplying information to publishers and others who are interested in the information. I've been in the city since March on a number of jobs, and I can assure you this is not the first job that's being done on a radio station. I'm sort of a leg man for some of these publishers who are interested in getting facts. One of them is *Confidential* magazine. Leeds, your telephone has been tapped for the past two days, but the tap was taken off yesterday afternoon. It's back on line now, but if we can come to an arrangement, it can be removed by seven-thirty tonight.''

Leeds leaned forward and stared at Jordan. ''I've checked the Alvin Hotel and you're not registered there.''

''You know I wouldn't call and give you my real name the first time we talked. It's Tony Bosco.'' He produced a press ID card, issued for 1958 by the Boston Police Department, identifying him as a reporter for a Boston newspaper.

''I'm wondering,'' said Jordan/Bosco, ''whether you know Bob Leder and Phil Dean who used to work at WINS, and whether these men left under other than friendly circumstances.'' We stared at Bosco in silence. ''Let me tell you,'' he continued, ''there are just reels and reels of tapes of all Alan Freed's conversations. Freed did all his business on the phone. It was stupid for him to have done that; most of his associates have stabbed him in the back. And there's been a huge tapping job going on at WNEW. Disc jockey's phones are being tapped. Leeds, if I were you, I wouldn't say more than the ABCs on the telehone. I can tell you that there is a spy at WINS who is funneling information out. It could be a man, it could be a secretary, it could be anyone. I know who this person is, and when you give me the two-hundred-fifty-dollar down payment, I will reveal that name. Let me give you an example of what I am talking about. There is a stenotypist for the Oren Hatch congressional committee on legislative oversight who has been reached. Her name is Delores Haddad, and she's leaking out closed testimony. She even has Bobby Darin's testimony; you know he's named two or three disc jockeys who have taken payola. Leeds, you're in an important position to pick music. I think you've taken a buck!''

Leeds leaned forward again. ''It might surprise you to learn that I have not.''

''Now, Mr. Leeds,'' Bosco continued, ''these wire tappers do not work in the building where your penthouse is on Riverside Drive. They work several blocks away. Once they locate the two proper wires in a large cable containing many other pairs of wires, they can do all the tapping they want.'' He pulled out a pack of

Come" / *Ruby and the Romantics* • "My Boyfriend's Back" / *The* cigarettes and tapped two of them up. "There are some investigators," he continued, "who work inside radio stations, who use recorders inside cigarette packs just like this. There are others who have microphones in the form of tie clasps. Now I am not bugged at the moment, but you'd better watch out. There's a Mr. Foley who might show up at the station. He could be dressed as a laundry or towel man.

"Leeds, I want to work for you. I want to help you. For two hundred fifty dollars down, I will see to it that the taps on your telephone are taken off and all the tapes made so far from those taps are destroyed. When you give me the money I will tell you who the spy is at WINS and I will even give you a signed receipt that will implicate me, and you can return that to me with another two hundred fifty dollars when the tap has been removed."

"Is that all?" Leeds asked.

"Oh no, the remainder of the job will be that I continue giving information about you and WINS to the people who are paying me for it, but it will be false information, and I will also let you know what I am doing."

"Excuse me," I asked, "what proof can you possibly give to back up what you are saying?"

"Well," he replied, "if you don't believe the tap is being removed, there's a certain telephone repairman who can check the cables. I'll tell you his name. I also want the money immediately, because *Argosy* magazine is coming out with a payola series and is interested in the information."

"I'll need the weekend to think this over," Leeds replied.

"Oh no," said Bosco, "you want the weekend to *talk* it over. Absolutely not. I want the money right now."

"Look," Leeds said, "I would have to get the money from someone else who is connected with WINS, and they are out of town and will have to be reached by long-distance phone."

"Suppose we make a deadline of seven-thirty Friday night," said Bosco. "I'll give you the room number where you can reach me at the Alvin."

Bosco left.

When we returned to the radio station, Leeds went upstairs and again called the police. He was on a first-name basis with many detectives at the Fifty-fourth Street station house; he had gotten his pistol permit there.

Angels • "Fingertips Part 2" / *Little Stevie Wonder* • "It's My

The detectives asked us to come down to a strategy meeting at the Criminal Courts building in lower Manhattan, where they suggested that Leeds call back Bosco and make an appointment to pay him the money. They suggested that Leeds be bugged and that he record as long a conversation as possible before handing over the payment. At that point, they explained, they would move in and make the arrest.

"Wait a minute," I protested, "we don't know who this person is. Suppose he doesn't want to be arrested and tries to shoot his way out of the situation? He'll think that Leeds turned him in and he might shoot Leeds."

"That's right," the detective in charge of the case agreed, "but what else can we do?"

"Maybe you can arrest both of them," I said.

"Good idea!" he said.

The detectives then asked Leeds to call the Alvin Hotel, using a telephone that was hooked up to a tape recorder. Bosco answered the phone and suggested they meet the following night at 8:30 back at Bob Olin's restaurant. Leeds agreed.

Getting the payoff money turned out to be the biggest problem of all. The police don't provide it.

"Get it from your employer," they said, "but copy down all the serial numbers of the bills."

Business manager Tony Soupious had to make several calls to Seattle to get Elroy McCaw's permission to release the money to Mel Leeds. The most annoying part of the situation was that the WINS Christmas party at Tavern on the Green was planned for that same night, and it now appeared that we would have to miss the festivities.

Friday afternoon, Leeds, his secretary, and I went down again to the Criminal Courts building. As we drove, snowflakes began sticking to the windshield of the car. By the time we got downtown, it was snowing heavily.

Once in the Criminal Courts building, we went to a room reserved for detectives, where Leeds obligingly removed his coat and shirt and had a miniature tape recorder taped just below his rib cage. A wire led through his shirt to a microphone on a tie clasp.

"Now, remember," the detectives explained, "keep him talking as long as you can, and when you are ready to pay off, hand him

Party" / *Leslie Gore* • "Louie Louie" / *The Kingsmen* • "Blowin' in

the money in an envelope—and after he takes it, you take off your eyeglasses. That will be the signal for us to move in."

Leeds nodded.

I got to Bob Olin's early and took up a position at the bar with Mel's secretary, Florence, who pretended to be my date. Restaurant manager Werner Baer was acting as bartender that night but knew nothing about the setup.

While we sat with our drinks, two detectives walked in and slipped into a booth near the side door to the restaurant. Two others lounged near the Central Park West entrance. Two more detectives appeared; one of them loitering near a door leading to the Mayflower Hotel lobby, while the other walked into the coat room, took over the concession, and began checking hats and coats. Unfortunately, he and the other detectives continued wearing their hats, and they looked exactly like six detectives on a stakeout. It seemed so obvious a setup; I wondered if Bosco would notice them.

My job was to nod affirmatively from the bar when the suspect walked in. I looked at my watch; it was 8:25. Just then the revolving door at the Central Park side turned, and Bosco walked briskly into the restaurant. Leeds was already seated. Bosco made directly for the booth. I nodded my head and the detectives at the side door nodded back. Time stood still. Leeds and Bosco seemed to talk forever. In fact, about thirty minutes passed. Then we saw Leeds reach into his jacket pocket, pull out an envelope, and hand it to Bosco. Leeds then took off his tiny reading spectacles and waved them in the air.

The six detectives converged on the booth. Bosco, who was busy counting the money, did not notice. A very large detective tapped him on the shoulder. Bosco looked up. The detective flashed a badge. Bosco's eyes immediately took in the situation. He was on his feet instantly with his hands in the air. He had obviously been through this routine before. Two detectives patted him down, then all six of them surrounded him and followed him to the door. Leeds, who had also put his hands up, now dropped them, relieved, and followed. Florence and I grabbed our coats from the backs of our bar stools and joined the procession while the astonished restaurant manager watched from behind the bar.

Outside, the snowstorm had become a blizzard. The temperature had dropped, and the wind was ferocious. The chief detective glanced around with a worried look and said, "Where's the wagon? Who called for the wagon?"

There was a brief exchange before all six detectives started yelling, "Taxi!" and waving frantically at the passing traffic. No cabs stopped. We fanned out. Everyone in the party began calling for cabs. The wind was so biting that my face began to hurt. Bosco looked around in alarm, then he too started to wave frantically, yelling, "Taxi, taxi!"

Finally the detectives used their badges to flag down some cabs. We all rode to the Criminal Courts building for the booking.

A few weeks later the case of one Elio Bosco was placed before the grand jury. His record included a string of arrests and convictions in Boston for similar activities. While waiting to testify before the grand jury, I was amazed to run into the executive staff of radio station WNEW also waiting to testify. Notations about the station had been found in Bosco's hotel room. He had been shaking them down, and they had been paying him for a number of months to buy his silence, fearful that he had something on the station's disc jockeys. A search of his belongings revealed that he had simply been operating from newspaper clippings, hunches, and the instincts of his "profession." The wire taps turned out to have been fictions.

Considering the nature of the music business and the widespread practice of payola, Bosco might well have succeeded in his scam had he not picked the unpredictable Mel Leeds for a victim. Beginning at the turn of the century, song pluggers had played the piano in the sheet music store windows, then had manned the front lines for the music business the way salespeople do in other industries. Like most other purveyors of products, they entertain, they cajole, they sell—and some of them bribe. Because the airwaves broadcasters use are in limited supply, somebody must play traffic cop and decree who shall broadcast on each frequency. That somebody is the government. With the pronouncement that the airwaves belong to the people, radio stations long ago fell under federal regulation and licensing, and their practices came under the scrutiny of headline-seeking politicians.

So long as only major labels made up the field, the plugging of records was a marginal phenomenon that drew scant attention. Rock & roll music changed all that. Hundreds of small, indepen-

Crystals • **1964** • "Hello, Dolly" / *Louis Armstrong* • "I Want to

dent, unknown record companies burst into the arena, challenging the industry's Goliaths with music that the major labels shied away from. In a business where airplay meant life or death to a new record, violation of the statutes on commercial bribery hardly constituted an obstacle. Even the rare conviction resulted in little more than a wrist-slapping.

As the big beat sound caught on and radio station ratings soared, the disc jockeys who controlled so much of the record airplay grew bold. Over Memorial Day weekend of 1959, twenty-five hundred of them held a convention in Miami Beach where record companies, large and small, fell over themselves to entertain the announcers. The result was a display of favor currying that caused leaders of more discreet industries to cringe, the public to gasp, and congressional investigators to get out their pads, sharpen their pencils, and then their knives.

A picture in *Life* magazine showed DJs in the lobby of the Americana Hotel throwing what appeared to be hundreds of dollar bills in the air like confetti. Other sources told of jocks returning to their rooms to find their beds occupied by hookers clad only in ribbons that read "Thanks for the Spins."

The convention simply brought together under one roof scenes that were going on regularly in every large American city. The "normal" business entertainment for a DJ or greedy program director was only just getting started when the music publisher or record plugger picked up the dinner check. From there it moved to a private suite where call girls, cash, expensive gifts, and drugs were available for the taking. For some, it became a way of life.

Considering those circumstances, one can easily see why Bosco thought he had come up with a foolproof scheme. His trial, however, never took place. He copped a plea and was put away for a year.

CHAPTER 8

Air into Money

After Bosco's arrest, I left for a previously scheduled Christmas vacation in Florida. Just before I locked my desk, Mel Leeds called me aside.

"You might see some unusual stories in the papers while you're away," he said. "No matter what they say, don't worry." He was no more specific than that.

New York papers are as common in Miami Beach as they are in Times Square, and I checked them every day. There was nothing for a week; then the *Daily News* reported that Claire Kaufman was divorcing Murray the K. A reporter interviewed a delicatessen delivery boy who swore that he knew what Claire Kaufman looked like, and that the woman opening Murray's apartment door when he rang with deliveries was not Claire.

When I returned to work, Mel Leeds did not look well. He informed McCaw that he was having a heart problem, and he stayed home for a week. Then he went on vacation, leaving me to look after the station in his absence. On January 26, 1960, I received a letter from Leeds saying he had resigned to take a job at KDAY, a station near Los Angeles. He said that being a "sentimental jerk," he found it hard to say good-bye to everybody and asked me to say his good-byes for him.

When I opened the letter, I was momentarily surprised. My first thought was, How will I keep the station operating? I told my secretary to move our files into the program director's office. I walked in and sat down at the desk Mel used to occupy. It had been cleaned out. I reviewed in my mind all of the operations that were underway and made a methodical list of everything that needed to be done in the upcoming weeks.

Then I called Seattle and told Elroy McCaw not to worry about the operation of the station. I assured him that everything would flow smoothly until he decided what he wanted to do about replacing Mel. He thanked me and told me to proceed.

On February 4, the *New York Post* broke a headline story that Mel Leeds had resigned because investigators were probing payola at the station.

"There have been rumors," McCaw told the papers. "Mel denied that he had done anything improper, and we have no proof to the contrary. We have been conducting a probe into the payola, and he resigned during the investigation."

McCaw was not the only one conducting an investigation. For three months, the chief district attorney of the City of New York, Frank Hogan, and his assistant, Joe Stone, had quietly been having their people go over the books of record company distributors and other industry businesses. Leeds knew from information leaked to him by detectives that his activities and those of employees at other radio stations were under surveillance.

On Thursday, May 19, 1960, a grand jury indicted five New York radio disc jockeys, one program director, and two former record librarians on charges that they had accepted payola. Hogan said the eight had taken illegal gratuities totaling $116,580 from twenty-three record companies over the last two years in return for playing certain records on their radio programs. Alan Freed was named on twenty-five counts charging that he took bribes, including a single payment of $25,000 from one record company. Mel Leeds was charged with taking $9,675 in payola while he was program director at WINS. WINS's former record librarian, Ronnie Granger, was accused of taking bribes. Other indictments named Peter Tripp, a WMGM disc jockey, along with WMGM's record librarian and some other jocks from some of the smaller stations in town that played only black music.

The *New York Post* got hold of a check from a record company that had been endorsed and cashed by Granger and printed it together with an interview in which Granger admitted that he had been collecting money during the time he was in charge of selecting extra records to fill out the program schedule. Granger also said that at his wedding reception he had received large payments from thirty record manufacturers and distributors whom he had invited to the affair.

McCaw called me into his office. When I entered, he got up, walked over to me, put his arm on my shoulder, and pointed to a small oil painting hanging on the wall.

"How much do you think that's worth?" he asked. I didn't know. "I'll tell you," he continued. "Art is worth whatever you're willing to pay for it." I waited for him to make his point. "Did you know that Mel Leeds bought an art gallery last year?"

I knew that Leeds was interested in art, and that his wife and sister-in-law had opened a tiny sliver of a store on the East Side called The Big Studio. I had visited it but was disappointed because most of the selections, while they were original oils, were of the mass-produced variety; the sort of pseudo-impressionist canvases one saw in suburban tract-house living rooms. They were the kind of paintings that were stocked more by subject matter than by artist. "Give me two more Eiffel Towers, another Champs Elysées . . . and how about a couple of Arc de Triomphes."

"Record pluggers and jocks have suddenly developed an appreciation for art," McCaw said. Then I remembered I had seen a painting of the Champs Elysées in Bruce Morrow's living room. I gulped.

"We have a lot of image cleaning to do," Elroy said.

Then McCaw informed me that he was going to look for an outstanding citizen to be program director, someone to help restore the station's image, but that until he found someone, I could continue the work I had started.

My first response to the payola indictments had been to stop playing music I thought was tainted by the scandal. I instituted a rotating committee to select music. The next week a WINS time salesman asked me what I was going to do about keeping the ratings high. I assured him that the quality of the programming was still high.

"That's not what I mean," he said.

He handed me a copy of a 1958 letter. It was from our sales department, confirming flight arrangements and discussing hotel and food costs on a vacation to Havana for employees of the rating company. I wasn't sure whether someone was tampering with the ratings or we had just been nice to them in the hopes of getting advance telephone reports before the ratings books came out. Of course, in the current atmosphere nobody would say anything.

I decided to concentrate on getting the station positive publicity and on improving the programming as best I could. Working with the sales department we hatched a publicity idea. WINS would deliberately plant what would appear to be a piece of an ancient Egyptian temple somewhere in the city. When it was found, there would be an uproar until the hieroglyphic symbols were translated. They would read "Everybody's Mummy Listens to 1010 WINS." A curator at the Metropolitan Museum of Art sketched the hieroglyphs for us. Two WINS time salesmen brought the sketch to an Astoria gravestone cutter.

"I do Latin, Hebrew, Old English, why not this?" he said. "I'll get you a nice piece of Hudson Valley granite."

When it was completed, it was delivered to WINS. The stone, five feet long, looked great, but not old. I got some dirt from Central Park and rubbed it into the rock. I hit it with a mallet until it chipped and finally cracked in half. Then I bound the pieces with Egyptian cloth and numbered the sections, taping on labels marked "Aswan Excavation Site 4—Quadrant B." I also pasted on arrows, indicating where to join the pieces. It looked very authentic.

Losing the stone was staged. The salesmen "lost" it in a taxi in front of 666 Fifth Avenue, making certain that the next occupant of the cab was WINS press agent and former *Daily News* editor Mortimer Matz. Morty "discovered" the lost slab just as the taxi was conveniently passing the Eighteenth Precinct station house. As the cabbie rushed in to report the find, the press agent called Associated Press, United Press, every TV station and newspaper, and all the radio stations—except WINS. Each call began with, "Hi, this is the desk sergeant at the Eighteenth Precinct. You've always been good to me. Now I've got a tip for you. A piece of ancient Egypt has been found in a taxicab and we have it here at the station house."

The press bit. *The New York Times* rushed the nation's leading Egyptologist, Brooklyn Museum curator John Cooney, to the police station. WHO LEFT THE SLAB IN HONEST ABE'S CAB was the headline in the *New York World Telegram and Sun,* praising cabbie Abe Kerner (who had already received one hundred dollars from the WINS press agent for turning in the stone). Every radio station in town fell for the story and used it in their newscasts. A picture of the stone made the *Daily News* centerfold. But alas, the Brooklyn Museum curator could not translate the Metropolitan Museum curator's hieroglyphs. He announced in *The New York*

Wah Diddy Diddy" / *Manfred Mann* • "I Get Around" / *The Beach*

Times that the stone was genuine Aswan granite but had been inscribed with an electric drill and was a fake. WINS station manager Hap Anderson then turned up to claim the stone and translate it, saying it was made for an advertising agency presentation. The "Egyptian stone" became the centerpiece of a coffee table in the Andersons' Washington, D.C., home when he later headed Radio Free Europe.

With promotions going full steam, I still had to keep the ratings going up. My big programming problem was the morning show. Al Collins's style was more suited to the nighttime audience. I decided to move Jazzbo to a more appropriate slot. Lee Gorman, who had been McCaw's payola investigator (and who looked like an Irish version of actor Telly Savalas), had been made sales manager of WINS and immediately began lobbying very hard on behalf of Stan Richards, a former Boston morning disc jockey with whom he was very close.

I agreed to listen to tapes of Richards. He had a warm resonant voice, a "breakfast table" personality, and he projected a cheerful image. We hired him, moving Jazzbo to a nighttime remote out of Mama Leone's restaurant, produced by Barry Farber, the young linguist acquaintance of Elroy's from North Carolina.

About a month later, when a mailroom clerk inadvertently opened a letter from Stan Richards's accountant, it became common knowledge around the station that he and Gorman had had business dealings.

The next day Gorman had a new friend—Murray the K. A few days later, the commercials began disappearing from Bruce Morrow's show. Then Gorman called a meeting with the station's current manager, Hap Anderson. He explained that he was having trouble selling the Morrow show to advertisers because Cousin Brucie's commercial delivery was so fast it was unintelligible. But the sales department saved the day. The solution was simple. All we had to do was move Murray the K down from his 11 P.M. time to the hallowed 7 P.M. period where Alan Freed had once held forth. Anderson knew Gorman would not make the suggestion unless he had already cleared the idea with Elroy McCaw. The expected edict to move Kaufman in to save the dwindling revenue was soon forthcoming from Elroy. Bruce Morrow was out at WINS.

Gorman also began lobbying with McCaw, Anderson, and me to

Boys • "A World Without Love" / *Peter and Gordon* • "House of

have the music list expanded. I had some acrimonious exchanges with him. He wanted a playlist of at least one hundred fifty records. He had met a great many music publishers and record company executives through Stan Richards and was telling Elroy that the more records we played, the better off we would be. I knew from my polls of record stores that less than four dozen records were selling well. Gorman had also fallen in love with our current record librarian, Judy Cross, who had been on his probe list when he came into WINS as one of Elroy's payola investigators. She also now favored a long playlist.

I stood my ground and refused to lengthen the list.

At this time I also began getting phone calls from former ABC announcer Hal Neal. Neal, now an executive, had been brought into New York from Detroit by ABC Radio to turn WABC, the last bulwark of radio soap-operadom, into a rock & roll radio station. We met several times for breakfast and lunch to discuss the possibility of my moving to ABC. Hal spoke about this in terms of the future, because he did not yet have a budget for a full-time program director.

McCaw, meanwhile, sensing that the time had come, put WINS on the market. He began negotiating with George B. Storer to sell the station to the Storer Broadcasting Company. Elroy worked long hours structuring a deal. From the day he bought the station, it had been Elroy's plan to someday sell WINS for the round figure of ten million dollars. Nobody had ever sold a radio property for anywhere near that price. He would bide his time and wait for the market to develop.

Now, as he worked out the details of the sale, a second piece of the deal had to be put into position. When Elroy moved WINS to 7 Central Park West to save the rent in 1956, he also purchased an option to buy the building. At the time, the option was only five thousand dollars. Now, if he could entice George Storer to keep WINS at its present location, he might just become a landlord. There was one problem—Storer went first-class, and WINS was a dump.

Elroy brought in a low-priced, nonunion, one-man contractor who came with his own truck, cement, and cinder blocks from New Jersey and slowly, over the next months, built soundproof walls and windows and made the floor into real studios.

The day after the construction was completed, a New York City building inspector came upstairs and walked right into one of the new walls that Elroy had built. I happened to be walking by when the incident occurred.

"Who's in charge of this place?" he asked me. "This wall isn't supposed to be here!"

I excused myself and said I'd be right back.

Elroy kept a retired attorney, Frederic A. Johnson, on a retainer. Johnson had been the world's leading authority on sports and the law. He had handled the famed case of the baseball players jumping to the Mexican league, where he traced precedents back to the Dred Scott decision. Now the aged Johnson spent his days sleeping in a small office near McCaw's, leaving it only at lunch time to walk to Lindy's Restaurant, where his bald pate and paunchy figure were familiar.

I woke Johnson, and he came out to see the building inspector.

"Look here," the building inspector said, "you have no permit to build walls here."

"I am sure there's been a misunderstanding," Johnson said.

The inspector looked up, squinted, and looked again.

"Fred?" he asked. "Fred Johnson?"

They hadn't seen each other in forty years, since law school. Elroy's building code violations were forgotten.

Then I got another job offer. This one was firm and required a quick decision. Art Tolchin called and offered me a contract to program WMGM. With WINS for sale and Neal still not ready with a budget at ABC, I decided to make the move. I went in to WINS on a Saturday morning to see Elroy and resign. Before I could say anything, he said to me, "I hear that Bob and Larry Tisch are selling their radio station to Crowell-Collier."

I was startled. Why would Tolchin be offering me a job now if his station was on the block? McCaw went on to discuss some of the terms of the sale as he had heard them. I thought the better of it and did not tender my resignation. Instead I called Tolchin at home and told him I wasn't coming to WMGM because the station was being sold. Tolchin was furious.

"Listen, sonny boy," he said, "when ten-million-dollar deals are made in this town, Art Tolchin knows about them. WMGM is not for sale. I think you're chickening out because you don't want to change jobs. If you change your mind between now and Monday call me. The press releases are already printed. I'm going to the World Series and enjoy the rest of my weekend.'' He hung up.

I sat for a long time with the phone in my hand. I didn't call back.

On Tuesday morning, *Radio Daily* reported the sale of WMGM to Crowell-Collier. I didn't see Tolchin until the following Friday at an industry luncheon. He spotted me, came right over, and said he had an apology to make. He had not yet known of the sale when he offered me the job.

Then, a month later, the FCC suddenly killed the WMGM Crowell-Collier sale. The commission had sought to persuade Crowell-Collier to leave the broadcasting business because of the questionable methods by which some of their broadcast properties were being operated. A recent incident in which a Crowell-Collier announcer had caused a near panic by broadcasting reports that there was ''an amoeba loose in San Francisco Bay'' had incensed members of the commission.

McCaw, who had been pleased when he first learned of the WMGM sale, now became apprehensive. He had good reason. WINS's license to broadcast had expired. Elroy's fears were realized when the FCC decided it was not about to renew his license so long as former employees were under indictment and questions of payola remained unanswered.

Elroy used every connection and implemented every technique that he could to get WINS's license reinstated. Employees took lie detector tests. He arranged for all his executives to come down to Washington to testify. To make certain that their presence at a critical hearing would not be stopped even by the weather, he bought a sleeper car and had everyone check in the night before at Pennsylvania Station, sleep on the train, and be ready to go when it pulled into Union Station the following morning. Of course, for most of the night the train was stationary, sitting on the platform in New York with all of us sleeping inside.

At that point, manager Hap Anderson had enough of Elroy McCaw and WINS, and he quit. In no time, McCaw's friend Irving Rosenthal was on the phone with a candidate for the manager's job—Palisades Amusement Park band leader Ted Steele. Elroy hired him. Steele insisted on a playlist of almost two hundred records and wanted to add every release that made the *Billboard* charts.

I was fed up. A playlist that long would drive away our audience. Elroy would either sell the station or lose it. I picked up the phone and called Art Tolchin at WMGM. He was continuing to manage the station now that the sale to Crowell-Collier had been canceled. I asked if he still had an opening for program director. He told me he had already hired Art Wander, a program director from Ohio, but that he would make Art his assistant and that the offer was still open if I wanted to join the organization. At that point I resigned from WINS.

The commission refused to renew Elroy's license, and his deal with George Storer fell through. After the deal collapsed, the FCC decided they had punished McCaw enough, and they granted him a license renewal. It was like handing Elroy a ten-million-dollar bill. He commenced negotiations immediately to sell the station to Westinghouse, and the eight-figure deal was consummated.

With the money from the sale of the station, Elroy exercised his option on 7 Central Park West and bought the building for little more than he had originally paid for the radio station. He then sold it as the site of a skyscraper for almost as much as he had received for WINS. Elroy McCaw had parlayed his $25,000 down payment on WINS into almost $20 million in only seven years.

There was a footnote to the WINS saga. While Alan Freed pleaded guilty to some counts of commercial bribery, the trials of former WINS employees never took place. Nobody else from WINS, including Mel Leeds, was ever found guilty of taking payola.

After WINS was turned over to Westinghouse, most of the staff disbanded. The announcers whose names were written into the union contract were protected and continued to work there. Newsman Tom O'Brien was recruited by Hal Neal to head ABC Radio News. Paul Sherman, the "Crown Prince of Rock & Roll," stayed on for well over a decade before retiring to Florida where he later passed away. The voices of former DJs Stan Z. Burns and Brad "Battle of the Baritones" Phillips continued to be heard well into the eighties, broadcasting news on WINS.

Murray the K stayed on at WINS until 1965, when the station changed to its all-news format. A year earlier, when the Beatles became famous, Murray called himself the "fifth Beatle" and tried to do as many interviews as he could with the quartet. When the first wave of psychedelic clubs caught on, Murray opened his own version. Called The World of Murray the K, it used multimedia projectors to transform the Long Island airplane hanger where Lindbergh had kept *The Spirit of St. Louis* into a communal acid trip. In later years, Murray worked as a DJ on WOR-FM, the first New York FM station to play pop music. He also landed a part in a fictitious film about the Beatles' first trip to New York, and acted as an adviser on *Beatlemania,* a live show featuring Beatle look-alikes. Murray followed the show to Hollywood, where he married once again and, in his last professional work, hosted a syndicated radio show featuring music of the sixties. He died in 1982, and there were memorial services on both coasts.

Bruce Wendell, the mailroom boy, followed Mel Leeds to California, eventually replacing Leeds as program director of a Burbank station, and by the eighties Wendell had become vice president and a member of the board of directors of Capitol Records, with homes in Beverly Hills and Palm Springs, a Rolls-Royce and a Ferrari.

Alan Freed, who received a $300 fine and a suspended sentence after pleading guilty to a commercial bribery charge, saw his career ended by the scandals. After several years of heavy drinking, Freed died early in 1965 at the age of only forty-three in Palm Springs, California.

Clark • "I Got You Babe" / *Sonny and Cher* • "Stop in the Name of

CHAPTER 9

Changing Stations

With some of the profits from the sale of WINS and the windfall acquisition from the turnover of his building, Elroy McCaw, together with some of his former OSS buddies, embarked on a scheme to acquire the ABC Radio Network and move its studios to a low-overhead, nonunion location outside Syracuse, New York. Most of the national networks, ABC included, had been hemorrhaging dollars for over a decade and had been kept going in the fifties mainly at the insistence of the White House. President Eisenhower believed it was essential to national security for the federal government to have access to the radio networks so he could reach virtually the entire population in an instant in the event of a national emergency. Grudgingly, the large broadcasting companies had gone along.

McCaw's plan never materialized. Leonard Goldenson and Si Siegal, ABC's leaders in 1962, sensed a long-range potential in their radio network and had no intention of selling to McCaw or anybody else.

Elroy used some of his money on another unorthodox idea. He started the concept of cable television in New York City at a time when nobody had ever heard of the term. He went to City Hall and told Mayor Wagner's publicity aides that he had a system that would make it possible for the mayor to address every convention in town without leaving his office. He got permission to run a television cable network from City Hall to every major hotel in town. It was a simple understanding that McCaw could run cables through city conduits. Elroy did not stop with the hotels but continued to wire midtown Manhattan, concentrating on residential areas. In essence, he had talked himself into a free cable TV franchise. That system, then called Channel 6, eventually became Manhattan Cable Television.

I had my own challenges to face. It soon became obvious that WMGM was, for me, more of a way station than my next radio station. Loew's corporate management regarded the transmitter, studios, and license as an expendable property whose sales would help finance the construction of their rapidly growing hotel empire. They aggressively tried to sell it. Girders were already rising for Loew's Americana Hotel in New York when George B. Storer, still determined to get into the number one market after failing to buy WINS, bought WMGM from Bob and Larry Tisch.

Modern furniture gave way to early American as Storer took over and changed WMGM's name back to the original call letters of the thirties, WHN. In keeping with the Storer image of studied conservatism moulding was glued to the desks to make them look antique, prints of Independence Hall and the U.S. Constitution appeared on the walls, and modern lamps were replaced with period pieces selected by the company's vice president of interior decoration. A large oil portrait of George B. Storer was hung over the reception desk, and secretaries were given lessons in decorum and precise instructions on telephone etiquette and how to behave in every job-related situation, including how to eat lunch at one's desk discreetly.

Art Wander and I were welcomed to the Storer organization by their national program director, Grady Edney, and were asked to remain on staff and begin recording music for the new programming.

The transition to WHN programming took several months. A new format was to be installed featuring group vocal arrangements of songs like "Love Letters in the Sand," "Moonlight in Vermont," "Slow Boat to China," and "Wish You Were Here." It was all kicked off with a gala concert in the Grand Ballroom of New York's Waldorf-Astoria Hotel by Hugo Winterhalter and his orchestra, The Kirby Stone Four, and others on February 28, 1962.

After the premiere the new manager, who had come from Storer's Philadelphia station, informed Art Wander that he was no longer needed and then told me that he had already promised my programming job in New York to his programmer from the city of Brotherly Love. Art left for a job in Ohio, and I worked out a deal with Hal Neal while I negotiated a buy-out with Storer.

Neal had not yet gotten approval from ABC for a full-time program director's position, so he brought me in as production and community affairs director with a mandate to begin initiating and producing promotions for the radio station. He said he expected approval of the programming position later in the year. In order to be ready when the job was created, I reviewed WABC's progress thus far.

After my years of enjoying the double-digit shares—12, 15, and even 20 percent—of the audience that WINS commanded, it was hard to get used to the idea of starting with only the 5s and 6s that WABC had. As the flagship station of the ABC network, WABC had not made the early transition to music and news programming. Even now, two years into a rudimentary pop music format, the station still carried anachronisms like the live broadcasts of the Metropolitan Opera on Saturday afternoons! WABC was running almost a million dollars in the red, adding to the financial instability of the fiscally shaky fledgling American Broadcasting Company.

Earlier attempts at giving WABC a more contemporary sound had run into snags. Martin Block, having made his name establishing "The Make Believe Ballroom" on WNEW, seemed a good prospect and had been brought over to WABC in the late fifties to repeat the miracle. The music played on WNEW, however, was more like middle of the road, and listeners automatically turned to 1130 on the dial when they wanted it and didn't go near WABC's 770 spot. A brief flirtation with Alan Freed ended because he wouldn't sign the required corporate antipayola oath. The closest thing to pop music had been "The Robbins Nest," a potpourri of music and interviews with Freddie Robbins.

Most of the time listeners heard announcers who were old-school network types, well versed in elocution, but dull. On an overnight show called "Big Joe's Happiness Exchange," Joe Rosenfeld's early version of a call-in show consoled widows and others with advice. All day on Sunday traditional religious programs and public affairs shows filled the air.

A similar situation prevailed at most ABC-owned and operated radio stations. Only in Detroit, where former announcer Harold L.

Neal, Jr., reigned, was ABC Radio making any money. There, the studios that had formerly been home to "The Lone Ranger" and "The Green Hornet" now played rock & roll music. Thus, it was logical for Steve Riddleberger, president of the ABC Radio Stations to bring in Hal Neal to turn WABC around.

When Neal arrived in New York in 1960, he looked around for a program director for WABC. He called me and we had several meetings. But when Neal tried to get a full-time program director's position approved, nobody in ABC's upper management understood the need for such a position. Neal was told to have a disc jockey do the job part-time. He took another route and hired an outside consultant, Mike Josephs, so that he wouldn't need the approval of the personnel department. Josephs put in a format, but opted for a long playlist based on the 770 dial position. There were seventy records, seven hit albums, seven soaring singles, seven sure-shot albums, and a sleeper.

By Christmas, the middle-of-the-road jocks, including Martin Block, were gone. Block was bought out for more than it cost to bring in most of the new staff. WABC's first jingles went on. But the Mitch Miller versions of "Polly Wolly Doodle," "Daisy Daisy," and "Camptown Races" were hardly compatible with the music.

The new DJ lineup included WMCA's Herb Oscar Anderson as "The Morning Mayor of New York"; Charlie Greer from WAKR, Akron, Ohio; Jack Carney, Chuck Dunaway, Farrell Smith, Scott Muni (another defecter from WMCA); and staff announcer Bill Owen. As the year progressed, Carney departed and was replaced by Big Dan Ingram, a former Long Island DJ whose sharp satirical asides had shaken up audiences at KBOX in Dallas and WIL, St. Louis. Bruce Morrow, who had left WINS, New York for WINZ, Miami, returned to the city to take Chuck Dunaway's 10 P.M.-to-midnight slot. Puppeteer Fred Hall did fill-in work.

With the talent settled in, consultant Josephs ended his relationship with the station and Hal Neal, conforming to the wishes of ABC's personnel department, found a double-duty talent in DJ Sam Holman, who was paid extra to be part-time program director in addition to his on-the-air duties. He replaced Farrell Smith.

The station began to develop a distinctive sound. Scott Muni opened up his show with a sixty-minute nightly feature of solid gold, and WABC announced a very cleverly thought out audience promotion, "The Principal of the Year," which helped WABC build its audience base. The idea was simple: teens are the easiest listeners to lure from one station to another and, once recruited, would convince their parents, grandparents, brothers and sisters, relatives, friends, teachers, and entire faculty staffs to be part of a promotion that would force everybody to keep listening to WABC for so many months that their listening habits would change as they got used to the station. The promotion was used with deadly effect against WMCA.

"It's The Principal of the Year election," the voice of Dan Ingram boomed over the air. March music began, then faded down, and Ingram continued. "Vote for your principal to be WABC's Principal of the Year. Anyone can vote: Mom, Dad, little sister. Just write your principal's name on a piece of paper and send it to WABC, Thirty-nine West Sixty-sixth Street, New York twenty-three. Vote as often as you like. The winning principal receives a color TV set and a special award assembly."

The idea of permitting people to vote more than once was easily explained. The more you loved your school, the more times you would want to write your principal's name. The idea clicked. Before the balloting ended, more than three million pieces of paper had been delivered to the studio. Ratings jumped as listeners tuned in daily for the latest vote count. Hal Neal was elated. Hundreds of schools had participated. A nun who was principal at a parochial high school in New Jersey was the winner. "The Principal of the Year" contest gave the station the momentum it had lacked.

WABC DJs were called "The Swinging' Seven," but Neal didn't like the name so he changed it to "The Good Guys." The result was an ambivalent attitude in the studio. Some of the jocks used the phrase and others did not. Neal had heard about the phrase from his sales reps, who picked it up in Los Angeles, where it had been used by program director Chuck Blore on KFWB, Crowell-Collier's first rocker.

Across town at WMCA, program director Ruth Meyer and manager Steve Labunski thought "Good Guys" was a great name. When WABC began using it only as an occasional slogan, they lifted the phrase and went all out with it. WMCA produced spot announcements about *their* "Good Guys." They had "Good Guy" ads and jingles. WMCA also began giving out expensive long-sleeved "Good Guy Sweatshirts." The orange-yellow garments became coveted status symbols among teenagers who wore them. Pretty soon every time a DJ at 770 on the dial mentioned ''Good Guy,'' it was associated in listeners' minds with the station at 570 on the dial, WMCA, and they began getting credit when listeners told the rating companies they listened to the ''good guy station.''

With the ''Good Guy'' battle going full tilt, Hal Neal welcomed me to WABC.

CHAPTER 10

Beating the Drums with Salvador Dali

On June 11, 1962, I walked into the former Central Park stables at 39 West Sixty-sixth Street, now part of ABC's New York complex, looking for WABC Radio. The station was scattered over several floors in the building, which it shared with the news department. Hal Neal and the WABC sales force were housed in makeshift offices in the former Blue Network studio on the second floor, and the broadcasts originated from a converted soap opera studio on the fifth floor.

As director of community affairs I spent my first months on public service campaigns. ABC's famous opera announcer Milton Cross obliged me by recording announcements to raise funds for free opera in Central Park. I instituted news tip awards, and the first one paid off the next day when a tornado hit Paramus, New Jersey. WABC scooped the world when a listener phoned in the story. We recorded speedboat enthusiast and bandleader Guy Lombardo doing boating safety announcements, and I took all the DJs to the police department shooting range to tape police recruitment spots.

Then I began producing promotions for the station. Due to ABC's financial state, WABC had a tiny promotional budget at that time. ABC was the struggling third TV network in an era when there was only enough national advertising to support two and a half networks. The big question at ABC was how to find a way to finance the conversion from black and white television to color. Every penny WABC earned was pumped into the corporate arteries to keep the company going.

Unable to give away large sums of money, we ran a search for the heir to an "international fortune"—a listener whose description most closely resembled one I had locked in the vault of a bank. That person would win the fortune: 100,000 Italian lira, 1,000 Indian rupees, 100 Japanese yen, 2 Hong Kong dollars, and a Swedish krona. The total came to $400 in American money.

That contest was successful and got us some Chemical Bank advertising from their Chinatown branch, so Hal Neal was willing to risk a thousand dollars on another promotion. We purchased a contest from Mars, Inc., Stan Kaplan's Connecticut-based radio contest company. It involved a "secret agent" who talked to the listeners by phone over the air every day for a month, telling them he would meet them at a location of their choice at the end of the month and give one person a thousand dollars. At the end of the month, following instructions that we broadcast, tens of thousands of people went to their locations after notifying us by postcard where they would be. Each person wore a makeshift card with the call letters WABC lettered on it to identify themselves. We had announced that the appointed hour was 3 P.M. on Friday the thirtieth. At that moment, dozens of people with WABC cards clipped to their clothing were standing in front of the information booth at Grand Central Station. Dozens more were at Cleopatra's needle in Central Park, and similar scenes were taking place at other public landmarks. We picked a winner who was standing outside a hotel near Gramercy Park.

Revenues began coming in from a contract Neal had negotiated to carry New York Mets baseball games, so I knew we would be able to continue offering prizes. (Neal had assigned a promising sportscaster, former attorney Howard Cosell, to do the warm-up show and locker room wrap-up to enhance the games.)

I produced jingles built around the theme "the Hotline of Hits." Our top records became "Superhits," and each had a numerical jingle introduction. We also introduced our version of a "Pick Hit of the Week"—a new record that we predicted would go all the way to number one.

As 1963 began, Neal became fed up with the WABC–WMCA battle of the "Good Guys." The term had been obviously preempted by WMCA, so Neal pronounced the WABC jocks "the All-Americans"—a name derived from the American Broadcasting Company. It is doubtful if any listener ever made the connection.

Of more immediate interest and excitement was Cousin Brucie's new theme. His "Big M" theme was retired when Frankie Valli and the Four Seasons recorded "Movin' and Groovin', Havin' a Ball with Cousin Brucie."

We came up with our first big promotion. I had been scanning the newspapers looking for an angle. Then I found it. Leonardo da Vinci's masterpiece, the Mona Lisa, was about to be flown from the Louvre in Paris to the Metropolitan Museum of Art in New York for a showing. This was big news for New York. There had to be a way that WABC could link itself to this story.

I thought that we might award a prize to the listener who painted the best copy of the Mona Lisa. Then I realized that most people can't paint very well; we would also have to award a prize for the worst copy of the painting. I decided to also award prizes for the biggest Mona Lisa and the smallest Mona Lisa. We would award one hundred dollars for the best, one hundred dollars for the worst, one hundred dollars for the biggest, and one hundred dollars for the smallest Mona Lisa.

We hadn't reckoned with ABC's broadcast standards department. They wanted to know who would decide which Mona Lisa was the best or the worst, and they insisted that we find an expert. With us saying the judge's decision was final, they didn't want anybody challenging the judge. I gave the problem to Mortimer Matz, who was now doing public relations for WABC. Within twenty-four hours he was back with a commitment from surrealist painter Salvador Dali. We now had our art expert, and we were free to proceed with the contest.

The hourly promotional announcements for the Mona Lisa contest were as classy as we could record. They were sung by Nat "King" Cole, featuring his rendition of the song "Mona Lisa," and were announced by Bruce Morrow. I crossed my fingers and waited for the results. We had no response during the first week of announcements, and only a handful of pencil sketches came in during the second week. I began to think that we had a real bust on our hands. What I didn't realize was that it took a long time to do a painting, and during that period our listeners were hard at work.

Honey" / *Herb Alpert and the Tijuana Brass* • "You Keep Me

We also had some help from an unexpected quarter—the newspapers. Virtually every metropolitan paper had decided to put a full-color photo of the Mona Lisa on the cover of the Sunday magazine section. There was a Mona Lisa in the *Sunday News,* the *Sunday Mirror,* and even the *Newark Star Ledger.* Now almost all of the sixteen million people in our listening area had a pretty good idea of what the Mona Lisa looked like.

Three weeks into the contest, we began receiving entries in quantity. Many were done with crayons or water colors on poster board, but more and more oil paintings—some of them really spectacular and framed—began arriving at our studios. Elated, I brought all of the entries into Hal Neal's office early one morning, before he arrived at work, and literally covered the floors, walls, and even part of the ceiling with paintings. Hal was ecstatic. Paintings continued to arrive in ever increasing numbers, and we began stacking them around the huge converted radio studio that served as the station's sales bullpen. Not all of them were on canvas. Mona Lisas of every size and description began pouring in, painted on eggs, glass, and every imaginable surface. Then the first large Mona Lisa arrived. It had come from a group of patients at a Pennsylvania mental hospital. We unrolled it. It was the size of a living room rug, but it was small in comparison to what was to follow. We ran out of space to display them. I borrowed a large television studio in an adjoining building, where I stored the entries. In the smallest Mona Lisa category, we actually received several pictures on microscope slides. Two of them had been done on microdots; fortunately one of the microdots was smaller than the other, so it was possible to render a judgment on the smallest Mona Lisa of them all.

The collection of Mona Lisas in the television studio turned into a visual fantasy so immense and incredible to behold that *Life* magazine asked to shoot the scene and use it for their famous "Speaking of Pictures" back page.

I decided to separate the judging into two events, since there was no way of dealing with the giant paintings even in our studios. Using the Polo Grounds Stadium in upper Manhattan, we laid them out on the playing field. A nasty wind hampered our work. We tried weighing down the corners of the paintings with steel scoreboard numerals, but there weren't nearly enough of these. Some of the paintings started to rip. In desperation I called the

Hangin' On" / *The Supremes* • "California Dreamin'" / *The Mamas*

radio station and one of our salesmen came to the rescue by having a sponsor, Bohack Supermarkets, divert a trailer truck full of flour that was enroute to one of their stores. The sacks of flour were unloaded at the outfield gate and were used to hold down the paintings. The largest Mona Lisa, done on newspapers pasted together, covered the entire infield.

All the other paintings were judged at the Arnold Constable department store at Fifth Avenue and Fortieth Street. They donated their entire second floor in the hopes of getting publicity. We had to display fifteen thousand Mona Lisas, but since we were a little short of space, those that we did not believe would qualify were simply stacked in a corner. Salvador Dali arrived, followed by an entourage of newspaper and television reporters. TV crews rigged power lines throughout the display, and Dali was followed by cameras as he set out to select the winning entries. He went up and down the aisles, peering at paintings through a giant magnifying glass that publicist Matz had provided. The smallest Mona Lisas were examined by microscope. Dali was thorough and painstaking. After several hours he said to me: "Is this all you have?"

"Well, yes, except for the rejects," I replied, pointing to the pile of sketches and pictures that we were unable to put up on the walls.

"I want to look at them," Dali said. He approached the heap of discards slowly, paused in front of it, dropped to his knees, and began picking through the pictures, throwing them into the air as he went. Suddenly he stood up, and clutching a small piece of white cardboard, shouted, "This is it!"

I rushed over, accompanied by Hal Neal, Morty Matz, and a half-dozen newspaper and television camera people. Dali was very excited. Peering over his shoulder, I was shocked to see that he was holding a black and white india ink cartoon of a Mercury space capsule with Mona Lisa's face gazing out of its window. It had obviously been dashed off in a few minutes by a cartoonist, and was far from the magnificent oil painting we had imagined he might select to win our contest.

"Are you sure?" I asked.

"Oh yes," said Dali. "This is it." He turned abruptly and headed for the exit.

"Wait a minute," I said. "You also have to pick the worst

Mona Lisa.'' Dali stopped, turned, and pointed to one of the discarded paintings propped up against the wall.

''This is the most tragic effort,'' he said. I continued to follow him as he started out of the door.

''But why?'' I asked. ''Why did you pick the cartoon?''

Dali turned around. ''Meet me on Wednesday at eleven A.M. at Leo Castelli's gallery, and I will show you why,'' he said. Then he departed.

After Dali left, Morty Matz and I looked at the winning cartoon. It had been signed by an air force sergeant who worked on the newspaper at a nearby air force base. Matz was on the phone in minutes to the base's public information officer, who became very excited when he heard that Salvador Dali had picked his cartoonist's sketch. He arranged for an awards ceremony to be held, at which the U.S. Air Force would roll out all the trappings of an honor guard and a few rockets.

On Wednesday morning, I drove over to the Castelli Galleries, which were in the Seventies off Madison Avenue, not too far from the Metropolitan Museum of Art. True to his word, Salvador Dali was waiting for me in the reception area. He led me through the galleries and into a rear storage room and turned on the lights. The room was filled with oil paintings done as cartoons. Some were hanging, others were stacked against the walls. There were comic strips, complete with dialogue, signed by Roy Lichtenstein. Paintings by James Rosenquist and Andy Warhol were on display.

''I have never seen art like this,'' I told Dali.

''This is going to be *next year*'s art,'' Dali explained. ''This is what the public will be buying in 1964. It is the new trend. It is the most important painting being done today.''

I walked around the room, looking at the paintings. Then Dali asked me if I could drop him off at the St. Regis. We got into my car and I drove back slowly and very carefully through the midtown traffic.

After getting Dali safely back to his hotel I returned to the station, where Hal Neal was waiting.

''You'll never believe it,'' I told him. ''Next year they're going to be selling oil paintings of comic strips to the public. If you want to clean up, buy some now!'' I had been treated to a preview of pop art.

* * *

As 1963 progressed, Hal Neal told me he wanted to repeat the successful Principal of the Year election. I decided to use the same type of announcement, but this time I added the phrase "second annual" to the title. All of us at WABC had underestimated the popularity of the promotion. Most of the students and faculties who had participated the first year automatically assumed that the award would be an annual event. Many of the schools that had lost in 1962 decided to get the jump on their rival schools. Their students had been writing votes all year. Vote writing had also commenced at hundreds of other schools that hadn't entered candidates the first time around. To further complicate matters, the word was spreading in some educational circles that being voted Principal of the Year was a sure ticket to the job of superintendent of schools. Vote writing activity was feverish and widespread, beyond anything we could imagine. In gymnasiums and lunch rooms throughout the listening area, votes had been piling up for nine months. And because WABC's nighttime skywave signal bounced all the way down the coastline of North America there was a college in Virginia that had a trailer truck loaded with votes ready and waiting. When we decided to repeat the Principal of the Year, we were totally unaware that any of these developments were taking place.

At WABC, preparations went ahead for the second contest. A dozen secretaries were assigned to aid in the vote counting. To stimulate entries, I took Bruce Morrow by helicopter to visit suburban high schools. Not until a story broke in a West New York, New Jersey, paper did we have any inkling of the importance of the promotion among educators. One candidate for a superintendent of schools office had accused a rival principal of keeping his students after class and forcing them to write tens of thousands of votes. Charges and counter-charges filled the headlines for a week. Still we had no hint of the size of the deluge that was about to descend on us.

As the voting deadline neared, caravans of station wagons, pickup trucks, and vans filled with votes began arriving at WABC. They were driven by parents, teachers, students, priests, rabbis, and nuns; some were driven by the principals themselves. Within a week, the studio set aside for the vote counting contained so much paper and had become so disorganized that it was impossible to work there. We diverted the vote deliveries to St. Nicholas Arena further down the block.

Throughout the last week of voting, the parade of vehicles was unending. The piles of cartons of votes were staggering. On the final day of the contest, West Sixty-sixth Street was blocked all day and night by moving vans, trucks, cars, and school buses delivering votes. Friday night at midnight, the deadline for deliveries passed.

On Saturday morning I walked into St. Nicholas Arena and was instantly overcome with feelings of both elation and terror. Cartons of votes covered the floor and overflowed into the grandstands. The votes counted thus far were minuscule compared to what lay ahead. We undoubtedly would have a ratings triumph in the spring, but somebody would be counting votes for months.

On Monday morning, there was a crisis meeting in Hal Neal's office. The ABC attorneys charged with safeguarding WABC's license arrived. WABC was worth tens of millions of dollars, and the lawyers wanted to know how we proposed counting the votes. We suggested weighing them, but the lawyers pointed out that the votes were on paper, cardboard, and oaktag and came in all sizes and shapes. Neal became very concerned. This was going to cost a lot of money.

He assured the lawyers that all the votes would be counted, and then he called a closed-door staff meeting. We evaluated the problem. The award date was a month away. Our business manager quickly estimated that it would take eighty people working in two shifts around the clock to count all the votes in a month. The cost would be close to $100,000—more than the entire promotion budget for the remainder of the year.

WABC didn't have eighty people on its entire staff. We couldn't spare anybody to count the additional votes. Calls went out to firms that supplied office temporaries. They recruited college students, substitute schoolteachers, stenographers—and eventually began hiring drifters off New York's skid row, the Bowery.

The mix of people working in St. Nicholas Arena counting votes was a sociological powder keg. We were less than a week into the counting when the keg exploded. One of the Bowery derelicts touched an attractive young schoolteacher. She protested. A college student at the next table went to her defense, and the hobo hurled a chair at him. The student swung and hit the man, knocking him down. His buddies rushed to his aid and in a few seconds the scene resembled a brawl in a Western. Chairs, tables, and votes were flying everywhere. Our supervisor frantically called for ABC security guards, but by the time they broke up the fight there were votes scattered all over the floor.

It took over two months to count the votes. In the end we tallied over 176 million ballots, more than had been cast in the previous United States presidential election, and Teaneck, New Jersey, high school principal Helen Hill was the winner. The $100,000 was buried in the bookkeeping, and the ratings went up enough for us to raise our ad rates and more than make up the loss.

After the smashing success of The Principal of the Year 1963, I was approached by Mark Olds, General Manager of WINS, and asked to return to my old station, which was now owned by Westinghouse. We had one negotiating meeting at the boat basin in Riverside Park. Since Neal had not yet acted on my promotion to program director of WABC and time was going by, I seriously considered going back to WINS.

The next week however, Steve Riddleberger, president of the ABC-Owned Radio Stations, was appointed vice president of ABC News. Hal Neal was immediately promoted to Riddleberger's job and, in a typical radio industry move, Neal appointed an old friend from Detroit, Walter Schwartz, general manager of WABC. When I heard the news, I wondered what would happen next, because Schwartz had been assistant general manager of WINS and knew about the talks I was having with Mark Olds.

As his first move after joining WABC, Wally Schwartz appointed me program director.

Franklin • "Ode to Billie Joe" / *Bobby Gentry* • "I'm a Believer" /

CHAPTER 11

Genesis of the Giant

When I started to program WABC in 1963, it was the third-ranked rock & roll station in New York, trailing far behind WINS and WMCA in the ratings. Rock station managers never want to be number three in the format because the advertising agencies rarely put commercials on more than the top two stations.

There were many reasons for the low ratings. Not only was the extremely long music playlist holding us back, but the station's commitment to broadcast various mutually incompatible programs supplied by the old ABC Radio Network was crippling my attempt to build a consistent music audience. Five-minute newscasts interrupted the music flow twice an hour despite research that said that once the morning drive period ended our audience wanted only music. From 10 to 11 A.M., we had to carry Don McNeil's "Breakfast Club" live from Chicago. It wasn't even breakfast time in New York! A large portion of the audience we had amassed during the morning Herb Oscar Anderson show dissolved under the syrupy servings from the Windy City. Music got underway again at eleven on WABC, but it was interrupted half a dozen times a day by another of the network's offerings, "Flair Reports," chatty features on fashion and cooking that broke the music's continuity. WABC had to stop the music yet again to carry a lengthy block of network and local news programs, complete with commentaries and editorials, from 5:55 P.M. to 7:20 P.M. nightly. WABC also carried a full season of play-by-play baseball with the New York Mets, and two football schedules: the New York Titans (the team that later evolved into the Jets) and Notre Dame college football.

It was a very frustrating situation for me because I had to answer for the station's ratings. Music was our show. Every time non-music programming came on, the music audience tuned out en masse and dialed up a competing music station. There they stayed until something happened on *that* station—a poor record or too many commercials or a newscast—that drove them back to us. It was as if we were running a movie theater where we started the feature with a full house, waited a while, and then turned up the lights, opened the exit doors, and ushered the audience into the street. It was no way to do business.

General manager Wally Schwartz and our attorneys told me repeatedly that not only could I do nothing about the network commitment, but that our FCC obligations required us to carry lots of local news as well. And because we were the ABC Network flagship station, we also had to broadcast every U.S. presidential address live, as well as other happenings of public importance.

I felt that I was not entirely in control of my own destiny, but I told myself that such an attitude was self-defeating. I still had authority over substantial portions of our air time in key periods, and perhaps we could make up for those network handicaps with better local programs and more local promotion. I also knew that nothing lasts forever, and if we made a good case, someday we could get out from under some of those network constraints. Our clear-channel, 50,000-watt transmitter had powerhouse potential if only it was used correctly. I was determined to make WABC number one.

In order to achieve a breakthrough in the ratings, I would have to use the strongest weapon I had—the music itself. Tracing back the development of the music, a strategy began to evolve in my mind. I knew, of course, that when Alan Freed began playing the first rock & roll music in Cleveland, there had been a distinct difference between that beat and all that had gone before. And by now I appreciated the implications of that difference. The new music was so unusual that only youthful ears could accept the change. As a result, a clear demarcation in musical preferences had arisen between young listeners and older listeners. Nineteen-fifty-four was the last year *without* a music generation gap. The big songs were "Little Things Mean a Lot" sung by Kitty Kallen, "Wanted" by Perry Como, and "Oh, My Papa" by Eddie Fisher. Anyone who listened to the radio at the time can hum "Three Coins in the Fountain" or "Hernando's Hideaway." They can still hear Rosemary Clooney belting out "This Ole House," Dean Mar-

• "Snoopy vs. the Red Baron" / *The Royal Guardsmen* • "Gimme

tin singing "That's Amore," or Tony Bennett's "Stranger in Paradise." Patti Page fans could choose between "Cross Over the Bridge" and "Changing Partners" for their favorite. The first hint of the change that was to come could be found further down the charts, where Bill Haley had slipped in a different beat on a song called "Shake, Rattle and Roll."

Only one year later, Alan Freed had made it to New York, spinning his records on WINS, and Bill Haley had the number two song of the year, "Rock Around the Clock." True, it was sitting there between Perez Prado's "Cherry Pink and Apple Blossom White" and Mitch Miller's "Yellow Rose of Texas" in the number three slot. But the first rock & roll smash had arrived.

By 1956, Elvis Presley had exploded onto the scene with five of the top fifteen records of the year, including the number one and two songs, "Heartbreak Hotel" and "Don't Be Cruel." Youth was having its way. A rash of former unknowns had infiltrated the pop charts on all levels, and the teen/adult music schism was widening. Young people found that the new music expressed their thoughts and feelings. Their parents hated it, called it noise, and stuck with the familiar.

The years that followed split the audiences even further. It was adult pressure that drove Freed off the stage and caused the police to shut down his rock & roll concerts. The deepening wedge between the age groups gave rise to more specialized programming, and to demographic time buying by radio advertisers. The sponsors were afraid of the new music. Teens were listening to Jimmy Gilmore and the Fireballs' "Sugar Shack," the Beach Boys' "Surfin' U.S.A.," Skeeter Davis, the Cascades, the Chiffons, Paul and Paula, Bobby Vinton, and Little Stevie Wonder on WINS, WMCA, and WABC. WINS's top ratings in this market hadn't brought top dollars from the agencies, who simply bought air time cheaply in order to sell pimple cream to the kids. To reach adults in New York, they went to WNEW, where Andy Williams and Nat "King" Cole could be heard.

My strategy crystallized. I would devise something that would give WABC both enormously high ratings and a top-dollar rate card. It went against every basic rule of radio, but I felt I had no choice if I wanted to win. It would also be very difficult to accomplish. I decided to build WABC's ratings on a *coalition* of audiences. My targeting plan was to go after everyone. I wanted the black urbanite and white suburbanite, the rich and the poor, and everyone in between, the young children, the teenagers, the parents, and even the over forty-nines. I wanted all of them to think of WABC as *their* station. If I had my way, someday I would be able to walk along the sand at Coney Island or Jones Beach and hear WABC continuously, as the radios spread a blanket of sound along the water. We would dominate the market.

To achieve this control of the dial would require extreme selectivity on our part. I would have to find universally appealing music that would attract almost everybody. Each record would have to do triple demographic duty, or I could not afford to play it. Every air personality would have to appeal to three or more types of listeners. The jingles, news presentations, and the contests and promotions would have to please multiple groups of audiences—each group would perceive the station as its own.

No management in its right mind would have bought such a strategy. Fortunately for us all, nobody asked what the strategy was.

Two months into the job, I realized that more and more often I was saying no to people.

"No, we won't play this record," to 295 out of every 300 records. "No, we can't use you as a disc jockey," to 1,999 out of every 2,000 applicants. "No, we won't do this promotion. No, we can't run that commercial. We won't lengthen the newscasts; we won't add another network feature. No, you can't plug that unknown act on your show. No, you can't deviate from the format."

I wasn't making too many friends. As the playlist got shorter and shorter, tempers at the record companies got hotter and hotter. They began to pressure the disc jockeys who attended the music meetings. Some jocks wanted to pick the music for their own shows. Others wanted to rotate music differently. I met individually with the performers and reasoned with them. Not all of them were happy about the situation. Sam Holman left, and I replaced him with Bob Dayton from WIL in St. Louis. (Since Holman had a part-time shift and Dayton was hot I gave him a full shift, moving Charlie Greer to the overnight.) The jocks agreed to try it my way. I knew that in order for my plan to work I needed their cooperation, but I also needed the strongest possible control over WABC's music.

Music was the key ingredient of WABC's programming. Over

the years people wondered if we had a secret formula. If there was any "secret," it was in the painstaking work of the selection and exposure of each of the records. To generate the biggest ratings in radio, I used the shortest playlist in the business. Most new songs just did not appeal to all the diverse groups that made up our target audience, so I refused to play them. Once a song *did* meet our highly selective criteria, it would be played with increasing or decreasing frequency as its popularity changed from week to week. Each record was in its own rotation, like a planet in its own orbit. Each of the most important songs had its own countdown clock, timing the minutes to its next airplay.

I played the songs that were the most popular with the most people. If, as a result, we played five female ballads in a row, that was fine with me, although I'm sure our rival stations could never bring themselves to violate accepted good programming practice in quite that way. I didn't care. My idea of what constituted good programming worked better—it got bigger ratings.

Because there were so few records making up the current playlist, we had to pick the right ones. If one of our selections was a mistake, that mistake would repeat itself again and again—such was the nature of the format. (The same pattern of airplay that drew in the audience could, with the wrong records in place, disperse it.) To find the best records to program, I designed a self-correcting research-and-decision process that culminated each week in a WABC music meeting, similar to the one at which "MacArthur Park" had been selected. Each meeting was preceded by a week of data gathering that included phone calls to record stores to track sales of singles. Some record companies gave key stores free boxes of records in return for a pledge from the store managers to report extra sales of those records to us. By rotating our sales survey among 550 stores, and studying the weekly report patterns, we were able to pinpoint such "hyping," disregard the inflated reports, and eventually make it unprofitable for the companies to continue the practice.

The WABC music meetings were held on Tuesday mornings and were preceded by the arrival of a stack of new records on my desk. These represented the most promising among the hundreds of singles released that week, as well as those record releases of recent weeks that showed consistent upward movement on a consensus of independent surveys. During the meeting, one or two of the tunes would be approved for broadcast on WABC. A few of the older songs currently on the station might be dropped. Top songs that had run their course would move into the permanent library and would continue to be aired, though less frequently. Some of those songs would stay on the air for over a decade, becoming "classic gold" records in the process. All these decisions were made at this meeting.

Because WABC developed the biggest audience in the country, and because its share of the market remained consistently high, year after year, the WABC music meeting eventually became the most closely watched decision-making process in radio. Hundreds of other stations watched and waited until WABC added a record before they moved on it. Record companies knew that a WABC "add" automatically guaranteed sales of tens of thousands of copies of that record in the metropolitan area alone. With so many other cities' stations playing copycat radio, hundreds of thousands of additional copies, sometimes millions, were sold nationwide. The stakes were high. The artists listened to WABC. Their managers listened to WABC. And the entire music industry listened to WABC. The WABC music meeting began to be regarded as the launching pad for gold records.

More than once, recording stars who had grown up in New York listening to WABC told me that their big dream was to have a record on the station. Barbra Streisand, whose music sold mostly in album form at first, never believed that a single of hers would crack the Top Twenty and get on WABC. In 1974 when "The Way We Were" became our number one single of the year, it was a tremendous kick for Barbra, because WABC was her old hometown station. Tony Orlando has spoken many times of the feelings he experienced when WABC took a chance on "Knock Three Times" and "Candida." When WABC went on a song called "Cowboys to Girls," it helped change the life of Kal Rudman, a $10,000-a-year special education teacher at Bucks County, Pennsylvania's F.D.R. Junior High School. Using money borrowed from a Philadelphia clothier, Rudman and Kenny Gamble had started a record label and produced the recording by the Intruders. When the record took off nationally, Rudman made almost $100,000 and quickly gave up teaching to publish "The Friday Morning Quarterback," a national music industry tip sheet for programmers. It became a phenomenal moneymaker, joining other tip sheets like the "Gavin Report" published by Bill Gavin in San Francisco.

Sensing the sessions' uniqueness, *The New Yorker* magazine twice covered the music meeting. The *Wall Street Journal* gave it page one, column one in a profile story on me, and *The New York Times* made it a feature story in their Sunday Arts and Leisure section.

Selecting music that would appeal to vastly diverse groups of listeners was difficult. Songs usually were played occasionally over a period of weeks locally before our adult listeners became comfortable with them. But if we waited too long before going on a genuine "hit," the teens would tire of it. Our timing had to be just right.

I rotated the attendance at the meetings among members of my staff, the talent staff, and station department heads. Usually we would have six to ten people present. A typical music meeting might include my production director (Jeff Berman and Julian Breen were two of the best over the years), disc jockeys like Herb Oscar Anderson and Cousin Bruce Morrow, perhaps the station's sales manager or promotion director, my secretary, and our music librarian, Sonia Jones, who prepared copies of all research on record sales and national chart popularity for everyone present.

We generally scrutinized the current air playlist first, dropping records without hesitation if they showed no gains after two weeks on the station. (A record once dropped might be brought back if there was a resurgence in sales.) We received many telephone calls and mail requests, but we never called listeners to ask them what records they wanted to hear. Instead I researched how they spent their money on the music. That way, I was measuring people's actual behavior instead of measuring what they *said* about their behavior. As a result, the data was more accurate.

When it came to the newer records not yet on WABC, we first listened to the stack of songs performing well in our own listening area and then evaluated other national hits. Big names did not impress us. When it came to getting a hit record, the top stars flopped more frequently than might be believed. During the music meeting I would also set the frequency of broadcast for each record. A record could be number one in the market, but if it was a fad novelty tune like Ray Stevens's "The Streak," I might slow the repeat play time down to once every 125 minutes instead of every

70 or 80 minutes. To really impress us, a record would have to make a series of large upward moves on the charts. When that happened, the disc would be aired on WABC. Each record was voted on, but if I believed the group at the meeting had made a mistake I would explain why I thought so and call for another vote. The group usually reversed itself.

Lyrics were sometimes a problem, and we discussed them. In those days a word like "crap" in the opening line of Paul Simon's "Kodachrome" would cause us to start the record on the air only at night, in teen time, and slowly move it to earlier dayparts where the more sensitive adult ears predominated. Some songs never made it to the morning. Once, a man who identified himself as King of the Gypsies called to protest Cher's song "Gypsys, Tramps and Thieves." The call was put through to the music meeting, and as I spoke to the man, I realized that he might have a legitimate beef.

"I'll take it under advisement and call you back," I said.

"I'll have to call you," he said. "Gypsies don't have phones."

But I never heard from him again. There were laughs at the meetings and there were tense moments when arguments broke out. As a result of the little weekly playlist adjustments, the meeting acted as a massive stabilizer to keep the sound intact and consistent.

When I began the music meetings in 1963, the record library was small, but after a few months there was enough music in it, along with hits from past years, to enable me to establish categories of records and rotate them for maximum audience impact. I used color codes, actually marking the tape cartridges with dots to indicate usage patterns.

When the library was completed and all the cartridges were on revolving wire racks in the studios, I realized that we didn't have any music to play in a "change-of-mood emergency"—a situation in which a tragedy or disaster that affected the entire nation would render our rock & roll offerings inappropriate.

Over the next few weeks I devised an additional library, divided into sections, that I called quiet and transitional music. The quiet music was selected to be used in those very rare instances when an audience is plunged into emotional shock. Included were several requiems and instrumental mourning music. In the three transitional phases, the music was more familiar. Although the melodies would be known by our listeners, the arrangements might be versions by artists not normally featured on WABC, "The Shadow of Your Smile" interpreted by Andre Kostelanetz, "Walk Away" and "Mr. Lonely" as played by Frank Chacksfield, for example. The transitional music might be played a few days later as the mood of the public slowly returned to normal. In the first phase of the transition, jingles would not be used. In the second phase we would start using the slower jingles, and by phase three the station would be back to normal.

Unfortunately, we had to make use of this format almost immediately. On November 22, 1963, President John F. Kennedy was assassinated. I ordered WABC to stay with the radio network coverage after they broke the first bulletin, and we remained with them for five hours. When the programming reverted to local control, we were ready. The quiet music phase began immediately. Across the nation, while other program directors searched frantically for suitable selections, WABC personnel followed the plan. Over the next few days the programming went slowly through its phases, and by Thanksgiving Day, with the city turning its attention to parades and turkey dinners, we were back to normal. In the years to come, songs like "Homeward Bound" by Simon and Garfunkel, "Safe in My Garden" by the Mamas and the Papas, and even "As Tears Go By" by the Rolling Stones found their way into the library of quiet music.

The amount of news on the station continued to bother me. Since there was nothing I could do to change it—the station's license required specific amounts of news, and the ABC attorneys were reluctant to amend it until after the renewal hearing the following year—I decided to use it to my advantage. I scheduled all news five minutes *before* the hour and half-hour so that when our competitors began their news and the music listeners started turning their radio dials searching for music, we would already be back, playing records. Each WABC newscast began with the phrase "News, five minutes sooner on WABC, New York."

Now I turned my attention to the jingles. WABC jingles were built around a musical theme from the song "I'll Take Manhattan." Neal paid five thousand dollars a year in royalties to use it, but his jingles didn't match the music. I flew to Dallas where the PAMS jingle company was located. (Dallas was the radio jingle capital of America. A combination of cheap real estate for studios

Pipers • "Harper Valley P.T.A." / *Jeannie C. Riley* • "(Sittin' on)

and favorable Texas right-to-work laws drew jingle companies to the Big D and as a result the city was soon rich in vocal talent. The singers went from one company to another doing sessions.) PAMS boasted vocalist Glenni Rutherford, a Cherokee woman whose vocal range spanned several octaves. Her high notes were to become a unique characteristic of WABC jingles.

In Dallas, I worked directly with PAMS President Bill Meeks. Bill was a former musician who still participated in some of the instrumental tracks for the jingles. He was multitalented. When budgets were tight, Meeks thought nothing of engineering his own session and playing most of the musical parts himself. He would start a tape recorder and then go into the studio and play the saxophone part. Then he would rewind the tape, go back into the studio and do the clarinet section. Eventually he had a full music "bed," and when it came time to record the jingles, even the typists and the receptionist sang. (Meeks had played sax for Jack Ruby in Ruby's nightclub. When Ruby shot President Kennedy's assassin, Lee Harvey Oswald, nobody was more surprised than Bill Meeks. He described Ruby to me as a man of tremendous energy who would spend long periods of time swimming laps in the pool for recreation. It was a strange time to be doing business in Dallas.)

Studio sessions to record WABC's jingles began with my rewrite of PAMS's lyrics for more impact. As the singers recorded each number, I would send it through an echo chamber and play it back on a two-inch speaker that approximated the sound of the small transistor radios that most WABC listeners owned. I would suggest changes in the arrangements and the male-female vocal mix until each one sounded right. PAMS series 27, the first jingles for WABC starring Glenni Rutherford (and also featuring PAMS sales manager Jim West, who sold by day and sang bass by night), became the most famous set of radio jingles ever recorded. It spawned imitations everywhere. There were special jingles for the morning, the evening, for each DJ, and others for weekends. The theme was "77 WABC, where the action is."

With the Manhattan music as the base, the singers also recorded a series of record intros for our top-ranked Superhits. On the air, the listener was led into the top hit record by a production spot that went like this:

The Dock of the Bay" / *Otis Redding* • "Angel of the Morning" /

CHORUS:	77 WABC with the Hot Line of Hits
MUSIC:	(Staccato beats like a Morse code)
ANNCR:	This week, this song is Superhit number five.
ECHO:	Five five five five five (fade).

PAMS's outside sales director, Gary Edens, sold variations of the series to stations everywhere. The action jingles and the hotline of hits (including the New York–oriented melody line "I'll Take Manhattan") were used to identify stations in every major city in the United States within a year, and were even sold to so-called pirate radio stations broadcasting rock radio into London from ships offshore (commercial radio was still illegal in Britain). Ten years later, some cuts were still being played, in English, to identify Paris stations. Only the call letters had changed.

At WABC I used jingles on a massive but carefully programmed basis throughout the day and night. There were jingles to introduce the weather, the sports, and the traffic. The special jingles that introduced the records by rank were recorded directly on the individual cartridge of each of the top fourteen songs every week. Fortunately for me, WABC had a crew of engineers whose lunch and relief rules in the air studio gave us surplus technical help when we needed extra manpower in the production studios to do all that recording.

I also instituted slogans that the disc jockeys delivered live, promoting the station. The Most Music—WABC and Musicradio WABC were the two that were used the most.

We probably mentioned the call letters almost four dozen times an hour. WABC was mentioned several times in most jingles, was in every slogan, and was even worked into the service information (temperature was given in W A B C Degrees) and news ("the congressman told WABC newsman Tom O'Brien . . .").

I believed that each mention was critical, and followed a mathematical strategy. If WABC averaged 250,000 listeners in a given quarter-hour of listening, and there were 168 hours in the week, and 4 weeks in the rating period, and another 8 weeks in the crucial habit-forming period prior to the rating sweep, then each additional call-letter mention per quarter-hour during the 12 weeks would gain us 2,016,000,000 additional call-letter impressions! I ran a minimum number of commercials and a maximum number of records as well so that the odds were greater that a person scanning the dial for music would find it on WABC. With that music chosen from the shortest, most popular list of records in radio and introduced by real personality disc jockeys, we were ready to take on the world.

CHAPTER 12

Tales of the Early Morning and Halftime at Big Shea

In radio, the battle for winning ratings begins with the station's morning show. Morning is radio's "prime time" for the same reason that the evening belongs to TV. More people listen to the radio in the morning than at any other time of day. They listen to find out what the weather is going to be. They need to be constantly reminded of the time of day. They tune in to find out if the world is still there. They want to know if the schools are open or closed, if the parking regulations are in effect, and generally to find out what's new around town. I would begin building my permanent audience base in the morning. Its most important format ingredient, apart from the music, would be the weather.

Weather is the most universal topic for radio. It affects virtually all listeners. Even shut-ins are interested and enjoy hearing about it. Since most people listen on and off over a period of only thirty to forty minutes in the morning, weather forecasts are usually given every fifteen minutes, interspersed with weather briefs. (I know a station owner in Phoenix who devotes five minutes of every hour to a full North American weather roundup. "We have lots of listeners who moved here from Canada," he explains. "They like to hear how their ex-neighbors are freezing.") Time and temperature are the names of the game in the morning. We would give them after every record.

/ *The Rolling Stones* • "Get Back" / *The Beatles* • "Crimson and

I also decided to rework the news approach. In small towns, people listen to morning radio for the latest gossip. In big cities they tune in braced for the day's hassles. But they *all* listen apprehensively for news that affects *them*. They want all the information that can help them get through their day.

For example, a newscast that begins, "There has been a severe flood in the interior region of Brazil and much of the fall coffee crop has been ruined," will not get the station better ratings. Opening the story with this lead: "You're going to be paying more for that morning cup of coffee starting next month, because the Brazilian coffee crop has been destroyed. Manuel Gomez told WXXX News that it looks bad down there," not only gets the listener's ear but also links the station's call letters to the story. Result—bigger ratings in the morning.

I knew that people also listen in the morning to be entertained, and for companionship. A high percentage of morning radio listening is done around the breakfast table, so the morning is one daypart that is "multidemographic"—it delivers more than one target audience group, sometimes the entire family. In those situations the youth are likely to be controlling the dial.

A great deal of morning radio listening is also done in cars. The 5-to-10 A.M. time has been dubbed the "morning drive" period and is AM radio's best time. Not all car owners have FM radios, and those who do sometimes experience reception problems and switch to AM. FM's high fidelity and stereo capability is also less important here because music takes a back seat to news and information in the morning.

During morning drive, I allowed the sales department to schedule more commercials. The spots blend in more easily with the expanded news and information content than with the music in other dayparts, without as great a risk of tune-out and ratings loss. The combination of more commercials and more people listening creates that "prime time" bonanza for radio. Some stations pack in over eighteen minutes an hour without hurting their sound. In resort areas dependent on seasonal business, twenty to twenty-two minutes of commercials are not uncommon in the morning, during the peak season. With all that money coming in, it's no wonder that the morning air personalities command radio's highest salaries and are at the top of the disc jockey pecking order. The morning voices are frequently the only DJ "names" that listeners actually remember well enough to report to the rating services.

My big morning competition was the "Rambling with Gambling" show with John Gambling—now a dynasty with the reins passing from father to son, and with a grandson in the wings. The Gambling dynasty started by accident. In the twenties, stations were owned by big department stores that were trying to sell those new devices, "radio music boxes." One of those stores, Bambergers in Newark, New Jersey (part of the New York radio market), founded the Bamberger Broadcasting Service and started each morning with a physical fitness exercise show featuring Bernarr MacFadden. The health cultist became sick one day, however, and the show's engineer called the store owner and asked what to do. "Turn on the microphone," he was told, "then go over to it and try to do the show yourself." Engineer John Gambling did the show. His style was unique and the public loved him; he was a hit. Bambergers, in the best tradition of show business, gave the show to the stand-in, and "Rambling with Gambling" was born.

Against John Gambling, WABC started the day with Herb Oscar Anderson—HOA he called himself—"The Morning Mayor of New York." Herb had the softest touch in radio. His contract specified that he did not even have to keep the log—that is, write in the times of each event and the titles of the songs he played. He commanded a full-time producer. Herb sat behind the microphone reading *The Farm Journal,* a tractor catalogue, or the New York *Daily News.* As each record ended, the producer, Murri Barber, put a piece of commercial copy in front of Herb, pointed to the first word, and Herb was off reading the commercial. Then Murri would write out the name of the next record on a piece of paper and hold that in front of Herb Oscar.

"It's the Beatles, the Beatles, the Beatles," Herb would say in his incredibly warm and friendly air voice. "If no one has said it as yet to you my dear, good morning." Herb had roughly six phrases that he used. "If no one has said it as yet," was one of them. There was also, "I got up bright and early to say 'I've Got a Song for You,'" and "The Call of the Great Northeast, W-A-B-C." He also used to say, "Girls, let's see some bright colors this morning," when it was gray outside. There was a joke at WABC, hypothesizing that if HOA ever failed to show up one morning and we just played the six phrases on cartridges between records, nobody would know he wasn't there. Herb sang on his opening theme song, ''Hello Again,'' and then played a hymn. At eight the rock music was interrupted for a ''march around the breakfast table.'' Herb projected a studied ''square'' image, and was terribly predictable. He was perfect for the morning.

When Herb's routine was broken, however, the results were anything but predictable. One day, Herb Oscar had to put in an appearance at an advertising agency after his show. Normally HOA didn't shave in the morning, but that day he brought in an electric razor. As the last hour of his show began, he got out the razor and looked around for an electrical outlet. He spotted one on the floor. It had a plug in it. Herb reached down, yanked the cord, plugged in his razor, and began to shave. WABC went off the air. The studio engineer jumped to his feet and began pushing buttons. Across the river in Lodi, New Jersey, at WABC's powerful fifty-kilowatt transmitter, another engineer grabbed the phone and began frantically dialing up the studio in New York to report the outage.

''Will you guys get things fixed?'' Herb yelled over the sound of the razor. The engineer in the studio ran out the door and raced around the floor to the radio station's transmission room, where he feverishly began checking out all the broadcast line connections. The connections were fine.

Five minutes later Herb finished shaving, reached down and unplugged his razor, replaced the other plug, and the program went back on the air. He was unruffled when he found out what had happened. It would take something far more explosive to shake up his routine. It took Wally Schwartz's yacht to do it.

After station manager Wally Schwartz, a man with flair and style, had appointed me program director with a mandate to move the station from the middle of the pack up to first place in the ratings, his next step had been to impress the advertising community by getting a station yacht to cruise the New York City waters entertaining clients. (The prospect of weekend use by station execs and their guests was also on his mind.) Yachts are costly propositions, and Schwartz had no budget for a boat. He opted to save some dollars by trying to get a seasonal charter instead of a purchase, and to reduce costs further by giving free advertising time to the boat dealer in return for the boat.

Schwartz still had problems. No one else at ABC had a yacht. No one in television had one. No one at the network had one. There was no company yacht. If ABC couldn't raise money for color TV cameras how could radio justify its own yacht? Schwartz knew that ABC was a lean corporation. The frugal policies of Simon Siegal, who along with Leonard Goldenson had started ABC on a shoestring, were still in effect. And Siegal was known as "the man who says *no.*" Siegal would say no to anything that smacked of extravagance the first time around. He would also say no the second time. If you came back three times, he would know that you were serious and that there might be a reason that made sense for the request. Such prudent policies served ABC well. But this kind of a request was not one you brought back to Siegal even the second time.

Wally Schwartz really wanted that boat. He didn't know how to get it, but Schwartz had a shrewd promotion manager who had saved some other "hopeless" situations. For example, he had swung a New England ski lodge for WABC brass in return for commercials and by letting the lodge owner phone a daily ski report to the station. Ski reports on Musicradio WABC would have caused instant tune-out and been deadly to the ratings, so the reports never got on the air. All winter the ski lodge owner was broadcasting over a loudspeaker in the sales office of WABC and not over the air. The ski lodge was out of range of the WABC signal and he was never the wiser; besides, he got his commercials. Schwartz now turned to that same promotion manager for help in getting a yacht.

The promotion manager's ploy was ingenious. WABC would announce a new service for the boating public—marine weather reports from the new WABC cruiser. Marine weather reports actually came from the Coast Guard and had nothing to do with WABC or its yacht. But this fact got lost in the gobbledygook of intercorporate communications, and the yacht was approved.

The *Music Power* sailed daily from the Seventy-ninth Street boat basin on the Hudson River, complete with catered meals and a steward. (Schwartz became known as "the admiral" around ABC, an image that was later to help propel him to the top of the radio network and finally to the presidency of the television division.) But once Wally Schwartz had the boat, WABC had to come up with marine weather reports on weekends. To assign a union writer to do them would have been costly. Instead we hired a part-time stenographer from an office temporaries firm called Kelly Girls.

Kelly Girls sent us Vera. Vera's job was to sit outside the studios on Saturday and Sunday mornings, listening to a Coast Guard radio and writing down the boating reports for Herb Oscar Anderson. The idea was a good one. What we didn't know was that tall and stately Vera, with her high cheekbones and jet black hair, was an out-of-work striptease dancer.

Vera got the hang of the job very quickly. By the second week she had the boating report typed in five minutes and was spending most of her time sitting in the studio enjoying the records. In those days we played the number one song every hour on WABC. That week the song at the top of WABC's Silver Dollar Survey was a David Rose instrumental, "The Stripper." Since "The Stripper" came up in rotation every sixty minutes, it wasn't long before the song went on while Vera was in the studio. A few beats into the record Vera's ears perked up. Another beat and she was on her feet.

"That's my music," she said, bumping and grinding to the music. "I have a whole routine that goes to that song."

There were three other people on the fifth floor in the studio early that Saturday morning: a newsman, an engineer, and Herb Oscar Anderson. Vera needed only the slightest encouragement to go into her routine. She started to prance back and forth in front of the startled morning crew.

First the skirt fell, then her blouse.

Unknown to Herb, his uncle and aunt from Brainerd, Minnesota, and their small children had been driving all night on the final leg of a trip to New York. As the sun rose, the Manhattan skyline came into view through the bug-spattered windshield of their station wagon. A thrill went through the family. This was the big city. They tuned in the radio and got another thrill—Uncle Herb was on the air. They decided to surprise Herb with a visit to the studio.

As Vera's bra came off, the station wagon was rounding the corner of West Sixty-sixth Street. As she dropped her panties, the station wagon was pulling up to number 39, the building housing WABC.

The kids scampered out of the car first, eager to stretch their legs, and raced into the building lobby. A red-jacketed page boy sat alone at a desk. The rest of the family followed. They introduced themselves to the page, who rang the studio. Herb answered.

"Your family from Minnesota is here," the page said. "They're on their way up in the elevator."

Herb leaped to his feet screaming. "There are KIDS COMING UP!" he yelled. "We have less than ten seconds. Cover up."

Vera grabbed for her blouse and was wrapping her skirt around, just barely holding it in place from the back as the studio door flew open.

"Uncle Herb! Uncle Herb!" the kids squealed as they raced for HOA's outstretched arms.

The engineer had his hands on the control board volume control "pots" (potentiometers). The news announcer was staring at his script. Vera stood unnoticed in the corner, one hand behind her back and the other holding the boating report, while Herb had his reunion.

On Monday two announcers applied for the weekend morning announcing shift and an engineer used his seniority to bounce the Saturday morning technician so he could work the shift. Management was bewildered. Staff people wanting to give up their weekends?

On Wednesday a concerned Herb Oscar Anderson confessed all to his colleagues, saying that we were better off hearing the story from him now rather than getting an exaggerated version later on and second-hand.

Kelly Girls was called, and Vera was discreetly replaced by a substitute schoolteacher.

The morning show settled down, and my attention was drawn to management's decisions to mix rock & roll music formats with play-by-play sports and sports promotions. In the early, dollar-hungry days at WABC, before the ratings got really big, the big-money sponsor contracts dangled in front of the company by the sales department carried a lot of weight and overpowered good programming practices. One such sponsor was Sonny Werblin, whose New York Jets had moved into the new Shea Stadium that had been built along with the New York World's Fair in Flushing Meadow. Werblin was a master showman. He signed quarterback Joe Namath to a headline-making, big-bucks contract. Every type of razzle-dazzle was employed to try to lure loyal Giants fans to the new team that had been built on the wreckage of the New York Titans who—along with *their* ballpark, the Polo Grounds—were only a memory. Why not come to the borough of Queens to see football? And as an added inducement a special halftime show, different each week, was dreamed up to entertain the fans.

It was with trepidation that I entered a meeting called by the sales department to discuss some sort of promotion involving the Jets and the Jocks (our disc jockeys). The ace salesman on the Worsted-Tax account, Larry Wynn, was there. Worsted-Tex sponsored the halftime show. We had pregame shows, postgame shows, and locker-room wrap-ups. It was a wonder we got any music played on Saturday nights.

"We can cross-promote our jocks to the football listeners," the sales manager explained. "They all bring radios to the game anyway."

Before we could get any further into the meeting, another salesman walked in. This one represented the Chrysler-Plymouth Dealers of New York. In a few minutes, the promotion had been laid out. At halftime WABC and Worsted-Tex would sponsor a fashion show. All the DJs would be fitted with new custom suits. Each one would ride in a new Chrysler convertible. The parade would start from behind the scoreboard and proceed around the stadium. Each air personality dressed in one of Worsted-Tex's latest fashions would receive a salute from the stadium announcer as his outfit was described in glowing terms to the fans. I started to protest, but I knew that the ball games were bringing many sorely needed dollars to the station. While I couldn't wait until the day came when we canceled sports I knew I had lost this round before it began.

The disc jockeys actually became excited about the idea. The free suits turned them on. They spent hours selecting styles and being fitted. Pictures were taken for publication in the Jets program supplement.

Unknown to us, previous attempts to attract fans by giving away refrigerators and appliances at halftime had not worked. The people wanted football. But the Jets public relations staff assured us that we had a winner in this show.

On the night of the game all the WABC announcers were seated in special VIP boxes next to the press boxes. We watched the first half of the game from unobstructed fifty-yard-line seats. We saw the Jet drives stall again and again. We saw one Namath pass after another intercepted. Suddenly the Jets were behind. A few more plays, a fumble, an opposition field goal, and the stands erupted with boos. Then it was halftime.

"I don't like this," I said to Herb Oscar Anderson as we headed down to the playing field.

"What's not to like?" he replied. "The crowd, the lights, the excitement. It's a beautiful night."

"They're losing," I answered. "The crowd is ugly, Herb. Ugly. They're angry."

"No, they're not. They're just football fans. Have a beer."

The high school band that had been talked into playing for free, finished their performance and the booth announcer began to talk:

"Ladies and gentlemen! When you entered the park tonight you were given a special program that will guide you through our next event. WABC Radio and Worsted-Tex Clothes together with your local Chrysler-Plymouth dealer are proud to present the WABC All-Americans in the first ever football fashion show. You will see the latest in Worsted-Tex fashions and the first showing of the new 1965 Chrysler convertibles." A low murmur swept the stands.

The band played a fanfare from the sidelines. Herb Oscar Anderson stood up in the lead car's back seat, braced himself with one hand, and told the driver he was ready. The car moved out from behind the scoreboard and headed for the stands.

"Ladies and Gentlemen: Wearing a new three-piece Worsted-Tex houndstooth pattern with the new wide lapels, the morning mayor of New York, Herb Oscar Anderson."

Herb raised his free hand high and waved it at the crowds as he had seen Douglas MacArthur do in an old newsreel years ago.

For a moment he basked in the crowd's adulation. Then the first beer can struck. Then another and another. The moment the car was within firing range of the stands the crowd had opened up on HOA. The driver bravely continued foward as Herb Oscar Anderson, bobbing and weaving, tried to dodge the oncoming missiles.

Waiting behind the scoreboard, we had no way of knowing what was happening. And on cue the announcer began again.

"The finest in evening wear by Worsted-Tex is worn this evening by Big Dan Ingram."

The second car rolled and then the third.

Jock after jock, they went like lambs to the slaughter. The angry football fans were venting their full frustration on the hapless targets. By the time they got to the last car we were well aware of what was happening. My driver stayed out in the middle of the field, made a quick turn, and nobody ever got to see my new raincoat.

The next time I saw the inside of that stadium, it would be packed with fifty-five thousand hysterical Beatle fans.

Salvadore Dali and I examine a listener's entry in the Mona Lisa art contest held by WABC in 1963. Dali clutches a cartoon, depicting the Mona Lisa looking out of a space capsule, which he later declared the winner. The contest, which offered $100 for the biggest, smallest, best, and worst copies of the painting, drew over 15,000 entries. *(Bill Mitchell Photography)*

''Biggest'' Mona Lisas are judged on the playing field of New York's Polo Grounds. Scoreboard numerals are used as weights to hold the entries down against the wind. *(Bill Mitchell Photography)*

Left: Disc jockey "Cousin" Bruce Morrow (left) boarding a helicopter with me to visit high schools for the "Principal of the Year Election" on WABC. *(Bill Mitchell Photography)*

Below: Sacks of mail surround me as entries pour into WABC Radio for the "Principal of the Year Election." Votes on cards are counted by Tickometer machines. Students could vote more than once, and over 176 million votes were cast. *(Bill Mitchell Photography)*

We scooped every other station when Bruce Morrow interviewed the Beatles at the Warwick Hotel, New York. Here Morrow talks to Ringo Starr, as George Harrison looks on. *(Rick Sklar, private collection)*

Left: Huntington Hartford (at bottom, on the ladder) views a Beatle sketch submitted during a WABC contest and displayed here at the New York World's Fair of 1964-65. WABC general manager Walter A. Schwartz (closest to sketch) and fair officials look on. *(Rick Sklar, private collection)*

Below: Bruce Morrow shows Paul McCartney the "Order of the All Americans" medal awarded to each of the Beatles by WABC in 1966 for their contribution to popular music. Looking on are WABC disc jockey Dan Ingram (left) and Rick Sklar. *(Rick Sklar, private collection)*

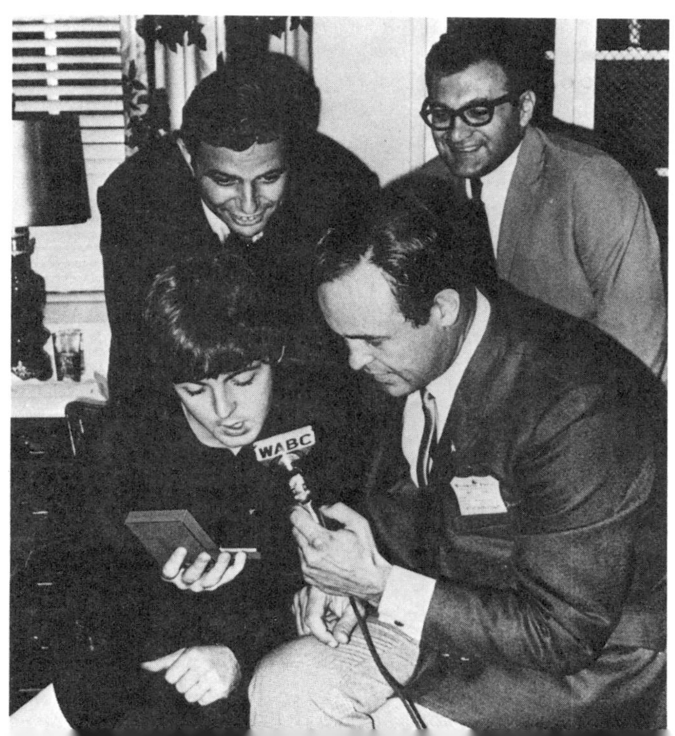

ABC Radio president Hal Neal with me in Neal's 38th-floor office in the ABC headquarters building in New York, thanking Tony Orlando for his impromptu performance at an ABC Radio sales meeting. *(Rick Sklar, private collection)*

I show cartoonist Charles Addams and WABC general manager Walter A. Schwartz the fans' banners at WABC's Superman Fan Convention in 1966. *(Bill Mitchell Photography)*

CHAPTER 13

W A Beatle C

I decided to make my music audience base as large as possible and go for the cume (cumulative audience) as they say in radio. When the baseball and football games, the seventy-five-minute newscasts, and the network features drove away the music fans, we tried to get them back into the listening pool as quickly as we could. Music, jingles, jocks, contests, slogans, and even our WABC Action Central newscasts all were produced so as to have magnetic entertainment value for optimum impact on the ratings.

The strategy worked. New York's monthly Pulse ratings books changed dramatically. In March 1964, WABC pulled alongside WOR, long the leader in the morning. We tied them with a breakfast time share of 16. Middays and at nights WABC was first that month. By May WABC was pulling a 22 share at night, taking much of it from WINS, which dropped to a 7 from a previous share of 15. A new factor sweetened the picture. WABC's exciting programming had pushed nighttime radio listening up. The number of homes where radios were tuned in at night increased by almost a third throughout our listening area. Not only did we have a bigger slice of the pie, but the pie itself was bigger.

In the midst of all this forward movement, the Beatles came into our lives.

Politicians have nothing on program directors when it comes to riding on the coattails of a winner. Radio execs are constantly scanning the headlines for people and events that will make for good tie-ins with their stations. Nevertheless, first reports of the hysteria generated in England by a group called the Beatles were greeted with some skepticism by an American radio industry numb from years of record company hype. Even concert promoter Sid

Bernstein, who brought the Beatles to this country, was cautious and opted for Carnegie Hall over New York's 18,000-seat Madison Square Garden rather than risk playing to a half-empty house.

But when the Beatles' first major release in this country, "I Want To Hold Your Hand," shot up the charts like a rocket and "She Loves You" did the same, my interest focused sharply on the new British quartet.

The Carnegie Hall concert set aside any remaining doubts. Fan adulation of the type lavished on rock groups in the eighties, or even by the swooning Sinatra fans of the forties, pales in comparison to what happened in Carnegie Hall that night. The Beatles' first American concert was a happening to end all happenings. When the predominantly female teenage crowd caught sight of the four fragile-looking, neatly attired young men who had let their hair grow to what was then an unheard-of length, an outpouring of desire to mother, protect, worship, love, and devour them exploded into the loudest continuous shriek imaginable, punctuated by the brilliant, unending explosion of flashbulbs, a surging of bodies down the aisles, faintings, and a mass ecstasy that continued during the entire time that the group was onstage. Not a single note of the entire concert was heard by anybody. The legendary acoustics of the hall served only as a sounding board for the audience itself, totally drowning out the concert. The scene left no doubt that American fans would attach themselves with fierce loyalty to anything they perceived as a part of the Beatle phenomenon.

When I left my box in Carnegie Hall that night, I decided to make the Beatles' success our success. WABC became W A Beatle C.

I flew down to PAMS jingle company to write and produce new jingles and production slogans built around W A Beatle C. Those jingles were tagged onto every Beatle record we played, and the slogans were shouted out by the jocks. All our contests became vehicles to tie us to the Beatles. We ran Beatle look-alike contests. A Ringo look-alike prize was won by a woman who, incredibly, had the same face as the Beatles' drummer. A WABC Beatle poster contest was staged in the Coca-Cola Pavilion at the New York World's Fair (emceed by A&P grocery heir Huntington Hartford as a way of ending a running feud between himself and fair creator Robert Moses over a giant A&P sign nearby that was ruining the fair vista).

While WABC normally waited until records became established hits before playing them, Beatle records were programmed as soon as they came out—before they started to sell. Often we didn't even wait for a new Beatle song to be released. Advance pressings or taped dubs of new Beatle records mysteriously found their way from Capitol Records pressing plants to WABC where, to the anguish of competing stations, they went on the air after the close of business Friday night—too late for competitors to badger Capitol for copies. Further, jingles that said "W A Beatle C Exclusive" were dropped in every fifteen seconds over the record, making off-air dubbing by competing stations difficult. WABC would have an *exclusive* for the weekend, and still higher ratings as fans learned to stay with WABC for the newest Beatle hits. As a result, the Beatles rode our coattails too. WABC's night signal covered half of America and was of inestimable promotional value to the group and their label.

Our most intense efforts at tying in with the Beatles were reserved for covering the group's visits to New York. When word came out that John, Paul, George, and Ringo would be staying at the Warwick Hotel on Fifty-fourth Street, our coverage was planned with the thoroughness and precision of a military operation. We rented a suite directly above the one in which the Beatles would be staying. Radio lines were installed back to our studios across the street. Instead of simply setting up the WABC suite for a remote broadcast with microphones and a control board, I also had our engineers rig up an RF (radio-frequency) receiver that could pick up wireless microphones that I borrowed from Julie Barnathan, head of ABC Broadcast Operations and Engineering.

The RF microphones gave us a terrific advantage over competitors because we could wander around the hotel with them, broadcasting from anywhere we found a Beatle. The signal would go back to our suite where it would be mixed into our console and then be carried by radio lines to the station for broadcasting. We could feed the network and the world from one wireless microphone. The method would give our ABC affiliates in other cities exclusive feeds that would help them build ratings along with WABC.

Nonetheless, all the equipment in the world wouldn't help if we couldn't get within talking distance of a Beatle. That meant that we would have to have freedom to roam the lobbies, hallways, elevators, and even access to the Beatles' own suite. Security on the day of their arrival was intense. Groups of fans had begun gathering in the street the night before, despite the fact that the group would not be landing at JFK Airport until the afternoon. Police protection was so tight that even traditional press badges were not enough. Never would a back entrance or freight elevator prove more valuable. Our production people, armed with bottles of Scotch and ten-dollar bills, worked their way up to the Beatles' floor, making friends with plainclothesmen, hotel staff, and floor guests—we tried to meet anybody who seemed worth the effort.

By mid-afternoon, the streets around the Warwick Hotel were like a war zone. Hundreds of police were posted around, trying to keep about fifteen thousand teenagers from reaching the hotel. The crowds were contained behind wooden horses across the street and spilled back for four blocks along Sixth Avenue (Avenue of the Americas). Our engineers, producers, and DJs, led by Cousin Bruce Morrow, were already in the suite as registered guests of the hotel. From our vantage point we could see down Sixth Avenue, and Bruce could also view Fifty-fourth Street by leaning way out the window while I held him by his trouser belt. Then it became a waiting game.

Periodically the crowd would surge, hysterical shrieks would erupt, police on horseback would rush down the block, and then the crowd would subside. By monitoring our other team covering the arrival at the airport, we tried to time the trip. We were actually relaxing and away from the window when the really loud yelling began in the street. Bruce Morrow bolted to the window and we spotted a Rolls-Royce coming up Sixth Avenue. It headed right for the Fifty-fourth Street corner and turned in front of the hotel. The closest crowds broke through the barricades screaming and shrieking. Hysterical girls surrounded the car as police seemed confused by what was happening. I called for an air feed and Bruce tilted so far out the window that I was afraid he would fall. Morrow peered down at the scene and broadcast a brief description. The door to the Rolls-Royce's rear compartment opened. One young man, then another, then two more, bolted from the car into the lobby. Bruce had a puzzled look on his face as he described the scene. Even from eight floors up, something didn't look right about it and he cautioned the audience. Moments later we learned that we hadn't seen the Beatles at all, but another singing group called the Teddy Boys who were trying to cash in on the excitement of the moment in the hopes of getting some publicity.

At least forty-five minutes passed. In the interim the police began shunting all traffic off Fifty-fourth Street and soon the block was clear all the way to Fifth Avenue. Then, very unexpectedly, a motorcycle-escorted motorcade appeared at the almost deserted corner of Fifty-fourth Street and Fifth Avenue and proceeded west up the one way *eastbound* street, pulling up in front of the Warwick before the fans realized what was happening. For an instant the bulk of the crowd was caught completely off guard. Then the realization hit. This was it! The four living gods were within the crowd's grasp. Before the first police escorts had jumped from their own cars to surround the Cadillac limousine carrying the group, a wave of teenage girls poured across the street, bowling over the barricades, and surrounding the car. The car doors flew open on the hotel side. The car's occupants bolted out. For a moment the leading edge of the human wave touched the group, then the police lines re-formed and the Beatles were in the hotel.

We were in their rooms faster than we had hoped. While hotel guests were kept two floors away and detectives flushed fans out of the broom closets in the halls, our now familiar faces were waved in by the plainclothesmen, and a knock on the door brought an immediate response. Yes. We could come in almost immediately. In fact there was a problem. Ringo needed our help.

Bruce Morrow, Scott Muni, and I walked in. Paul McCartney and John Lennon were padding around the room, walking off the after-effects of a long flight and the motorcade. George Harrison was stretched out on a bed, resting. Ringo sat in an overstuffed armchair, looking dazed. His face was flushed, his jacket and shirt ripped. He had been the last out of the limousine, and by then the crowds had closed in, overwhelming the police. His clothes had been torn and a Saint Christopher's medal on a chain had been ripped from his neck.

Bruce turned on the wireless RF microphone and called for engineer Bobby Ryan to put us on the air.

"We're in the Beatles' suite, Bobby. Bobby, get this."

In seconds Morrow was describing the scene in the room both to the WABC audience and to listeners at ABC Radio Network affiliates across the country. Once he realized the microphone was live, Ringo managed a smile and said, ''Hello, how are you? Good to be back in New York, anyway. The only thing is the medallion. I haven't had it off me neck since I was twenty-one. That was three years ago. It's sort of a keepsake. It's just a gold Saint Christopher's medal.''

''Gold?'' Bruce asked.

''It's gold. I only wear gold,'' Ringo assured him.

Scott announced that he and Bruce were going to go down into the crowd to try and find the medal, but also asked that anyone having the medal or knowing of its whereabouts come to the WABC studios. Since virtually every person in the crowd below had a transistor radio, it didn't take long before a girl arrived at the WABC studios with the medal. Her name was Angie McGowan and she couldn't really explain how it had come into her possession. She said that the moment of the arrival was confusing, and that she had reached out to touch Ringo and somehow found herself with the medal.

Elated, I brought her into the executive offices and thought quickly. The loss of the medal was becoming a cause célèbre. It was a moment of drama. The longer we could prolong it, the longer the listeners would stay with us and the higher the ratings would be. I asked if she could call home and tell her parents that she might have to stay overnight to meet the Beatles. We reassured them that she would be safe, and kept her locked in the WABC hotel suite while we continued to broadcast appeals for the medal. By the next day, the entire city and Ringo were frantic. After twenty-four hours of melodrama and suspense, Angie McGowan appeared before our microphones. Ringo and his Saint Christopher's medal were reunited on the air, and the ratings went through the roof.

Other memorable moments punctuated our coverage. There were the afternoons when the crowds below could be orchestrated into a frenzy by the simple act of jostling a closed venetian blind or letting anybody in our group with long hair brush against a window. But my most vivid recollection involved the second day of coverage when Paul McCartney was to accompany me to the WABC suite to do a formal taping. I picked him up at the Beatles' suite below and rang for the elevator. Because we were nervous

Cone • "What's Goin' On" / *Marvin Gaye* • "Don't Pull Your about staying out in a public hall, I pressed both the up and the down buttons. The Warwick elevators were manually operated in those days, so a down elevator could be reversed mid-trip. Sure enough, a down light came on and an elevator door opened. A uniformed female attendant rolled back the inner steel-grating door. Inside the elevator stood a distinguished-looking man in a business suit, one hand gripping a briefcase and the other the hand of a teenage girl, probably his daughter who had persuaded her dad to take her with him on a business trip in the hope of meeting the Beatles. She was staring down at the floor. "Excuse me," I said to the elevator operator. "I know this elevator is going down, but this is an emergency. Could you take us up *one* floor?"

At that moment the girl raised her head. She was staring into the face of Paul McCartney, less than twelve inches away. "It's him. It's HIM!" she said. The elevator operator stared, uncomprehending. "I'm sorry," she replied. "This is a down elevator. You'll have to wait for the next up car." And she rolled the steel grating shut between the girl and McCartney. "Let him in!" the girl screamed. The outer door closed. The elevator continued its descent. We could hear that girl screaming all the way to the lobby.

New York was the jumping-off point for almost every Beatles American tour. Between visits, I kept the link between the group and the station intact in the hearts of the fans. No angle was overlooked. When the Beatles appeared on an ABC television show, I secured the giant photo that was used as a backdrop for the program and gave it away over the air. Responding to a United Cerebral Palsy request for a charity idea, I talked the Beatles into doing a concert to raise funds and also got the New York Paramount Theatre donated. Listeners who bought tickets to the event at the elaborate Times Square movie palace also stood a chance of being picked for a backstage champagne reception. (The girl who won was rushed into the Paramount dressing room as I broke open a bottle of the bubbly and poured drinks for George, Paul and John, while Ringo ruminated from a corner chair.) The Paramount was sold out in hours, and the scene was a repeat of Carnegie Hall with the screaming and flashbulbs. ABC's chairman, Leonard Goldenson, personally welcomed the quartet from the Paramount stage, managing to overcome both the noise levels of the crowd and the faux pas of a scriptwriter who thanked "John, Paul, Jack, and Ringo."

By the end of the year we were able to run an ad that read "In 1964 More People Listened to WABC Than Any Other Station in North America."

For the next Beatle visit to the States, I was offering ten box seats for the Beatles' return engagement at Shea Stadium to the listener who designed the most appropriate medal to honor the group for their contribution to popular music. (Its real purpose was to further cement the image of WABC as the "official" Beatle station.) The winning design, a torch rising from a clef, was inscribed on a bronze medallion and was called "The Order of the All-Americans" after our disc jockey team. Neither the WMCA "Good Guys" nor the "Fifth Beatle" (as Murray the K was calling himself on WINS) had anything like it.

When the second Shea Stadium event rolled around in 1965, W A Beatle C was so firmly fixed in the heads of the teens that twenty thousand of them, packed into a five-block stretch of Park Avenue, sang along with every jingle and Beatle record when WABC staged a remote broadcast from the Delmonico Hotel where the group was staying. I recall dozens of other images of Beatle-related moments, but none surpasses that afternoon at the Delmonico. The fact that the huge crowd was singing in unison meant that just about every person in it had a transistor radio tuned to WABC. We had won. We were the official Beatle station. We didn't have to wait for the ratings books to find out.

Even after the Beatles left town, the sense of excitement remained. As the year rolled up record ratings for WABC, the four long-haired lads from Liverpool could point to seven top hit records on our charts, all from the biggest album of the year, *Meet the Beatles*. Ironically, they did not have the number one song of 1964 on WABC. That song was "Hello Dolly" by Louis "Satchmo" Armstrong. It was on our playlist for twenty-two weeks, a run that was never exceeded by any other single. It dramatically proclaimed that WABC's audience included a segment of men and women even larger than the segment of teenagers, a spectacular accomplishment for the station that was also first with teens. Beatle songs did take number two ("I Want to Hold Your Hand") and number three ("She Loves You"), overshadowing Frankie Valli and The Four Seasons (who were having one of their best years ever with "Dawn" and "Rag Doll"), the Supremes ("Baby Love"), and the Shangri-Las (with "Leader of the Pack").

More rumblings began to be heard from Britain. Great Britain was "in" with its new fashions and music. Other English groups were springing up. We tried out a record by one of them, the Dave Clark Five. It quickly demonstrated the reach and influence of our signal. A Philadelphia record chain sold 3,500 records even though the record was only on WABC. Groups like the Dave Clark Five were talented and exciting, but the Beatles were an unprecedented phenomenon.

CHAPTER 14

Happy Birthday, Baby

The WABC of 1965 was a different station than the one that had welcomed John, Paul, George, and Ringo when they made their American debut. We had moved from the stables on Sixty-sixth Street to more extensive studios and offices on the fifth floor of 1926 Broadway, a sturdy old loft building facing Lincoln Center. (A historical note for engineering buffs: The move was delayed almost two months by a classic engineering miscalculation. Almost a thousand cables ran from the main studio control board through floor conduits to rack panels at the other end of the block-long building. During the installation process these cables were pushed into the conduits and pulled up at the other end by construction engineers who discovered to their chagrin that each cable was two feet short. They had to painstakingly splice two feet of wire to each cable, a costly blunder.)

There were other changes besides new studios. I had tightened the music policy further and the ratings zoomed higher. As the audience grew larger and the playlist grew smaller, the pressure from the record companies and the music publishers intensified. The disc jockeys attending the weekly music meetings were buttonholed in the streets, repeatedly telephoned, and taken out to lunches, clandestine meetings, and dinners, and urged to do everything they could to add certain records. Some of the jocks were not pleased with my strict music lists, and we had heated exchanges. When "Hello, Dolly," the antithesis of rock & roll, clung to the number one playlist position week after week—a rank that meant it got played every sixty minutes—Scott Muni became furious.

"Get that song off my show," he demanded.

I refused.

Eventually Scott Muni challenged the record store sales data secured by my telephone researcher. "How do we know that she writes down what the store clerk is saying at the other end?" he demanded. He threatened to go to the FCC and punch holes in the integrity of our system.

I stayed calm. "No problem," I said. "We'll tape the calls." I immediately added a beep sound and a soundscriber tape system to the research phones.

Next week he was back again, complaining to me in front of my staff, about the short playlist.

"I haven't declared war on you yet," he warned. "But when I do—"

"You have," I said. "The war is over."

Scott left. He was a very talented jock with a unique voice that got ratings, but the situation was untenable. Later on he went to work as a DJ and then program director at WNEW-FM. (It was a long time before Scott and I began talking again, but in 1982, when almost all pop music had moved from AM to FM and Musicradio WABC gave up the format and became Talkradio WABC, Scott devoted an entire evening on WNEW-FM to a documentary salute to Musicradio WABC that featured me and the jocks and tapes of the station in its heyday.)

With Scott Muni gone, I moved Cousin Bruce Morrow into the early evening "teen jock slot." This left our 11 P.M. period open. I started listening to our competitors. I really wanted to do something different and scanned the high end of the dial where more specialized stations were located. One of those stations was WWRL with a predominantly black music list and DJ roster. I heard Chuck Leonard and liked his smooth sound. I wasn't sure whether he was white or black, but I guessed he was probably black. No major New York station had a black disc jockey then. We met and agreed to a contract. When we notified the company that we were about to hire WABC's first black jock, the word came down from the top of the company. Leonard Goldenson, ABC's chairman of the board, was delighted.

As 1965 progressed, more and more music came from the other side of the Atlantic—the British Invasion continued. Music was either by British groups sounding like the Beatles or American groups sounding British. We had the Rolling Stones (whose single, "Satisfaction," ended up being the number one song of the year),

Sammy Davis, Jr. • "Lean on Me" / *Bill Withers* • "First Time Ever

Herman's Hermits, Gerry and the Pacemakers, the Kinks, Freddie and the Dreamers, the Searchers, Peter and Gordon, and the Moody Blues—all of whom had hits.

Then WINS dropped out. They were the first of our competitors to give up their music format. Westinghouse management, in a bold move, became the first major-market station to go to an all-news format. Scoffers throughout the industry doubted that the idea would work in a Top Ten city, but WINS would eventually go on to become a high-rated, nonmusic station with a unique format that could almost be called Top Forty news. (The top story got the most plays.)

Having knocked off WINS, I continued to be very strict and methodical with the music and slowly phased in another jingle package based on the theme "Go-Go," after the go-go dancers in a new type of club called a discotheque that was becoming popular for the first time.

Competition continued with the other music hit station, WMCA. Program director Ruth Meyer received an advance copy of the Beatles' "Paperback Writer" from Capitol Records' Pennsylvania pressing plant, causing us to retaliate with more Beatle exclusives. The press became increasingly intrigued by WABC and our goings-on. *The New Yorker* sent Renata Adler to sit in on a WABC music meeting and do a story.

By the summer of 1965, we had enough gold records in our library to give our radio listeners a treat. I ran a "Summer Solid Gold Spectacular"—every other record was from our gold collection. It was another blow to WMCA and their "Good Guys."

During WABC's summer of solid gold, almost a third of a million people listened to the station every quarter-hour. Over 100,000 of them were women, almost 60,000 were men, and there were 150,000 teenagers and children as well. On a brilliant sunshiny day in August, with the Summer of Solid Gold in full swing and all those people listening, disc jockey Bob Dayton crossed the line of good taste and on air responsibility.

It was the twentieth anniversary of the atomic bombing of Hiroshima, and Dayton marked the event by playing the song "16 Candles" by the Crests. The lyrics begin with "Happy Birthday, baby." Protest calls from listeners poured into the station switchboard, and Dayton never did another show on WABC. Had this been his first misjudgment or even the second, we might have forgiven him. But with Dayton it was an epidemic. We had barely escaped a lawsuit on the previous Election Day when Dayton led into a Republican commercial in what he termed his "creative" way. The spot announcement had been recorded by a housewife. Here's what the listeners heard:

DAYTON: "I'm feeling good today. Yeah. Had a nice time last night. One of the most beautiful women I go out with and I . . . well we were in my spacious bachelor apartment. Everything was perfect. The wine was poured. The music was soft and low. The candles were lit. Very romantic. And I whispered sweet nothings in her ear. And do you know what she said? She snuggled up to me and she said . . ."

WOMAN: "My name is Mrs. Edward Burke. I live in Astoria with my husband and three children in a community which we moved to in order to give our children a better life. We have a school there that's the pride of the city. My children are happy there. But now they want to bus my children to schools outside our community. Don't my family and I have any rights? I'm voting for Barry Goldwater tomorrow."

DAYTON: "So the only thing I could say was . . . the preceding announcement was paid for by the Woman's National Republican Campaign Committee."

Charlie Greer was rushed back into daytime to take Dayton's place. For the overnight spot, I once again reached back to the station that had spawned Dan Ingram and this time came up with WIL's cherubic "Wile Chile," Ron Lundy. I put Lundy on the overnight spot to train him in the format. He caught on quickly.

The Dayton upheaval was the talk of the station until November, when the Northeast was hit by its first power blackout. The outage occurred during the Dan Ingram show and first manifested itself as a drop in power that caused studio lights to flicker and music cartridges to play at slow speeds. As reports came in to the newsroom of city after city along the coast being blacked out, the newsmen began to speculate that it was possibly a Russian invasion. Nobody could imagine what was happening. The then unknown concept of a regional power grid failure was the last thing in anybody's mind.

America • "Nights in White Satin" / *The Moody Blues* • "I Can See

Many stations went off, but when all the power went, WABC was still on the air because the station's transmitter was in Lodi, New Jersey, and that state was on a different electric grid. Telephone service continued so we could broadcast voices by phoning the transmitter. Since we couldn't play music from New York we rushed Dan Ingram to Lodi with a stack of records and continued the show from there.

The next day we ran an "In the Dark" contest giving transistor radios as prizes for the most outlandish explanations for the blackout.

Clearly Now" / *Johnny Nash* • "Saturday in the Park" / *Chicago* •

CHAPTER 15

Fail-Safe

The blackout helped focus my attention on technical reliability. A station can have the best mix of music and the top jocks and jingles, but if the tapes break, the cartridges jam, or the music fidelity is off, the ratings begin to evaporate.

Periodically, I noticed that some of the songs weren't being played, even though they were important to the ratings, because a cartridge had disappeared or a tape had jammed. I began to think about ways to eliminate such problems.

While I was pondering the solution to that annoyance, another technical difficulty arose. Some of the songs we were broadcasting inexplicably began sounding muddy over the air. The high notes had disappeared! I spent several weeks troubleshooting that mystery only to discover that the culprit was one of our own management engineers. WABC's transmitter had been cited by the FCC for splattering high frequencies across the radio dial and disrupting the sound of neighboring stations. Some old parts had malfunctioned. Rather than spend the money to fix things, the engineer had come up with a quick and dirty solution. He had placed a high-frequency filter across the recording circuit on the machine where our records were re-recorded onto tape cartridges. All the high notes were being filtered out of the songs before they ever reached the air. This clandestine tampering had been going on for six weeks before I uncovered it. Listeners were turning us off in droves, disgusted with the sound. I finally had a maintenance man simply go to the circuit and cut it off.

A few weeks later, the same management engineer who had cut the highs out of the music again interfered with the on-air sound. This time he installed an experimental console in the main air studio. This monstrosity was supposed to automatically fade down the music when a disc jockey began to speak, mix channels without the touch of a human hand, and join the network at just the proper loudness.

It was a disaster. The music drowned out the jocks, commercials blurred into records, and finally the machine played two songs at the same time. When that happened I wanted to run into the studio and tear the thing out, but I had to go through channels. The broadcast operations and engineering department had gone on record endorsing the new control board. I found myself battling internal bureaucracy trying to get the device out of there. After several weeks, a political compromise was reached, typical of the face-saving scenarios that have been devised in large companies to deal with situations like this. The guts of the unit were removed and replaced by a normal control circuit. The outside facade of the unit was left in place so it appeared that the new automatic control board was still functioning. There it remained until, in a comedy of errors, an engineer hitting a stuck button on the unit caused it to short out. As he reached into the panel racks to fix the short, a heat-warped printed circuit-board crumbled. When he tried to replace the board, other parts fell away and the station went off the air. We literally operated out of a suitcase (using gear built for remote broadcasts) for months. A new control board could not be ordered because our studios and offices were about to be moved again, this time to the new ABC corporate headquarters building at 1330 Avenue of the Americas.

Loss of signal is a terrible ordeal for a program director. Once listeners hear dead air, they go over to the competition in about two seconds. The longer a station stays off the air, the greater the likelihood of a negative impact on the next ratings book. Radio stations try to minimize the chances of these outages. One way is by having two transmitters. However, no system is perfect. WABC once went off the air because a bulldozer on a road building job sliced through the conduit containing the underground cable that carried our signal from our studios in New York to our transmitter in New Jersey. I had been assured by our engineers that we had a backup cable.

"What happened to the backup cable," I asked.

"It was in the same conduit," the chief engineer replied. Frantic calls to the phone company got us a temporary circuit to replace

Me Softly With His Song" / *Roberta Flack* • "Tie a Yellow Ribbon

the cut cables. After that debacle, WABC's programs were beamed to the transmitter from a microwave dish atop our new forty-story home. It was a dandy line-of-sight signal direct to our tower across the Hudson River. This remedy worked until the new fifty-story Burlington House began to rise across the street. The day Burlington construction reached the forty-first floor and steel girders were swung into place in the path of our microwave signal, WABC went off the air. This time our engineers puzzled for three hours before noticing the construction across the street. Hurriedly they angled the microwave dish southwest and bounced the WABC signal off the J. C. Penney building on the next block, deflecting it around the Burlington building. WABC went back on the air.

The three-hour signal loss bothered me until I head about an engineer at an FM station who had turned the power down from 100,000 watts to 25,000 watts to save on the electric bill. The following year, the Federal Communications Commission froze all FM signals at their current operating strengths and the station never got its power back.

Equipment failures also plagued us. I had told the engineering department that we needed five cartridge-playing machines for the format to work. The rapid intermixing of jingles, songs, commercials, and promotion spots demanded at least that many different sound sources. But every day one or two machines were broken and the pace of the station slowed down, damaging the audience appeal.

Before I got that problem resolved I found out that copper poachers were endangering our ratings by weakening the signal. A powerful AM station like WABC sets up its tower in the center of a wide, "moist" field. The "wetter" the better. AM stations depend on electrical conductivity to help generate a strong ground wave to supplement the air signal. To achieve this conductivity, two hundred and forty copper cables, each one as long as the transmitter tower is high, are laid out, radiating from the base of the tower, every degree and a half in a circle. There is a lot of copper buried in the field surrounding the WABC transmitter. To thieves, the site at the intersection of I-80 and Route 17 in New Jersey was a copper mine. When the price of copper rose, the WABC signal would diminish. They would dig a hole in the middle of the night and pull the copper out of the ground. It took round-the-clock security patrols to end the thefts.

'Round the Ole Oak Tree" / *Tony Orlando and Dawn* • "Crocodile

The first years on the job, I was often frustrated by the technical obstacles standing between WABC and number one ratings. Nevertheless, I persisted in my efforts to achieve a near fail-safe technical plant for the station. It took five years to accomplish this goal. One source of reassurance and inspiration was the discussions I had with scientists who had worked on the Apollo project.

When the plans were announced for the first flight that would actually land men on the moon and bring them back, I decided that I was going to be there when they lifted off from the earth. From a historical perspective, this would most likely turn out to be the most significant event to occur in my lifetime, not unlike Columbus's setting sail on the first voyage to India and discovering the New World. I flew to Cape Kennedy with my eleven-year-old son. For a week we lived at the Holiday Inn in Cocoa Beach, whose facilities had been taken over by NASA and ABC Radio News. Some of the astronauts' families and astronauts from earlier space voyages were staying there along with key Project Apollo scientists. By then it was mostly a matter of waiting out the days for the launch and we all spent a lot of time soaking up the Florida sun and swimming. What do you say when you come out of a wave and collide with Wernher Von Braun? In our case, we both laughed.

I was fascinated by the assurance with which the NASA people spoke about the coming mission. They were virtually certain they could land men on the moon and bring them back safely. My own technical hassles seemed insignificant by comparison. Nevertheless, I was as strongly motivated to make WABC number one as they were to reach the moon and return. I wanted to have that same sense of confidence about our equipment and systems as they had about theirs.

I wondered whom to talk with. Fortunately, newspeople were everywhere. If you ever want an answer, ask a newsperson. If they don't know the answer (and they usually do) they know someone who does. At the Cape they could point out the best restaurants, Alan Shepard's daughter, or Deke Slayton walking by.

"Talk to the guidance experts," one ABC newsman told me when I asked about the people in charge of fail-safe operations. "They're the reason that we're going to the moon before the Russians. When we invaded Germany, we captured the guidance scientists and the Russians got the propulsion experts. Hell. Anybody can do propulsion. But guidance . . . that's something else!"

So my son and I went down to the beach and spread our towels next to those of Walter Häusermann, who had designed the guidance systems for the V-2 rockets as well as those of the Apollo command module. Häusermann had a beach party going. The other guests were all middle-aged men, mostly paunchy and wearing ill-fitting black boxer trunks. They were all speaking German.

We introduced ourselves, and he said he would be delighted to talk with me. But first the formalities. I met this former German general, and that former commandant, and heard how they had built a little German town at the Redstone Arsenal in Alabama. Standing around on the Florida beach, it suddenly dawned on me that my son was talking baseball with former generals who, for all I knew, might have been slapped on the back by der Führer himself after they pulverized London with their rockets. Looking carefully at their faces for a few moments, I could imagine a metamorphosis backward in time and see them as they were in 1943. It was hard to accept the fact that these former enemies were behind Amerca's space race.

Häusermann bore an uncanny resemblance to the Dr. Strangelove character portrayed by Peter Sellers. When he spoke, he emphasized his points with jerky arm gestures, and his teeth, some of them capped in silver, European style, seemed to give a biting harshness to his accent.

"How can you be so sure you can get them there and back?" I asked him.

"We use triple measurement and triple backup on everything," he told me. "If two of the three readings on any measurement agree, we assume that it is the third meter and not our readout that is at fault."

We went over the launch control precautions where four hundred technicians sat at four hundred consoles in the launch control room. They had an additional four hundred technicians in an exact duplicate of that room next door, in case anything went wrong in the first room. There was a third room ready to go, into which the technicians from the first room would move to back up the second room if the first room went down. There was even a fourth control room just for good measure.

I didn't turn WABC into another Kennedy Space Center, but I had many of the concepts and procedures duplicated. I had eight cartridge machines built in the studio; three of them were there in case of failures. We duplicated every one of the two thousand-odd cartridges that made up the WABC sound, and we built an exact duplicate of the main air studio. A third partial backup was constructed in the production studio. Land lines to the transmitter were augmented by nonduplicated north and south versions that took different routes and were backed by the microwave dish on the roof of the building that sent still a third signal to our towers in Lodi, New Jersey.

Double sets of trouble reports were instituted. Whenever anything went wrong, both the announcer and the engineer on duty had to write up their own versions, which would be circulated to all department heads. Each instruction to the disc jockeys would now be issued three ways—verbally, via a posting on the studio bulletin board, and by sending a sealed, personally addressed memo to each performer. There would no longer be any way errors could be ascribed to ignorance.

The physical setup of the studios was redesigned. No glass separated the announcer from the engineer. The two now worked in the same room as a team, with the jock permitted to operate certain timing clocks and a few switches. With the main studio in its final configuration, the operation of Musicradio WABC was a joy to behold. It was as perfect a mating of men and machines as the cockpit of the most advanced two-seat fighter bomber. It was a formidable weapon. The new studio design was "human engineered" like the inside of a space capsule. Placement of signal lights, countdown clocks, slogan boards, writing surfaces for the logs, and locations of the copy books all took into account the peripheral vision, physical mobility, and anatomy of the engineers and announcers. The disc jockey and engineer faced one another across a double console set in the center of a large blue and silver room. A table wrapped around each of them on three sides. Color-coded audio controls, knobs, buttons, and switches sat on an angled, black master console bearing a proud plaque attesting to its pedigree—it was built by Rupert Neve of Cambridge, England (no American firm would bid on the custom job). Each button was opaque and glowed when pressed. Faders controlled the volume on each sound channel using a beam of light rather than relying on mechanical systems that wear out. The cartridge playback machines were stacked to one side along with a skimmer cassette recorder that enabled me to have a recording of whatever was said when the mike was activated.

All the jingles, commercials, and the other announcements were housed in continuous-loop cartridges stored in four large circular revolving racks located behind the engineer. The music was housed in four additional racks located behind the announcer who selected songs and handed them across to the engineer. The jingles were also kept in cartridges here under control of the jocks. (Each DJ guarded his own jingles carefully and sometimes, late at night, a jock would come back to WABC and have an engineer mix parts of different station jingles with his own name jingles to create jingles different from the ones other WABC jocks had.)

WABC had the finest microphones made. They were so highly directional that they picked up only the sounds directly in front of them. As a result, when the DJ mike was on, you did not have the studio speakers muted. Jocks could still hear a song if they were talking over the intro and not wearing headsets and this improved the sense of excitement in the room. State-of-the-art acoustic wall panels controlled the "liveness" of the sound in the room. (I had to replace them one year when painters touched up the room, and the paint destroyed its acoustic properties.)

There were other useful features. Automatic lights reminded the jocks when it was time to repeat specific records. Built-in telephones allowed DJs to tape listeners who called in to win prizes. Both the announcer and engineer faced identical clocks whose faces were marked with colored gels denoting time periods when competitors were broadcasting news or commercials. Those were ideal times for WABC to be playing songs to snare listeners who were doing button pushing of their own, hunting for music. Slogans were mounted in movable large letters on a simple menu board appropriated from the company cafeteria. Nothing more complicated would have done a better job. One famous feature, a hinged one-inch board that could be folded out and snapped into place to widen the writing surface for oversize announcers was put in at the request of Big Dan Ingram and became known as "Ingram's Added Inch."

In short, we had enough redundancy, and had built so much self-correcting feedback into our operating systems, that very few things went wrong. After several months of smooth operations, I began to wonder how many of our systems would have to fail simultaneously for something significantly bad to occur.

It happened on a Friday afternoon at around 2:30. WABC actually broadcast the sound of a taped religious show being played backward at double speed instead of "The Dan Ingram Show." This blooper continued for almost nine minutes. When I traced back the sequence of events that had gone wrong in order for this major error to occur—and continue to occur for such a relatively long time on what was then the number one radio station in America—I counted thirteen mistakes.

That morning the microwave dish on the roof of the ABC building had malfunctioned. That was error number one. While repairing it, the engineers had to turn off the monitoring system that enabled disc jockeys to hear the actual broadcast in their headsets as it was received on a listener's radio, instead of listening to the studio version. That was error two. They taped a note to the mike boom that read MONITORING SYSTEM UNDER REPAIR. WHAT YOU ARE HEARING IS NOT WHAT IS ON THE AIR. Later in the day the monitoring system and the dish were repaired. But the engineers forgot to take down the note. That was error number three.

Error four had been a design error in the console. A bank of push buttons, which controlled the feed of the sound and which could switch programs from one studio to another and to the transmitter, had been poorly located, only one inch above the floor on a side panel next to where the engineer sat. They were so low they could be accidentally activated if an engineer's shoe hit them. The error in design had been discovered, however, shortly after the studio was built. A metal bar had been made to extend in front of the buttons to protect them from being kicked, but the man assigned to install the bar never got around to putting it in, even though he had checked the job off on his assignment sheet. The booby trap sat around for years. That was error five.

The sixth mistake was made by the maintenance engineers. They had pushed the section of the console containing the bank of push buttons out of its normal position to make some of the repairs that morning, and had neglected to return it to its proper position. Bob Ryan, one of our crack engineers, had just come on duty to ride the board for the Ingram show. Ryan, a determined and strongly motivated young man, was almost totally blind. He had triumphed over his affliction using his keen sense of hearing and touch to run the controls. He was a terrific technician, so good that some of the DJs, including Bruce Morrow, insisted that Ryan do their shows whenever possible. On this particular day, Bob Ryan came in, sat down, and rolled his chair into place. Since the console had been moved by one of the repair crew, who forgot to put it back in place, one of the chair legs momentarily brushed a button on the console panel (error seven). It was only for an instant, but it was long enough to switch the broadcast feed from "The Dan Ingram Show" to a production control room where another engineer was duplicating a radio program by recording it backward at double speed, an approved industry practice. (The tape had come in from a church, so it had not been recorded by a union engineer. This dubbing was required by the union contract to give the tape a legitimacy. Had the engineer doing the re-recording wanted to, he could have taped it at normal speed and run up overtime, but this was Klaus Gruber, and Gruber prided himself on efficiency.)

At that instant the audience listening to WABC in cars, at home, and at work suddenly heard the incredible sound of the double-speed tape playing backward. Ingram also heard the sound, but staring him in the face was the sign saying WHAT YOU ARE HEARING IS NOT WHAT IS ON THE AIR, so he ignored it and took off the headsets he had been wearing. Error number eight had occurred.

An engineer at the transmitter also heard the tape, but thought it was the latest rock & roll song. Error nine. I normally monitored the station myself, but at that moment I was at La Guardia Airport. My own absence was the tenth link in the chain. My assistant who had the primary daytime monitoring responsibility had just turned down his office loudspeaker to concentrate on a phone call. Error eleven.

Of course, our listeners heard what was going on and began phoning the ABC switchboard. The first call came to my new secretary, who had been on the job less than a week and was unfamiliar with procedures. Seeing an engineer hurrying toward the studio, she assumed he was on his way to correct the situation. She turned her attention back to the phone and thanked the listener for calling.

"They know about it and they're fixing it now," she told the caller. Had she followed the engineer, she would have seen him walk past the studio door and continue rapidly down the hall toward the men's room. Error twelve. By now hundreds of calls were pouring into the ABC switchboard. Rather than continue annoying executives upstairs, the switchboard operators fielded the calls themselves, thanking each listener and assuring them all that the problem was being corrected. Error thirteen—and that's why WABC broadcast a tape playing backward at double speed for so long.

After almost nine minutes, another engineer who had been working in the production studio where the tape was being dubbed walked into the air studio and remarked that the sound on the monitor speaker was originating in the production studio. Ryan immediately realized what was happening, reached down, felt for the culprit button and reset it. "The Dan Ingram Show" was back on the air.

Years later Bob Ryan and I reconstructed the incident. (By then, Ryan had lost what vision had remained. He had also left radio to begin a new life in a new state. Entering politics, he rose quickly and became a Nevada state senator.) We talked about the chain of events leading up to the mortifying minutes, and we decided that our systems weren't so bad after all. If it took that many misjudgments, malfunctions, and errors over a period of years to stop our sound for nine minutes, our safeguards had more integrity than we could have hoped for. Even Apollo had to turn back on one mission!

There is more to redundancy than backup equipment, of course. The final touch in any quest for "fail-safe" involves having backup *people*. Nowhere was this better demonstrated than an event I witnessed at the 1975 convention of the Radio Television News Directors Association in Dallas.

As part of the festivities, the convention program committee scheduled an outdoor barbecue and Western hoedown at a dude ranch outside the city. It was equipped to feed hundreds under tents. Delegates arrived to the sight of steers roasting on spits and gunslingers demonstrating their skills. Square dancing commenced on a large floodlit floor under canvas. The bravest among the reporters were invited to rope baby calves and wrestle them to the ground. Virtually every radio and television news director in America was there, along with the chief editors and some top anchor people who had wangled invites to Texas.

• "Can't Get Enough of Your Love Babe" / *Barry White* • "Rock

At the height of the festivities, the telephone in the dude ranch office rang. A delegate who had stayed behind in Dallas was calling his editor. The editor reluctantly pushed back his plate filled with roast prime rib and made his way, somewhat annoyed, through the table-filled tent to the ranch office, which was in a small building nearby.

When he picked up the phone, he couldn't believe what the voice at the other end was saying. The FBI had captured Patty Hearst. The story they had all been waiting for—the biggest news of the year—was breaking, and he was thirty-five miles outside Dallas at some damn dude ranch. He gave his reporter the best instructions he could manage by phone and bolted for his car, stopping just long enough to shout the news into the tent.

That lone office telephone was the ranch's only link to the rest of the world. Dignity and rank were forgotten, as almost a thousand of the nation's most senior news chiefs, editors, reporters, and announcers stampeded out of the tent. For a moment they began to form a line at the door of the ranch office, but then they realized the futility of the situation and ran to their cars; some chartered buses for the race back to Dallas.

Once they returned to their hotels, they discovered they were too late. Their backups—subordinates in newsrooms throughout the country—had handled the story very well without the "indispensable" news directors, editors, and anchors.

CHAPTER 16

The Money Machine

By 1966, WABC was more than a well-functioning technical facility. It was a super money machine. Although it was number one in the ratings, I was concerned. WMCA was pounding away at us with music, while our heavy commitment to hours of dull network programming cost us dearly in listeners. I knew the network wasn't making money with that programming. There had to be a better way to make networks more compatible to the sound of a particular radio station. I sent a memo to the president of ABC Radio, Hal Neal, describing a new, farfetched kind of network that I had thought up. It was based on space satellites. I envisioned four simultaneous feeds of music programming, compatible with the needs of different types of stations, including Top Forty, middle of the road, and country formats. The stations would get what they needed and become more profitable. I realized it was a dream, but I hoped it might inspire some new thinking about our current problems. Neal circulated the memo, and I got some positive feedback. Eventually this idea played its part in the evolution of the new multiple radio networks that began at ABC and spread throughout the industry.

For now, however, I would have to hone the station, keeping it finely tuned. After Ron Lundy's training period ended, I moved him from the overnight show to a midday schedule, and Charlie Greer returned to the all-night show. Not satisfied with the ''Fun City'' jingles developed by PAMS, I created a new jingle package around a more exciting theme, ''Music Explosion.''

The Vietnam War was on everyone's mind. The audience was looking for escape. Our tapes were being played daily on Armed Forces Radio, and the big song of the year was ''The Ballad of the

Green Berets.'' The time was ripe for comic strip superheroes who clearly knew where they stood in the Good Guy versus Bad Guy conflict. The big new TV series was ''Batman.'' WABC played Batman records and sent listeners to Hollywood to visit the set, meet actor Adam West, who played Batman, and ride in the Batmobile. I began looking for a superhero worthy of WABC, and I soon found one.

Broadway producer Harold Prince had announced his new musical. *It's a Bird . . . It's A Plane . . . It's Superman*, starring Jack Cassidy and a cast that included Linda Lavin, had begun rehearsals and would start previewing in a few months. I decided to ask Prince to give WABC the first preview performance of *Superman* as a joint promotion. My idea was to fill the theater with Supermen. I could see 750 men sitting there, each super at something. I wanted the best fisherman, the top chef, the super lumberjack, the best lover. They would be nominated by, and would bring along, their Lois Lanes—their wives, their girlfriends, or their daughters. We would set up a row of phone booths outside the theater where each Superman would be given a cape to wear to the performance. I could see the theater full of Supermen on the front page of every paper and on every TV show. I thought the idea was so great that it couldn't miss.

Armed with enthusiasm, I made an appointment to visit Broadway's wunderkind, producer-director Hal Prince. I would persuade him to give me the 1500-seat Alvin Theater and a free performance of the show.

I found Prince cordial and friendly. With an expansive wave of my hand, I began to lay out the details of the WABC Superman promotion. Prince listened attentively as I described his theater filled with Supermen and Lois Lanes. I talked about phone booths, capes, and lots of publicity. Finally I finished my pitch, saying, ''And I'd like the first preview performance for the promotion. What do you think?''

''No,'' he said. He shook his head. ''No,'' he repeated. ''It could kill the show.''

''Kill the show?'' I didn't understand.

''Shows can live or die on the reviews,'' he said. ''Critics are very sensitive to hype.''

He went on to explain how the promotional hoopla could alienate the critics and set the wrong tone for opening night. He wanted

Steisand • "I Honestly Love You" / *Olivia Newton-John* • "Hooked

the show to be judged on its merits. My heart sank. Prince was right, of course. He knew his business. If we did that promotion, it could damage the show's reception.

Prince stood up, and we shook hands. My encounter with the mastermind of Broadway triumphs was ending. I saw the promotion evaporating as I rose to leave. My mind raced as he walked me to the door. We shook hands again. Just as I thought it was all over, an idea hit me. I paused in the doorway and turned back.

"You're right," I said to Prince, who had returned to his desk. "We don't want to do that promotion."

Prince looked up, surprised.

"We can't possibly focus on the show. We need to focus on the public out there that is Superman-crazy. We need to stage a Superman Fan Convention. We can invite Superman fans from all over the country. They are behind this Superman craze. And what's more logical than to hold this convention in the Alvin Theater, where you're going to open *Superman*? We'll have a keynote speaker, banners, a platform, and, as the climax of the convention, you can put on the first New York performance of the show. Every Superman fan in the country will want to come to New York to see that musical."

Prince jumped to his feet. He thought for a moment. "That's a great idea," he finally said.

My exit speech had lasted all of thirty seconds, but it brought the first performance of a Broadway musical to WABC. Our promotion director, Joe Cook, swung into action, and the convention was a huge success. Delegates were selected by cartoonist Charles Addams on the basis of the originality of their convention banners. Doubletalker Al Kelly gave the keynote address, and the audience, many of whom had never seen a Broadway show before, loved every minute of it.

Prince later sent me a personal note saying it was the best piece of promotion he had ever seen.

Superman provided a lift in a disquieting year. Values were shifting, and the big changes that were to come were heralded in popular music. Listener complaints about lyrics and artists kept radio stations on the defense. The Rolling Stones' "Let's Spend the Night Together" never reached the airwaves of most large music stations, including WABC. (Of course, in later years it had no problem being added to the record library.) "They're Coming to

Take Me Away,'' by Napoleon VIX, a gag record lampooning mental illness, was yanked in the wake of a public uproar, and for a brief time we even had a hold on Beatles tunes after a remark by John Lennon comparing the Beatles to Jesus Christ.

As a final send-off into the new year, the American Federation of Television and Radio Artists struck ABC, and we had to replace our jocks and newsmen with executives. Having been warned earlier that the negotiations were going sour, I had recorded a series of strike jingles for WABC. Thinking it would be a short strike, I wanted to keep our listeners abreast of what the absent jocks were doing. Using the basic ''Manhattan'' melody line, we had jingle singers doing lyrics about the ''Strikebound Sound of 77 WABC,'' while we broadcast humorous spot announcements inviting our listeners to see our jocks walking the picket line along with ABC television personalities.

Meanwhile everyone at ABC wanted to do an on-air stint. I had my hands full keeping divisional presidents and vice presidents off the air. In response to a talent recruitment sign in the lobby of the ABC building, dozens of top executives showed up at my office claiming prior experience as disc jockeys. Most were absolutely awful. Tactfully, I auditioned myself first, turned myself down as a jock, and then was able to tell them they would be better off doing newscasts or nothing at all. I did news; so did Hal Neal. Engineer Bernard Koval became a DJ—"Bernie the K.'' Publicity man Marty Grove took over Cousin Brucie's slot; ABC Chicago programmer John Rook was ''Johnny Roe'' in the morning, and salesman Dan Aaron was ''Billy Joe'' in the afternoon. Secretaries replaced the engineers who refused to cross the AFTRA picket lines.

As professional as our replacements were over the air, the basic rhythm of the station was off, and the consistency of the familiar voices was gone. Listeners became uneasy and started to tune us out as the strike went into its second month. When it finally ended, I waited for the ratings books to come in so I could survey the damage. We still came in first, but there had been some audience erosion, most noticeably to Gary Stevens's show on WMCA.

I redoubled my efforts to recoup the audience and created a new jingle series called ''Musicpower.'' I thought up new promotions, the biggest being the ''Truck A Luck.'' It involved painting a delivery truck gold and sending it around town to make surprise deliveries to listeners. The WABC "Truck A Luck" would pull up to somebody's driveway and drop off a new car, a mink stole, or a gold watch. Our listeners went wild because all they had to do was send in their name and address on a postcard and hope that theirs would be drawn.

WABC still kept to its policy of playing only the hits, but now the top songs had more obscure lyrics. Popular music was becoming psychedelic. The Beatles released the *Sgt. Pepper* album; Jefferson Airplane had "White Rabbit" and "Somebody to Love" from their album, *Surrealistic Pillow*. The Doors released their first album. Some records were unusually long: Artists and record producers were trying to break out of accepted patterns. I thought that WABC's listeners would get bored by the overly long tunes, so I limited the length of records we would play to three and a half minutes.

In October, the engineers went out on strike. This time we were more than ready. Engineers are not essential in a music format, and many stations don't have them. Our air personalities, who had been reluctant strikers during their own union's walkout (which had been mostly over television issues), now refused to honor the engineers' picket line. We picked the jocks up by limousine and drove them into the basement garage of the ABC building every day so they wouldn't be seen outside crossing the lines. The strike ended, and we were back to business as usual.

In keeping with my plans to have WABC perceived as a friend to the community, I began an ongoing project called "The Big Break" to give local amateur musical acts a chance at stardom. Every night we played a tape of a different group over the air, then invited the best of these to be judged by musical experts. The prize was a contract with a record company.

The year 1968 arrived with terrific news for WABC Radio. ABC announced it was shutting down the old radio network. In its place, ABC Radio would present a totally new concept in networking, and Wally Schwartz would run it. He was replaced as general manager at WABC by Don Curran from San Francisco. Gone were "The Breakfast Club," the long newscasts, "Flair Reports," the evening newsblocks, the commentaries, and the mandatory play-by-play sportscasts. In their place would be four radio networks. The group vice president for radio, Ralph Beaudin, not yet having a satellite to work with, had figured out that if ABC abandoned all

McCoy • "Love Will Keep Us Together" / *The Captain and*

long network radio programs, four networks could share the time on the one network line, and share the cost as well. Different networks would use the distribution line at different times during the hour. At the beginning of the hour the ABC Information Network would offer a newscast designed for talk-, information-, and all-news-formatted radio stations. At a quarter past the hour the ABC-FM Network would present news specifically written for so-called beautiful music stations. The newscast at half past the hour would be designed for middle-of-the-road stations and country stations and would be on the ABC Entertainment Network. Five minutes before the hour, the ABC Contemporary Network would present news for rock music stations. Headline and newsbrief services would also be given to those stations that wanted shorter newscasts. For the concept to work, ABC would have to have up to four affiliated stations in each city. Since the stations delivered different types of audiences who used different products and services, advertisers would love the concept—targeted delivery of demographic audience groups. For ABC's part, the network would quadruple the number of commercials it could sell. All they needed was government permission to have multiple affiliates in each market. Because network radio had been a bust as a business, the government saw nothing wrong with scrapping the old anti-monopoly rules and letting ABC go ahead with the experiment. A four-year plan was laid out, and twenty-eight million dollars were committed to the project. For WABC it meant the lines that tethered our airship had been cut. We were free. For the first time since I had come to ABC over five years before, I had control of all my own air time. We would carry a brief network newscast five minutes before the hour, and that was all.

Our new jingle package told the story: "The Most Music." Our new set of slogans proclaimed: "All the Music All the Time on WABC," and our ratings took off as never before. Bruce Morrow had the highest rating of any jock in New York. I wondered how long rival WMCA could hang in.

With the extra time in our schedule, I brought in another air personality, Florida DJ Roby Yonge. Roby, whose surfing exploits had earned him the title of The Big Kahuna, spent his first weekend with us heading upstate to see how different snow skiing was from water skiing. He put on a pair of skis, rode a lift to the top of a slope, and quickly found out.

Monday Roby showed up for his new show with his chest and arm in a cast. His opening months suffered as a result.

Another problem was Herb Oscar Anderson. The Morning Mayor of New York walked into my office one morning with tears rolling down his cheeks and announced he'd had it with getting up at 4:30 every morning and racing in from Connecticut. He had decided to retreat to a house in Minnesota. The sales department went into a panic. I assured them that even in the morning, the format would carry the station and I would find an appropriate replacement. No one in the sales department believed me. I was told that the station would not survive Herb's departure. Herb Oscar Anderson had been sold to the sponsors and their ad agencies as a very special personality. We were paying him a bonus of a thousand dollars a quarter rating-point per hour per month. The sales people now expected the morning ratings to take a severe drop.

Harry Harrison, the midday air personality on WMCA, was my choice to replace Herb Oscar Anderson. Monitoring WMCA, I had concluded that if you sat Harrison down at almost any breakfast table, he would fit right in as an extra member of the family. Harry Harrison was "plain folk." He was corny. He didn't sound overly slick, and he had a tremendous believability in his voice when he spoke about products. His lack of "extreme personality characteristics" was actually a plus at that time of the morning, when the widest cross-section of people, young and old, was sharing the same radio set in the kitchen. His heavy, somewhat nasal voice also cut through the AM ether and penetrated; like our own station echo, it was a distinctive sound. I felt sure he would get better ratings in the environment of WABC's sound than he did at WMCA.

Just after Harry arrived, one of his lungs collapsed. Instead of being on the air, he was in a hospital with a sandbag on his chest as doctors sealed a pinhole in the lungs. I had some anxious weeks. Fortunately for all of us, Harry recovered. The ratings didn't miss a beat; then they continued their upward ascent.

Six months later, Herb Oscar called from Minnesota. The snow was piling up on the roof and his wife was mixing martinis. "Do they miss me back there, Rick?"

"Of course we miss you, Herb. But I have someone else under

God" / *Frankie Valli* • "Lady Marmalade" / *Labelle* • "My Eyes

contract now.'' He asked if the ratings were holding up. I said they were. The format, and Harry Harrison, were carrying the day, and I had Herb, a top star, as a backup if I needed him.

Before the year ended, Hal Neal asked me to do some work on ABC's New York FM station. The FCC had decreed that FM stations had to be programmed separately from their AM counterparts at least half the time in major cities where the same company owned both. I began experimenting with WABC-FM, using some of the same disc jockeys, including Dan Ingram (who called his FM show ''The Other Dan Ingram Show'') and Bob Lewis. Playing more progressive rock, a mixture of music including Jimi Hendrix, Cream, Joan Baez, Bob Dylan, and Janis Joplin, it was in sharp contrast to the bubble-gum sounds prevalent on WABC-AM that year.

We kicked off 1969 with an enhanced version of ''The Big Break.'' Once again we offered local music acts a shot at immortality. Listeners who belonged to bands were asked to send in tapes. Bruce Morrow broadcast the best tapes on his show each night, and after a dozen weeks we brought the finalists to a playoff concert in the grand ballroom of the New York Hilton. There, a blue-ribbon board of experts would award an ABC Records contract to the best group performing that day. We received over seven hundred tapes. Some showed a great deal of promise.

To make the playoffs exciting and to inspire the amateur groups, we invited ABC recording stars Steppenwolf to appear at the midpoint in the competition. We made the event a Police Athletic League benefit and hoped to fill the 4,500-seat ballroom. But three hours before the doors were to open, there were already over ten thousand teenagers in line. A hurried call to the police brought reinforcements to handle the crowd. Luckily they did not riot, and we placated those who could not purchase seats by giving them free WABC souvenir playlists and posters.

The show was about to begin when an officer who had supervised the dispersing of the overflow audience sought me out. ''Our men didn't expect this crowd,'' he said, ''You didn't tell us. We put in a lot of extra work. I think we should be taken care of.''

''ABC's not getting a cent from this,'' I told him. ''It's all going to the people on stage, but I don't think . . .''

He was already on his way to the stage. He had one foot on the steps when he recognized the deputy inspector of police next to the police official who headed the Police Athletic League, both wearing civilian clothes. He smiled, saluted them, and left.

The show began on time, but after a few numbers it became obvious that the performers' stage presence left much to be desired. The tapes were better than the bands' in-person performances. The amateurs could not sustain the concert on their own, and there was no sign of Steppenwolf. While emcee Bruce Morrow tried to keep the crowd happy, I called ABC Records and was assured that Steppenwolf had landed and that the group—and their instruments—was fighting its way through midtown traffic to the Hilton. After almost another hour had passed, the instruments arrived. We called an intermission, rang down the curtain, and rushed the equipment, speakers, and instruments on stage. The roadies, sensing the impatience of the crowd, did one of the fastest setups in history and rushed through a superficial sound check.

When the intermission ended, Steppenwolf appeared backstage. They sort of floated around, still seeming to be at thirty thousand feet. I don't think they knew what city they were in. I'm sure they didn't know if it was day or night. The curtain rose. Steppenwolf began to play. The crowd leaped to its feet, cheering. Now they would get some real rock & roll. The organ player, who was performing standing up, was too far from the keyboard of the electric organ to reach it. His hands and arms moved, but they weren't hitting the keys. With each note he lunged forward, then tilted back further and further from the organ. Finally he simply fell over backward, his head hitting the floor with a thud. For an instant his boot tips went up toward the ceiling and then crashed back down. The other members of the band just kept on playing. The audience, oblivious to everything but the music, didn't notice. I saw a pair of hands reach through the backstage curtain and begin to drag the organist by his feet. He vanished behind the curtain. The judges, including the music director of Radio City Music Hall, could be heard to gasp from their platform at the rear of the ballroom. I darted backstage. Bruce Morrow's father was slapping the organist in the face with a wet towel. The organist shook his head, sat up, and pulled himself to his feet. He heard the music. He looked around to locate the stage and, without another word, danced back out and took his place at the organ. This time his fingers reached the keys.

The afternoon was a success. A band from Long Island won. They went to Hollywood with a contract, but broke up in a disagreement over how to share the profits. They formed two groups, each with its own manager, and never issued any records. So it goes in the music business.

In April of 1969, with the Labunski team long gone, WMCA abandoned its music format from 10 P.M. to 10 A.M. to go talk. It was the beginning of the end for them. They put Frankie Crocker on in the evenings against Morrow, but couldn't dent Bruce's numbers. Rock was on WOR-FM now, using a tight Top Thirty format that had been perfected by Bill Drake, program consultant to the RKO group that owned the station. Murray the K was working there, and I wondered how he was surviving with such a tight playlist and rigid rules.

As the year progressed, I made one more talent decision—I would not pick up Roby Yonge's option when it came due. I let him know that he would be leaving.

Roby decided to go out in style. Ever since Woodstock, earlier that year, rumors claiming that Paul McCartney was dead had surfaced. A series of symbolic clues involving album covers and song lyrics were cited to support the fabrication.

One night after midnight I was awakened by a call from the WABC newsroom. Roby had seized on the McCartney death rumors and was broadcasting them over the air, promising listeners that he would try to get to the truth of the matter. At that hour of the night the signal of WABC carries over much of the United States, goes up the Canadian cost, rolls down to Guantánamo Naval base in Cuba and skips across the Atlantic to the African Gold Coast. For the first time, much of the world was hearing that Paul McCartney, the beloved and idolized Beatle, might be dead. Calls poured in from St. Louis, Ft. Lauderdale, Boston, and as far away as Albuquerque. Heartbroken girls wept over the air. I looked at the calendar. Roby Yonge's contract had less than two weeks to go. At many stations disc jockeys are not permitted back on the air after they have been given notice of termination as a precaution against just such grandstanding.

I phoned Les Marshak, a relief DJ, and asked him to meet me in the lobby of the ABC building as soon as he could. I also called security and requested a guard to join us. Marshak was there in twenty minutes, and we went up to the eighth-floor studios of

WABC. I put Marshak in a small auxiliary studio and had him put on the air. He began playing songs and doing a normal show, making no references to what had just transpired.

Then I walked down the hall and went into Yonge's studio. I told him his show had been taken off the air. We left the building together. I had no need of the guard. Marshak continued to do the show until I found a replacement a few months later.

Nineteen-seventy was a smash year for WABC. Harry Harrison's morning show hit an 18 share, compared to his biggest morning competitor, WOR's John Gambling, who had only a 10. The station had an average quarter-hour audience of 370,000 and was first in share all across the board, night and day. Our demographics spanned every age group; one month we were even first in the over-64s. WMCA gave up its remaining daytime music and went all talk. WABC's third annual ''Big Break'' was held at Carnegie Hall and featured Tony Orlando and Dawn. ''Music Is Our Message'' became the new slogan and jingle theme.

Even the nonmusic programming worked in the format now because it was directly geared to listener interest. Between the records on ''The Bruce Morrow Show,'' I ran a feature called ''The Drug Scene'' where teenage ex-users recounted the horrors of drug abuse. The show would win the prestigious Ohio State Award for me and WABC the following year. Even our Sunday morning religious programming got the music message across with Father Peter Madori, a rock music fan who was particularly effective in weaving his ideas around the songs.

WABC was cited by financial analysts as being the most profitable radio station in the United States. General Manager Don Curran left for television and sales manager George Williams took his place. My big goal had been achieved. WABC was far and away number one and had demolished the competition. The next few years looked as if they would be our best yet.

CHAPTER 17

Give Elton a Shot

During the seventies, ABC began expanding my responsibilities throughout the radio division. Our FM stations were now a separate group, trying to get off the ground. Their first attempts used automation and a national taped format for all their stations. Then I began consulting FM Vice President Allen Shaw in the fundamentals of live programming. Later I was promoted to vice president of programming for the AM stations by their president, Chuck De Bare. I recruited John Gehron from CBS-FM to become program director of our Chicago station, WLS, and consulted for them as well. Soon jingles proclaiming "Musicradio WLS" covered the Midwest. Like WABC, WLS was a clear-channel station that reached many states. They too added an echo chamber, a tight playlist, and more personality DJs, and soon dominated the Chicago pop music ratings.

At the same time I now had become operations manager of WABC with all departments except sales reporting to me. Those were heady times for the people who worked at the station. Ratings were soaring. Sponsors paid hundreds of dollars for thirty seconds of air time. Competitors came and went: WWDJ (screaming jocks from Hackensack), WCBS-FM (Solid Gold), WOR-FM (later WXLO then 99X, then WKYS) and WPIX-FM (the format of the month—or so it seemed). Murray the K had found his way to a weekend berth at WNBC. None of it mattered. WABC's audience cume hit another all-time high in 1972. Dan Ingram ran up a 22 share in afternoon drive.

As the ratings increased and the playlist contracted, I continued to maintain a businesslike and objective relationship with the music industry. The early lessons of Alan Freed and the fifties payola

Manhattans • "A Fifth of Beethoven" / *Walter Murphy and the Big*

scandals always stayed in the back of my mind. The record business was booming and entertainment of jocks and programmers was again lavish. I was an oddity. In a city where record pluggers plied their trade in the swank eateries by entertaining program directors, I would take *them* for cruises on *The Music Power*, WABC's yacht, this one an ocean-going 65-footer.

We would sail at noon and sometimes in the evening from the Seventy-ninth Street boat basin up the Hudson to West Point, around Manhattan or out to Long Island Sound. One summer evening, when I was entertaining David Cassidy, a thunderstorm caught us in the Hudson. The boat's generator went out, and water started to pour into the engine room. People on shore, seeing us lose headway to the tides, called the Coast Guard, who came to the rescue. Unfortunately, the Coast Guard reserve cruiser was manned by an older demographic. We offered them autographed Cassidy albums, but they wanted Tony Bennett.

As I continued my practice of reverse entertainment, picking up the tabs for the record pluggers who serviced our station, nationally syndicated columnist Jack Anderson was announcing that he had uncovered evidence of disc jockeys and program directors at other stations throughout the country receiving free vacations, cash, cars, and prostitutes as payoffs for plugging songs. He praised WABC for its ethics and its management for our sampling and monitoring system that made sure record stores accurately reported which records were selling best so that only authentic hits went on WABC.

It occurred to me that in a business that had coined the word *payola*, an honest program director presented a formidable challenge to record promoters who were trying to get exposure for their new product. I realized from my discussions with record company presidents that most of them detested payoffs for airplay and tried to discourage the practice. But I knew that the pressure to "break" a record—to get it started—was always present. So were the independent promotion men—the record promoters who are in business for themselves and who, by taking on individual records or assignments from the record labels, are a step removed from the corporate environment and its restraints. Some of these independent promoters function mostly as money conduits.

Certain cities are controlled by the independents. They get the ball rolling and break a new release by simply sharing their fee (in cash or cocaine) with a few key program directors whose "adds" are reported in the trade press. Some program directors fight fiercely to become trade reporters. Of particular significance are radio stations in certain medium-sized markets that start new records off and whose playlists are published each week in industry trade publications. Other stations and larger airplay charts then add those records. Because I went by research, a performer's previous track record, consensus opinions, and other data, and because I listened to the sounds of the records themselves rather than the pitches of the promotion people, the record pluggers considered me a brick wall.

Faced with this, some of the more determined promoters went to extremes that I had to admire. The challenge of the situation inspired a few bursts of sheer ingenuity over the years that once or twice almost bordered on the sublime. How could I get angry with New York promoter Herb Rosen when he went to the trouble of plastering every window of an office in a building across the street with signs proclaiming the progress of a new record that he was being paid to promote? And I always enjoyed the moments when a promoter snared the recording stars themselves and brought them around, together with their new album. But for persistence I have to give the gold medal to Buck Reingold.

Buck Reingold was one of the most determined record promotion men I have known. Buck worked for Neil Bogart in the early days, when Neil lived in New Jersey and launched Buddah Records. Buck covered every base ten times over. He was a very determined person. When Neil was married to his first wife, Beth, Buck was married to her identical twin, Nancy. When I didn't go on a record Buck was promoting, one he believed in strongly, he hired a limousine, mounted a loudspeaker on the roof, and parked it in the driveway of my Manhattan apartment building. As I walked to work in the morning, the beat of the latest Buddah release followed me as the limousine crept along behind. That night, as I sat in Madison Square Garden watching Muhammad Ali defend his title, the same song suddenly blasted at me again. Buck Reingold had found out precisely where I would be sitting in the 18,000-seat arena and managed to purchase the adjoining seats, one for himself and the other for a battery-powered phonograph.

Buck Reingold's phonograph turned up again a few months later. When WABC held off adding a record called "Put Your

Hand in the Hand'' by a group named Ocean, Buck camped out for three hours in the WABC men's room, waiting for my predictable appearance. When I finally walked in, the music started instantly. In this case, fortunately for Buck, ''Put Your Hand in the Hand'' turned out to be a hit, and as a result it became an automatic add on our playlists after meeting our research criteria. I didn't know if Buck claimed credit for the airplay. He probably did.

A more formidable challenge was faced by the promotion men who worked for Elton John. Elton, who had known slim financial times before success came, always operated with a fanatic determination to wring the last possible dollar out of each album. Elton worked every angle. You could tell when sales began to slump on a new Elton John album, because king-sized ads began to appear on the sides and back of New York buses. He wouldn't have spent that kind of money if the album was doing well. Elton also orchestrated the release of single records—the 45 rpm discs that were bought by music lovers who couldn't afford the album. He would insist on squeezing as many singles as possible out of each album. Sometimes the pressure for another single would persist even after the record company's artist and repertoire (or A&R) people had selected the last logical song for single release. I will never forget one of those situations.

This particular Elton John album, like most albums in the music business, contained some obvious hit songs, some ''turntable hits'' (records that get promoted onto the radio but never move up high on the charts), and some music that might be called ''filler material"—that is, added to make sure that both sides of the twelve-inch platter have enough musical inventory to sell as a legitimate album. Under intense pressure, the record company had released every potential song that might bullet its way up the charts. But the word was out that Elton wanted another hit from the album. Confusion reigned. The remaining songs didn't sound like Top Forty hits. Finally, in desperation, the record company reverted to an old practice that rarely works. Two different songs from the album were designated as ''potential'' singles. Half of the pop music stations in each city were given pressings containing a song entitled ''I Feel Like a Bullet (in the Gun of Robert Ford)'' and were told that this would be the next Elton John single. The other half of the pop music stations in each market were given a song called ''Grow

Manilow • "Welcome Back, Kotter" / *John Sebastian* • "If You

Some Funk of Your Own,'' along with a pitch about what a great new single this was going to be for Elton.

In New York, the thankless task of pulling this sleight of hand fell to promoter Ray Dariano. Unfortunately for Dariano, I happened to be talking to our Chicago program director that day, and when Ray gave me ''Feel Like a Bullet'' I already knew that other stations were being given ''Grow Some Funk.'' I instantly realized what was up. The A&R people, unable to pick another hit from the album were now sitting with their fingers crossed, hoping that maybe one of these two remaining cuts would catch on somewhere. In fact, not only was it unlikely that either song had the strength to make it as a hit single, but it was also possible that the mixed promotional efforts would result in the songs' canceling one another out. Certainly that was the effect at WABC. I put the record in a drawer and sat on it. I knew I had done the right thing by the radio station. And I also knew that there was a disappointed Ray Dariano across town.

The following Friday a large carton was delivered to my office. Measuring four feet by two feet, and a foot high, it was marked FRAGILE and THIS SIDE UP. The top was designed to lift off, taking the sides of the carton with it and leaving only the base. The carton had been delivered while I was out of the room and placed squarely on my desk. I lifted off the top. Inside was a huge rectangular white and blue cake. It was spectacular. I had never seen any cake like it. On top, along with a decorative border, was a plea in large letters that read: GIVE ELTON A SHOT! FEEL LIKE A BULLET IS A HIT! Below the inscription was a cake ornament in the shape of a pistol. Dariano had spent some money! Just after the cake came, the coffee cart arrived on our floor. The entire office was treated to cake. ''Feel Like a Bullet'' did not go on WABC.

''Feel Like a Bullet'' did not go on many other radio stations that week either. By the end of the week MCA, the distributors of Elton John's Rocket Records label, had given up on the song as a single and made the decision to try to bring home ''Grow Some Funk'' instead.

Having put such an effort into trying to convince programmers that ''Feel Like a Bullet'' was the next single, Dariano's credibility was about to be blown. How could he face me with another record? But Ray Dariano was resourceful. He had not always been a record promoter. Ray's first attempt in show business had been as a stand-up comic, and he came into the record business with his own album. The album had not sold well, and Dariano had not made comedy his career. But he still possessed that comic sense of timing and a sense of the situation. Faced with the unenviable task of admitting he had been touting a record that the record company had not been sure of, he now had also to convince me that the flip side, ''Grow Some Funk,'' was going to be released as the next single and would become a hit.

A week passed. Nothing happened. Then, just before the next Tuesday morning music meeting at WABC, there was a tremendous commotion in the station's reception area. Although no promotion people are permitted at the station on a ''music morning,'' two delivery men managed to get through the lobby and into the station, and made a beeline for my office. They brushed past the secretary, opened the door and, without a word, placed a carton as large as the one containing the ''Give Elton a Shot'' cake on my desk.

I was alone in the office. The staff had not yet arrived for the music meeting. I stared at the carton. I hesitated and then pulled off the cover. The bakery had outdone itself. This cake was even larger than the first. But there were no flowers, no ornaments, and no adornments. A simple inscription stretched across its full length. It read: DISREGARD PREVIOUS CAKE.

CHAPTER 18

The Singing Monk

While individual promoters conducted the music industry's front line assault on radio, the home office backed them with heavy artillery in the form of parties and dinners. These ranged from modest luncheons to the most elaborate events imaginable.

At the low end of the list was the impromptu dinner. A radio DJ or program director during the sixties needed but to appear at the bar of Danny's Hideaway or Al and Dick's Steak House on West Fifty-fourth Street, and a dinner invitation from a music publisher's representative or a record company promoter would be forthcoming. It was an unwritten law.

At the next level of importance were the planned events where advance invitations were issued. There were so many of these that in retrospect they seemed to merge into one another. Sometimes two or three occurred on the same night. One disc jockey went to so many openings at the Copacabana nightclub he eventually acquired a complete set of "souvenir" silverware. Invites to scenes like the Copa carried with them the obligation of a picture-taking session for the "trades" (recording industry publications) in the dressing room after the show. Jocks vied for ringside tables to see Bobby Darin, Engelbert Humperdinck, and Tom Jones. In an orgy of entertainment, one radio station's entire staff once sat through the Sammy Davis, Jr. show at the Copa twice, refusing to relinquish their tables and charging all their meals and champagne to the singer. Pop music columnists like Al Aronowitz of the *New York Post* let the public in on the doings.

A fascinating reception occurred at an early Melanie concert. Because of her gentle image, her record company staged a post-Carnegie Hall concert at the original Saito Restaurant, then housed in a serene wooden teahouse setting on West Fifty-second Street. (It later burned down.) Japanese restaurants were new and rare in America at that time. Their atmospheres were hushed, and their timid, kimono-clad waitresses—who spoke little English—bowed and smiled as they tried to please the patrons.

When the Melanie entourage arrived, most of the regular diners had left. The dozens of radio and record people were asked to remove their shoes and were led into the two-story main dining room, where they were seated on mats bordering the open rectangular area. Japanese music filtered in softly from overhead speakers. When drinks were slow to arrive, some of the record promoters began to shout at the waitresses. After a few sakis, two of them started chasing after the women, proclaiming that "they were geishas, trained to cater to man's every desire." DJs, uncomfortable from sitting cross-legged on the floor, went "tatami hopping" from one mat to another, singing. They drowned out the Japanese music as billows of marijuana smoke rose to the rafters. The restaurant manager appeared, a model of politeness, but he was soon reduced to the level of his guests, shouting and waving his arms. Several diners were unaccustomed to the food and gagged on it. The evening broke up in a fistfight between a busboy and some stoned promoters.

More lavish events, including some of those thrown by Robert Stigwood, usually were tied in with a motion picture soundtrack album or a premiere. Stigwood thought nothing of booking the entire Tavern on the Green or the vast Roseland ballroom to cater a party.

One of the most unusual receptions ever given was a black-tie affair that followed the premiere of *Tommy—The Motion Picture* at the Ziegfeld Theatre. It was held in the black marble concourse of Manhattan's newest subway station, at Fifty-seventh Street and Avenue of the Americas. The station was closed to the public that night. When the film ended, jet setters, socialites, politicians and industrialists, artists, record tycoons, radio personalities, TV and movie stars jostled one another as they poured out of the theater into stretch limousines for the three-block ride to the subway entrance. There, in a scene that outdid Times Square at rush hour, they got out and inched their way down a single subway entrance. Sequined dresses and fur coats were crumpled in the crush as the partygoers waited up to twenty minutes to make their entrances.

Almost a thousand people descended into a floral setting with hundreds of red-draped tables, spectacular pinball theme centerpieces, and a sumptuous buffet that featured fresh seafood and caviar, crepes prepared at your table, and roast beef carved to order. The wines and pastries had been flown in on Air France.

A similar party for the movie of *Grease* turned the midtown discotheque Studio 54 into a high school gymnasium where guests received white bobby sox and other fifties' souvenirs.

Invitations to a $100,000 Hollywood bash staged by Casablanca Records stipulated that all guests come dressed as characters from the Bogart–Bergman movie for which the record company was named. Company execs wore the original movie costumes used in the film.

The coddling of superstars occasionally demanded a more personal touch—a chief executive officer using his own residence for a private party or dinner honoring a recording artist. Since "label jumping" was the norm, and acts seized on the slightest provocation (insufficient promotion, disputes over royalties, or just the sense that they had been slighted, among others) as a reason to change companies, opening one's home to a star showed that a record company really cared. This technique went beyond the de rigueur limos and the five-star restaurant dining of those decades.

The party that then CBS Records president Clive Davis held for Janis Joplin at his Manhattan apartment following her Madison Square Garden concert was one such glittering, star-studded affair. While Bob Dylan spent the evening frozen against a wall (never taking off his gloves), there were also lots of press people, minor aides, and even some crashers who had to be escorted out. In the resulting crush, cigarettes, cigar ashes, and food were ground into the carpets and drinks spilled on sofas and chairs. I remember my wife asking me who was going to pay for all the damage. Sure enough, the cost of repairs were one of the items cited by CBS when they decided to part company with Clive.

The Joplin party was impressive, but the most memorable home entertaining I ever saw in the music industry was an intimate dinner party given in the sixties by Bob Crewe.

For several months in 1963, an unusual artist had dominated the record charts. A nun had risen to number one "with a bullet"—a fast jump to the top. Her song, "Dominique," seemed to owe its success to a combination of a beautiful melody, the French lyrics,

Theme" / *Meco* • "When I Need You" / *Leo Sayer* • "(Your Love

and the singer's vocation. The singing nun was in head-to-head competition with the Ronettes, whose ''Be My Baby'' was the top song of the year, and she had even topped the Chiffons's ''He's So Fine'' for a few weeks on WABC.

When the nun hit it big, record label presidents ordered their A&R people to check out talented clergy. Long-haired scouts wearing gold chains prowled choir lofts and appeared at pulpits of the nation's churches. If you could sing and wear a white collar, the boys from the Brill Building would give you a listen.

Producer, composer, and arranger Bob Crewe was in the top ranks of the music world in the sixties, collaborating on hit after hit for Frankie Valli and the Four Seasons. He had his own singing group, the Bob Crewe Generation, and he wrote and arranged for many of the industry greats.

One day his brother, Dan, got word from a Welsh monastery about a monk whose tenor voice was such that those who heard him sing believed they were listening to the voice of an angel. Determined to beat out their competitors, the Crewes went after the monk. It was only after the heads of the order were promised a share in any royalties that the monk was persuaded to leave his cell and go to America.

Bob Crewe had a long-established reputation as a party giver, dating back to the days when he owned a Taj Mahal-like co-op in the famous Dakota building in New York. His notorious party for the Rolling Stones was raided by police after live music by Mitch Ryder and the Detroit Wheels shook the staid edifice. Cops stormed in to find Mick Jagger and company surrounded by four hundred admirers, including Leonard Bernstein, Murray the K, and an unknown ukelele player (whom Crewe had found in a Greenwich Village bar) named Tiny Tim.

Now the monk was on his way to America and a rendezvous with Bob Crewe. When he landed at Kennedy Airport, he was met by Dan Crewe and whisked in a Cadillac limousine through the darkening streets, headed for Crewe's latest residence.

Bob Crewe is a man of imaginative tastes, and the massive royalties that poured in from his music gave him the wherewithall to turn his fantasies into reality. Crewe had designed his latest environment out of three penthouses, stacked like layers of a wedding cake and joined by internal staircases, atop an apartment building on Fifth Avenue at Sixty-seventh Street, overlooking Cen-

Has Lifted Me) Higher and Higher" / *Rita Coolidge* • "Nobody

tral Park. The lower penthouses were ringed with landscaped terraces. On the main level, curving panoramic windows were framed with archways above built-in window seats where concrete shelves paved with tiny stone tiles supported pillows covered in soft brown kangaroo skin.

To cover the walls of the main salon Crewe used carved wooden panels that had lined the interior of the Indonesian Pavilion of the New York World's Fair. Walt Disney had wanted those walls very badly for his Anaheim amusement park but Crewe outbid him and the panels went up in the penthouse on Sixty-seventh Street. Entering from a private elevator, one heard rushing water pouring from a small stream into a pool. To the right a hanging staircase wound its way up to the next level against a wall of colored glass blocks. Recessed lights illuminated paintings and magnificent clusters of shimmering crystals, mineral rocks, and semiprecious stones set admist giant tropical plants. On either side of the room were life-sized wooden statues of Balinese dancers. With the push of a few buttons, the entire salon could be transformed into a screening room for motion pictures or an audition chamber for records.

Off to the side was a music room where Crewe's grand piano rested on zebra skin rugs. Exposed brick and modern semicircular lighting set another mood in the rear dining room, which was dominated by a huge brass-framed table that had a top of dark glass. Brass-trimmed leather chairs surrounded the table. Beyond the dining room was a kitchen whose massive ovens, gleaming overhead pot and utensil racks, and butcher block work tables outdid the facilities of many restaurants.

The second level housed Bob Crewe's office and a vast sleeping chamber. A platform bed with indirect lighting beneath it floated out from a wall whose arched niches contained oriental sculpture and plants, alternating with bookshelves lined with leather-bound volumes. The bed was covered with dozens of exotic fur pillows in a variety of textures and colors. The entire scene was reflected in the blue mirrored tiles that totally covered the ceiling. Crewe's office was visible through another archway. Beyond, the skyline of New York and the hills of New Jersey in the distance gave the composer an inspirational work setting.

Guest rooms and a gymnasium were on the third level. One of the rooms resembled an Arabian tent. Another room had a sleeping platform cantilevered out from a wall of granite boulders. The rooms were filled with exotic plants and paintings. The windowless gymnasium was stark, all white, and bathed in lights that illuminated the workout equipment.

Meanwhile, in brother Dan's limousine, on its way to the party, it had not been the best of days for the singing monk. The airline food had left him with indigestion. His ears rang from the changes in air pressure. This first flight of his life had been eight hours of cramped discomfort. He yearned for the straw mattress of his unadorned cell at the monastery. Heathrow Airport, with its illuminated yellow signs and long moving walkways, and now Kennedy with its chaos, were one blur.

The Cadillac's interior seemed enormous. Before him was a bar furnished with cut glass decanters, drinking glasses, and an ice bucket. He poured himself a Scotch but ignored a television set. Outside he was dimly aware of street lights flashing past.

The limousine glided to a stop in front of Crewe's home, and the chauffeur opened the door. Dan Crewe and the monk were escorted to a private elevator. It rose to the main penthouse level and the door opened. The singing monk had arrived in New York. He was surrounded by a dozen dinner guests chatting and making small talk. He asked for a sherry. Bob Crewe took him on a tour of the penthouses. The images tumbled on top of one another, assaulting the monk's senses.

My wife, Sydelle, and I were guests at the party, and at dinner she was seated next to the monk. They chatted amiably during the appetizer, but just as the main course was served, Sydelle, who has an unusual sense of humor, leaned over and whispered quietly to the monk, "You'll have to excuse these surroundings. Bob has had one stroke of bad luck after another. He hasn't done as well as most Americans."

The remark coincided with the arrival of the monk's roast beef entree. As the huge platter with its extra thick slices of meat was set before him, the monk's face grew pale. His hand gripped the armrest of his chair for support. He asked to be excused. Dan Crewe took him to his hotel.

The singing monk never made it to the charts. The clerical phase of pop music had ended.

Howard Cosell (right) and I prepared Muhammed Ali for one of his first radio interviews as world heavyweight boxing champion. *(Wagner International Photos)*

Howard Cosell (left) interviews John Lennon on the ABC Radio Network program ''Speaking of Everything.'' ABC's Sports president Roone Arledge (later to become president of ABC News) looks on with me. *(Rick Sklar, private collection)*

Stevie Wonder joking in my office, pretending to read WABC's ratings. *(Rick Sklar, private collection)*

Briefing Leonard Nimoy in 1968, as the supporting star of the television series *Star Trek* visits WABC after recording an album. Disc jockey Dan Ingram is sitting at left. *(Rick Sklar, private collection)*

Left: John Lennon and I react as security guards hold back stenographers seeking Lennon's autograph during one of John's visits to my office. *(Rick Sklar, private collection)*

Below: Neil Sedaka listens as I explain a lyric change on a special version of ''Breaking Up Is Hard To Do,'' which I rewrote for the United Way campaign. *(Rick Sklar, private collection)*

WABC disc jockeys at a station party in the early 1970s, ''hamming it up'' for the photographer. (Left to right: Chuck Leonard, Dan Ingram, Jim Perry, and Bruce Morrow.) *(Rick Sklar, private collection)*

The WABC ''$25,000 Button.'' Fourteen million were given out to promote the station. Button spotters awarded prizes ranging from television sets to $25,000 in cash.

Barbra Streisand gave me one of her rare radio interviews in March 1979 for an ABC Radio Network program. We talked at the MGM production building in Culver City, California. *(Rick Sklar, private collection)*

CHAPTER 19

John Lennon Meets Howard Cosell

Not all the excitement came from the music industry. We also had Howard Cosell. Howard originated three daily sportscasts and his weekend specials at the station. As a result, he became as much a fixture in my day-to-day life as the ABC shoeshine man. I was exposed to Howard Cosell almost every working day for fourteen years. I became genuinely fond of Howard. Some of his qualities were fascinating to observe close up. Cosell has an extremely high IQ and a computerlike mind with seemingly unlimited capacity. Over the years he has honed his sense of humor to a degree that enables him to demolish a colleague at a company roasting with the most biting and precisely chosen phrases imaginable. Howard's dismantling of DJ Cousin Brucie Morrow at Morrow's farewell party (Bruce went to rival station WNBC in 1974) ended in dire predictions of rating disasters that would reduce Morrow to "impoverished anonymity."

In the earlier years, before Howard Cosell became a national institution, we could have lunch undisturbed in the back room of the Office Pub on New York's West Fifty-sixth Street or at the Ginger Man, with Cosell cupping his hand around a dollar bill as he played liar's poker with the WABC executive staff. He taught me the subtleties of that game.

"Ricky," he used to say, "if you've got *two* of a kind, you've got to protect."

Howard's almost total recall was perfect for the game. He remembered every player's move and past strategy and outguessed

Wish" / *Stevie Wonder* • **1978** • "Boogie Oogie Oogie" / *A Taste of*

the table regularly. I can still see Howard pulling in dollar bills as he won hand after hand, or enjoying a free lunch on the hapless loser who had challenged a Cosell call.

But Howard had better uses for his memory than recreation. Cosell's recall was at its best during the taping of his five-minute daily "Speaking of Sports" program. Howard often worked without a script. Throwing a cue to the recording engineer, he would speak into the microphone. If he made a mistake three minutes into the show, he would sometimes start over again from the beginning and repeat the performance verbatim. He used the same timing, the same inflection, and the same pauses. It was an astonishing process to witness.

Howard Cosell's constant presence at the radio station affected everybody. Howard moved unseeing past many of the lesser functionaries. They watched and waited months, years in some cases, for an acknowledgment. Upper-echelon types were regularly accosted by Cosell, whose verbal zingers probed their insecurities and made light of their accomplishments.

Howard never did get angry with me, although I got him upset once. During the AFTRA performer's strike, Howard had to honor the picket line in front of the ABC headquarters building on Sixth Avenue. Howard didn't mind that so much, but then he was ordered by the union actually to join the line and picket. This was a terrible task for Cosell, torn between his friendship for Leonard Goldenson and Si Siegel, who were inside that building, and his contractual union obligations to picket. He walked glumly around the building along with the disc jockeys and the announcers.

Having anticipated the strike and trying to minimize its impact on WABC Radio's ratings, I had preproduced special spot announcements that invited listeners to come to Fifty-fourth Street and Sixth Avenue and see the most "star-studded picket line in the land." In one announcement we combined a line from a hit song with the name of each personality on our station's roster. We included Cosell. The announcement was a parody of our weekly "Superhit Rundown" spot. It went:

(timpany roll up and under)

ANNCR: This week you will see these superstars in front of All-American Radio WABC. Herb Oscar Anderson!

MUSIC: I'm walkin', yes indeed, I'm walkin' . . .

ANNCR: Dan Ingram!
MUSIC: I'll walk the line . . .
ANNCR: Bob Lewis!
MUSIC: These boots are made for walkin' . . .
ANNCR: Chuck Leonard!
MUSIC: Walk right in, sit right down . . .
ANNCR: Charlie Greer!
MUSIC: He's a walkin' miracle . . .
ANNCR: Howard Cosell!
SONG: I'm gonna walk like a man, fast as I can, walk like a man with youooo ooo ooo . . .

Howard had been listening to WABC on a small portable radio as he walked around the building. When he heard the Frankie Valli vocal he bolted right through his own picket line, ran upstairs to the executive offices of ABC, and demanded that the spot be yanked from the air. It was pulled off, but by then a *Time* magazine reporter had heard it, and the strike spots and jingles became news all over the country.

Despite being constantly surrounded by an environment of rock & roll, Howard seemed oblivious to the music. Though disc jockeys and record stars and the music itself confronted him at every turn, he usually moved through it without acknowledging the world of rock or any of its trappings in any way.

One Tuesday morning, however, after the weekly music meeting had gotten underway in my office, it became obvious that Cosell had been thoroughly aware of every last subtlety involving our music. The disc jockey staff, the music director, and my assistants were seated behind closed doors listening to new releases. Before each selection was played I would announce the results of our latest retail record store survey and then spin the record.

As usual, most records were getting the thumbs down. Since hundreds of new singles were released in those days by record companies and only a few became hits, it was only logical that we be very selective. I had just finished tabling a song for further consideration on a future week when suddenly the door to the office squeaked open just enough for Howard Cosell's head to appear in the doorway. Howard made a declaration:

"This is the room where the black man's music is being suppressed."

Gees • "Shadow Dancing" / *Andy Gibb* • "MacArthur Park" /

I looked up, startled.

''And this is the man,'' he continued, pointing a finger at me, ''who is keeping the black artist off the air!''

''Howard,'' I protested, more puzzled than anything else. ''What are you talking about?''

I knew that almost half the playlist was black music by black artists and that, in addition to having the largest white audience in the country, WABC also had the largest group of black listeners. Across the room, black disc jockey Chuck Leonard looked worried.

Cosell opened the door the rest of the way. He was not alone. Muhammad Ali was with him, and they barged into my office.

''Let's pick some music.'' Ali grinned. ''What's on the turntable, Howard?''

Muhammad Ali walked over to my desk. I had just cued up a song called ''People Gotta Be Free'' by the Rascals. The paper record jacket was still in my hand, and I was looking at the handwritten scrawl across the front. It said, ''Rick, this is a HIT, *please*. Sid.''—a plea for airplay from the Rascal's manager, Sid Bernstein.

Muhammad Ali smiled. ''Let's hear it.''

I started the turntable. It was a white group playing a white song, but it sounded black enough for Ali.

''I vote for that one,'' he said.

Every hand went up in agreement. The Rascals not only went on WABC, their song was voted the ''Pick Hit of the Week.'' It would get extra plays as a result. Cosell and Ali left the room.

The next week we voted to abolish Pick Hits.

Howard didn't say another word about the music until mid-1974, when I was honored at a testimonial fund raising luncheon at the Plaza Hotel for the Third Street Music School Settlement, a favorite music industry charity. John Lennon would be with me on the dais and would make the presentation. I asked Howard to tape a broadcast that we could feed into the ballroom where all the record company presidents and promotion people would be sitting.

With a little prompting from me, he took the room apart in two minutes. Here's how he did it:

''It was with sheer disbelief that I received the news that the recording industry was having a luncheon to honor Rick Sklar. I would have been less surprised to hear that Richard Nixon was giving a dinner party for Peter Rodino.

"It has been estimated that in the past twelve years at ABC Rick Sklar has rejected, turned down for airplay, and refused to broadcast over eighteen thousand new record releases, each of which, according to the promoters, would have obviously reached number one with a bullet. This very morning at the weekly WABC music meeting, whose record decisions are copied by hundreds of other stations across the nation, Sklar set a new world's record in the number of releases that failed the audition. He listened to and turned down thirty-eight songs in twelve minutes.

"One also wonders why he is up on the dais in the seat of honor. I don't know how he gets the courage to sit there surrounded by hundreds of hostile record company executives, music publishers, and promotion men . . . unprotected by bullet-proof glass, not even presenting a moving target.

"One also wonders why you the audience are here. The entire luncheon is a total mystery.

"But *you* know why you are here. It's waiting . . . waiting for that one chance to influence the incorruptible Rick Sklar. It could be a long wait. Jack Anderson says Sklar is unreachable. He never charged his kid's bar mitzvah to the company. He never even gave the kid a bar mitzvah. He's never taken money to play a record. In fact his playlists are getting so short he may not have any records left to play at the rate he's going.

"But let me assure you, in concluding, that this doesn't worry Rick Sklar. After all, there's nothing about empty airtime that play-by-play sports can't fill.

"Congratulations, Rick."

After that event I wondered if I would ever hear about music again from Howard. I did. After emceeing some Sinatra concerts, Cosell decided that there was more to broadcasting than sports. With the blessing of Roone Arledge, Howard set out to become the new Ed Sullivan. On the surface the idea seemed to have everything. Totally live television would be brought back to America. It would be a variety show. It would come from the Ed Sullivan Theater. The biggest acts would appear. Celebrities who were sitting in the audience would stand up and take a bow during the show. It would be "The Ed Sullivan Show" all over again with one exception: The emcee would be Howard Cosell.

Howard had never seemed as excited about anything as he was about this series. "Saturday Night," as the live program would be called, would be the biggest thing to hit television in years, and it would last for decades—even longer than the Sullivan show.

Howard asked me to help, and I joined the planning sessions at King–Hitzig Productions, where producer Rupert Hitzig and comedian Alan King worked with Howard to plan the programs. Howard wanted the opening show to be the biggest night ever on television. He conjured up visions of a jazz quartet featuring Woody Allen. He had animals, jugglers, and then the pièce de résistance.

"Ricky," he said to me, "get me the Beatles."

The Beatles! My heart sank. The Beatles had broken up in April 1970. Howard knew that. He was thinking of reuniting them with himself as the matchmaker. I knew that every rumor of a reconciliation made headlines, but I also knew that the reality of the situation made such a reunion virtually impossible. Howard kept talking.

"On opening night we're going to re-create the night that the Beatles first appeared on American television. And we're going to do it from the same theater, on the same stage."

"I'll make some calls," I said. "John is in New York."

Mid-afternoon the following week, Rupert Hitzig, Howard Cosell, and I were seated in the 21 Club lounge when John Lennon arrived, accompanied by a business adviser. Lennon was wearing one of his favorite black velvet jackets adorned with a large silver pin that said "Elvis" in script with diamonds set in each letter.

I handled the introductions. A waiter served drinks. We made some small talk, with Howard zeroing in on John as the perfect halftime guest for "Monday Night Football." Lennon seemed flattered by the fuss until Cosell began to explain the reason for the meeting.

"John, I want you guys on my show."

Lennon's smile evaporated instantly. "What do you mean 'us guys'?"

"You know, you, George, Paul, Ringo."

There was a long pause. Lennon stared down at the table. Then he looked up.

"I don't know," he said. "I don't know," he repeated. "After what's gone down, I don't know. I thought you wanted *me*."

I could see that Lennon was both hurt and disappointed.

Rupert Hitzig jumped into the conversation and talked quickly. This would be a first in more ways than one. The Beatles wouldn't even have to be in the same city. We could reunite them electronically using a four-way split screen. We could pick up George in India, Ringo in London . . . anything they wanted.

Lennon nodded. He began to think out loud.

"Well, sure, we've thought about it . . . getting together again. But we'd probably not do it. After all, what would people expect? What would they expect? We might leave them disappointed. Better to remember the memories. Remember us as we were."

Now Cosell began to elaborate about the TV show. The Ed Sullivan Theater; the restaging of the most electrifying moment in American television history. "I *do* want you," Howard said. "I want all of you. I want to reunite the Beatles in the same setting in which you first appeared on American television. It will be fantastic."

Lennon listened, then pointed out that in the unlikely event that the Beatles ever did get together again it would probably not be on a network television show. It would more likely be in a stadium the size of the Superdome with closed circuit TV to every other indoor arena in the world and theaters in every major city. The ticket price would be extremely high. The concert would also be filmed for a major motion picture and recorded for a very expensive album. The Beatles' reunion would be a financial bonanza. Yet even this, he said, was unlikely ever to occur.

We continued to talk, but Lennon could not be persuaded. Eventually he stood up and shook Howard's hand. A guest on "Monday Night Football," yes. A performance on Howard Cosell's "Saturday Night," no.

"I'll be going," he said. John and I spoke briefly about a new exhibit of Man Ray that had just opened at the Huntington Hartford Gallery of Modern Art in Columbus Circle, and Lennon wanted to take it in. The meeting with Cosell had ended far sooner than expected. John would go to the museum that afternoon, in fact.

Lennon, long separated from Yoko Ono, wandered through the galleries, taking in the paintings and photographs. It was late afternoon and the museum was empty. He could walk undetected like this at New York events, and he loved it. Lennon turned a corner.

Yoko was standing in front of a painting. They began to talk. They left the museum together hand in hand and began the reconciliation that was to last the rest of his life.

The next time John saw me he told me what had happened.

"You know, when that meeting with Howard ended so soon I thought I'd go see the Man Ray show, and you know who I met—Yoko. He brought us back together, Howard did."

Howard had not reunited the Beatles. He had reunited John and Yoko. "Saturday Night with Howard Cosell" opened with searchlights on Broadway, but no Beatles. Sid Bernstein now had another act, the Bay City Rollers. They came into the theater through a manufactured crowd of hastily assembled doormen, police, screaming girls, and passersby. But it wasn't the same.

CHAPTER 20

Jocks, the Extra Ingredients

That warm afternoon in the summer of 1974, almost a million radios were tuned to 77 on the AM dial. From the beaches of Southampton to the foothills of the Catskill Mountains, on every street in New York and every highway in New Jersey, and all along the lower New England coastline, the opening notes of Stevie Wonder's latest hit could be heard. The blind rock star began to sing. Something sounded wrong. Stevie was way off mike.

A thunderous voice interrupted. "No, no, Stevie. Over *here*. You're singing into a telephone pole." Dan Ingram's sardonic humor had struck again.

I was driving along, monitoring the station from the listener's point of view. Each disc jockey on WABC was different. Almost every disc jockey in America wanted to be on Musicradio WABC by now. Most of them hoped that they would be the next Dan Ingram. With twenty-five thousand announcers in broadcasting and only eight of the coveted time slots at WABC, it was a rare and distinctive breed that made it to New York and actually landed a contract with us.

Our jocks were very talented. No two had the same style. Yet no matter which one was on the air, the station's own personality always came through and was instantly identifiable. Slogans like Music Power, our jingles, that old WABC Chime Time that used to ring after every record reminding the jock to give the time and the EMT, that special six-foot echo chamber through which I fed all the programming, helped over the years to give the station such an unusual sound that even people tuning in during a commercial knew that they were listening to WABC.

Consistent sound characteristics like those had made it possible for our performers to project individual personalities without obscuring the station's own identity in the minds of the listeners. The payoff had always come as the audience first tuned in to hear the unpredictably outrageous remarks by the jocks and then remembered WABC by name when the rating companies came to call. The outrageous disc jockey was one of the extra ingredients that made WABC unique.

Our air personalities were not like those radio automatons we hear so often—the ones who have been trained to tell us the song title and artist, give the time and temperature, and read call-letter slogans from file cards (all in six seconds). Many program directors and station managers prefer these ordinary announcers. They get some ratings and they don't make trouble. But their ratings rarely exceed predictable minimums. Those robot DJs' remind me of the docile carriage horses who pull the hansom cabs in some of our cities. They may be fine for some stations in today's specialized radio marketplace where managements are satisfied with four percent of the listening audience. My goals were higher and demanded entertaining performers who had a keen sense of knowing just how far they could go to get a laugh.

WABC's listeners identified with the jocks and thought of them as amusing friends who could always be counted on for the latest joke. They enjoyed the risqué humor and the idea of being in on the fun. Who would be today's target? But for all the DJs' ad libs, brevity was their art. The practice of talking right over the music when a record began, all the way up to the start of the vocal, was not only permitted, it was expected. The jock would get in an extra zinger or joke that way. The station didn't sound "right" if that pattern wasn't followed.

Dan Ingram had gotten his WABC job by first taping the station, then splicing in his own voice in place of another announcer. The edited tape, now filled with Ingram's irreverent observations and double-entendre quips, was delivered to WABC. His success paved the way for other jocks who went after ratings by *almost* offending the audience. They were not supposed to go too far. Still, the on-air performances occasionally got out of control. With

/ *The Doobie Brothers* • "We Are Family" / *Sister Sledge* • "Rock

so much pressure to get ratings, even Ingram would slip over that fine line every now and then, creating an explosive moment.

To protect ABC from these situations, we had a clause holding the announcers liable for their own ad libs. In turn, most of the jocks carried insurance to cover themselves and we recorded all the broadcasts on tape. Dan, whose sharp sense of satire could be set off by a record title or a line in a radio commercial, seemed to spark more complaints than all the others combined. Hardly a ratings period went by without the familiar sound of his afternoon show being played back in the production studio, as I listened to recordings of the previous day's broadcast to find out why we had received complaint calls. Many of the protests were groundless, reflecting the taste of our most prudish listeners. Occasionally there would be fireworks.

An Indian tribe would protest Ingram's periodic impersonation of the Lone Ranger's sidekick Tonto. (Ingram often addressed his audience in pseudo-Indian dialect. ''Weather look bad, Kemo Sabe,'' he would say, using Tonto's affectionate term for the ranger.) A United Nations mission once called, outraged after Ingram, commenting on the supposed disappearance of Chairman Mao, observed that in a recent photo of the Chinese leader swimming, he looked suspiciously like his laundry man. One afternoon the traffic report that we normally received from a Throgs Neck Bridge tollbooth attendant did not come in. Ingram hypothesized that the attendant had been too busy pocketing coins to phone in the report. Dan went on to explain to his listeners that he himself had once worked the tollbooths on the Southern State Parkway in his early days, and that the toll takers were permitted a five percent leeway from the amounts registered as the cars went through. That week the toll collectors' union had been lobbying for parity in pay with the police and the right to carry arms. The remark caused an uproar and lawyers for the toll collectors were all over Ingram. Eventually Ingram and the union resolved the dispute.

Ingram was our most polished production voice and because his timing, delivery, and ability to take direction was so good, he was used on more contest and station promotion spots than the rest of the staff combined. He could usually knock off a spot in one take. It was easy for him to go from the air studio to the adjoining production studio while a record was playing and lay down a voice track for the weekly ''Superhit Rundown'' promotional spot announcement. He would do the track and be back in the air studio before the song ended.

''Superhit Rundown,'' like so many WABC concepts, was simplicity itself. It contained excerpts from the top records we were playing that week. They were our prime attraction, I reasoned. Why not promote the fact that we were playing them? The spot went:

INGRAM:	*(heavy echo)* This week you will hear *these* Superhit Sounds on WABC. The Fifth Dimension!
MUSIC:	''Let the Sunshine In'' *(excerpt)*
INGRAM:	*(heavy echo)* Tommy James and the Shondells!
MUSIC:	''Crystal Blue Persuasion'' *(excerpt)*
INGRAM:	Neil Diamond!
MUSIC:	''Sweet Caroline'' *(excerpt)*
INGRAM:	Jay and the Americans!
MUSIC:	''This Magic Moment'' *(excerpt)*
INGRAM:	*(echo)* Plus dozens of other stars in continuous entertainment. Remember: More minutes of the music you want to hear are on
JINGLE:	Seventy-seven W-A-B-C. *(trumpets sting)*

Because he was so good, I was concerned about Dan Ingram. His resonant and pliable voice with its great range of modulation got him so much freelance commercial work on television, radio commercials, and motion picture soundtracks that he had little time left for himself and desperately wanted Saturdays off. Just the thought of no Ingram on the weekend was too much to contemplate. The listeners had become so comfortable with that voice blaring out of portable radios in the parks and on the beaches that I couldn't afford not to have him on the air. I gave him everything else. More money. More publicity. But each year he negotiated a few more Saturdays. His vacation demands also increased.

One of the most important strategies in radio is consistency of sound. A station must present the same audio patterns as much of the time as possible. Listeners become comfortable with that sound and wrap themselves with it like a security blanket. If a different voice and style comes on, the listener feels uncomfortable and may try another station. As a result, I tried never to have any talent off the air for more than two weeks at a time. For top WABC air personalities, paradise was a three-week vacation. Ingram once flew away, ostensibly for two weeks. Then I received a cable from Tahiti that he had lost his passport and wallet and was stranded. We lost Ingram's "sound" for almost a month that time.

Each year there was just a little less of Ingram on the air. Just as we reached the point where I thought the ratings might seriously be affected, I received an unsolicited tape postmarked Tampa, Florida, from a young disc jockey who had aspirations of one day returning to his home town and working for WABC. He didn't ask for a job, only a critique. I listened to his tape and couldn't believe what I heard. The voice was giving Tampa-St. Petersburg traffic and weather reports, but it sounded like Dan Ingram. I continued to listen, fascinated. The vocal inflections were younger but so close . . . so close. Suddenly the idea of Ingram being off the air more and more frequently seemed less menacing to the ratings. The jock's name was Bob Morgan, but if he really sounded that much like Ingram the sound pattern could be maintained. If we were lucky, half the audience would never be aware of the substitution. I telephoned some radio program directors I knew in Tampa and had them tape Morgan's program just to make sure the tapes he had sent had not been processed or filtered to aid in the resemblance. They had not.

I flew the disbelieving Morgan to New York. He was handsome, with blue eyes and red hair, and was very personable. I quickly arranged to hire him.

Soon after, I received a congratulatory call from ABC's affirmative action desk. I had hired the first Puerto Rican disc jockey on a major New York station without knowing it. Morgan's name turned out to be Cruz. While his mother was Irish, his father came from San Juan. I was thrilled, having wanted to add a Hispanic jock ever since I brought Chuck Leonard in during 1965 as the first black DJ on WABC.

I used Cruz to cover when Ingram was ill or on vacation and on Saturdays. There were times I had to listen carefully before I was sure which one was doing the show. A record would end and a voice would say, "I'll get you, my pretty, and your little dog Toto." I would think it was Ingram and then realize it was Cruz. The arrangement didn't exactly overjoy Ingram, but I had to answer for the ratings and needed all the insurance I could get.

Ingram soon had another nemesis. A DJ in a small Southern city began calling himself Dan Ingram. Incensed, Big Dan sued, but quickly found out what happens to the star from New York and his lawyer in Dixie. Everyone from the judge on down knew who Dan Ingram was, and it wasn't our Dan. Ingram and his lawyer left the Southern town one step ahead of the tar and feathers.

Actually it was hard to zing Ingram. The other jocks tried. I sometimes joked with the jocks myself and even I tried to break Dan up. One April Fool's Day I let bandleader Sammy Kaye cut into the Ingram show from another studio and slip his own *Swing and Sway* selections on the air after Ingram announced the regular hits. Listeners were told what was happening but Ingram, of course, was not. Dan eventually caught on when he noticed that the needle on the volume meter in the studio was not moving in response to his own voice.

Another time, Ingram walked into the studio, handed his theme song cartridge to the engineer and discovered when the show went on the air that somehow the cartridge now contained the theme song of the "Listen to Lacy" show. Jack Lacy, a rival jock on WINS ten years earlier, had been the only competitor Ingram ever feared. Ingram broke up laughing over the air for ten minutes.

The ultimate Ingram breakup was elaborately orchestrated in 1969 by Bruce Morrow, whose show followed Ingram's. Late one afternoon, as Morrow and his staff drifted into the studio, Ingram was handed a revised weather report. Ingram looked at the new forecast, called for the mike, and said, "Watch out for brief showers." As he did so, everyone in the room showered Ingram with men's jockey briefs. Hundreds of pairs of shorts filled the studio. Ingram broke into hysterics and could not regain enough of his composure to finish the show.

Every new jock was a butt for the other DJs' pranks. You didn't join the team until you went through a sort of initiation. The overnight studio environment was usually the setting for this kind of fun, because I used this shift as a training slot for future daytime disc jockeys. Veteran WABC talent staffers and engineers regarded the night jocks as hayseeds who would have to prove themselves. In 1970 Jay Reynolds, who came from the Midwest, was hired for the all-night show. Somebody offered to teach him how to speak "NewYorkese," and one night I heard him doing a clothing commercial, saying, "So come to Dennison's Route 22,

/ *Pink Floyd* • "Upside Down" / *Diana Ross* • "Working My Way

Union, New Jersey. Old Man Dennison knows what you want. He's no schmuck!"

A few weeks after the "schmuck" incident, an overnight studio operations report arrived on my desk with a curious entry from the previous night. It read: 6:58 A.M. right candle went out. 7:15 A.M. left candle went out.

I later discovered a bogus memo purporting to be from me to all the talent staff on the topic, "Candle Contest." It stated that in connection with the showing of the movie *Bell, Book and Candle*, WABC was running a promotion that involved listeners guessing when two lit candles in the studio went out. The memo instructed all disc jockeys to watch the candles carefully and write down the time to the exact second each candle went out. The memo was signed with a copy of my signature and had been posted in the studio just before Reynolds went to work. As he arrived, jock Chuck Leonard had dashed out of the studio calling, "Don't forget to watch the candles." Reynolds walked in and found the lights out and two candles burning. All night long his eyes were riveted to those candles. At 6:00 A.M. the candles were still burning but Reynolds had to pick up his mother-in-law, so he persuaded morning jock Harry Harrison to watch the candles for him and log the time they went out. Charlie Greer had been the victim of a similar joke a few years earlier on the overnight shift.

When air personality Ron Lundy started on the overnight shift, nobody gave him a hard time. Word was out that Lundy was an old pal of Ingram's, and besides, his personality was so likable and friendly. Lundy started each show with a deep, "Hello, luv, this is Ron Lundy in the greatest city in the world." He soon moved to middays, where he perfected his warm style and became so well known that when the producers of the film *Midnight Cowboy* used a montage of radio programs in the film's soundtrack to indicate the passing of Jon Voight's bus across the country, they used Lundy to denote the journey's end in New York.

Ron worked any hours we asked, filled in during emergencies, and was so cooperative it was almost his undoing. When I offered a prize to the listener who could float the most seaworthy boat in the swimming pool of the then new Loew's City Squire Motor Inn, Lundy volunteered to splash around in a pool until he had sunk all but one of them. When we threw him into the water his thrashings were incredible. Thousands of ships went under in less than a minute. Then we had to jump in after Lundy. He had been too embarressed to tell us he couldn't swim.

The disc jockey I felt closest to and knew best at WABC was Bruce Morrow, because Bruce and I went back together to the mid-fifties at WINS and had shared so many experiences.

On one of his first remote broadcasts, from Ravenhall Pool in Coney island, a portion of the poolside stage collapsed suddenly during the broadcast. I had gone to the remote to work on improving the sound quality of the outdoor origination and was on the part of the stage that gave way. I found myself in the mud, and for a while I had to stand on an engineer's shoulders, holding up equipment that was in danger of toppling into nearby puddles of water. Bruce and I kept the show on the air and, from then on, knew we could count on each other. Stage appearances, and a close call we had during a helicopter take-off for a Principal of the Year promotional trip cemented the bond. I soon knew Bruce's mother, father and brother, and my wife and I often went out with Bruce and his wife.

Bruce too had that "extra ingredient." It was more than the uniquely identifiable sound of his staccato chattering and the high-pitched warble in his voice that he threw in just often enough to punctuate a point. Bruce never made himself into a "star" in front of his audience. He was never above his fans and was never a snob. Even in his thirties he still projected the personality of a James Madison High School teenager. (When Bruce started to make money, he didn't move to Park Avenue. Instead he took the two biggest apartments on the top floor of the most luxurious apartment house on Brooklyn's Ocean Parkway, joined them together and lived there, close to his roots.) The kids knew he was approachable, so they felt at ease around him, identified with him, and trusted him. Troubled teenagers could relate to Bruce Morrow when nobody else could reach them. They called him for advice when they couldn't talk to their parents.

Bruce's stage presence and ability to be disarming made him the perfect judge for audience participation contests as well. He could bring the most nervous contestants up onto a stage and get them relaxed and laughing.

Bruce had another quality. No matter what unexpected turn a promotion took, Bruce was never thrown. I remember vividly a promotion called the "Big Shot" contest. I had arranged to do a

Billy Joel • "Ride Like the Wind" / *Christopher Cross* • "Master

Cousin Bruce broadcast from the bridge of the new German cruise ship, the *T.S. Hamburg*, anchored near the Statue of Liberty in New York Harbor. It was a tie-in with Sylvania's flashbulb division. The exterior of the ship had been wired with ten thousand flashbulbs that would be set off simultaneously at 10:00 P.M. while WABC listeners, on cue from Brucie, opened their camera shutters on shore.

We boarded the liner at a Hudson River pier at 5 P.M. Six hundred travel agents from all over America, together with their spouses, had been invited to join our six hour minicruise. The ship was splendid and the travel agents, mostly over-fifties, wandered the decks and public rooms excitedly as waiters handed out glasses of champagne from trays that never seemed to be empty. Promptly at six, the bars opened and bottles of twenty-year-old Scotch were emptied like so many cans of Coke. At eight, dinner commenced with a captain's toast for which a shot of the most potent Russian vodka had been provided at each place setting. During the meal, the finest French red wines and German Rhine wines were served. After-dinner liqueurs followed dessert. At 9:30 P.M. the bars reopened and the waiters with champagne trays reappeared. By now the *T.S. Hamburg* was rolling in heavy seas off Asbury Park, New Jersey.

When the ship finally swung around and headed into position for the flashbulb event, the lavish offering of alcoholic beverages was beginning to take its toll on the travel agents. People were collapsing on desk chairs, folding up onto couches, and staggering along the corridors from bulkhead to bulkhead. Now bodies began crashing down the staircases. Women were heaving over the railings. Unconscious travel agents were everywhere. You had to watch where you stepped. The ship swung back and forth near the statue as the captain tried to hold it steady. Teetotaler Cousin Brucie, sober and splendid on the navigation bridge, called for the shutters to be opened. The ship was swinging wildly as the ten thousand flashbulbs went off. Every picture came out blurred.

Working with Bruce Morrow for over a dozen years at ABC, we created a special identity for his time period. Tuesday night became countdown night when all the records on the brand new "WABC Superhit Survey" were played. Saturday nights Bruce hosted "The Cousin Brucie Saturday Night Dance Party." We mixed the old with the new records and had a special golden oldies feature, "Bruce Morrow's Musical Museum." Bruce had several theme songs over the years, some that followed him from station to station along with his voice and promotional features. He had the "Big M" theme, the "Go-Go" theme, and others. The most famous was the one recorded for him by the Four Seasons. One night when an engineer hit a wrong cartridge start button, the Cousin Brucie theme was heard instead of the national anthem following a broadcast by President Lyndon Johnson about American marines landing in the Dominican Republic.

Although WABC was the number one station in all periods of the broadcast day, or "dayparts," as they are called on Madison Avenue, the numbers at night were staggering to behold because of the teens who listened to Bruce. Bruce Morrow's share of the market was regularly over twenty percent. More than one in every five listeners was tuned to Cousin Brucie. Frequently it was closer to one in four. The other three listeners were shared by twenty-six other radio stations. His 21 share of the 1968 March–April Pulse rating was typical.

Because we had millions of listeners, it was difficult for WABC to do "call in to win"-type giveaways. Most stations could offer free record albums over the air to "the tenth person to call" or "the next four callers." WABC couldn't do that. We tried once. Bruce offered Beatle concert tickets over WABC and the surge of phone calls knocked out the main trunkline between Manhattan and Brooklyn, Queens, and Long Island, cutting the borough off from incoming and outgoing telephone service.

Throughout his years at WABC, I let Bruce emcee all specials regarding the Beatles. (Ringo Starr said he always harbored a secret desire to be a DJ like Bruce, and during the early eighties did such a guest DJ stint on the ABC Radio Network.)

For years Bruce was a constant in a business that is known for change. Then, early in 1974 I became concerned while monitoring Bruce's show because I noted increasing periods of time when the music was segued from record to jingle to record with decreasing participation by Bruce. I knew he had grow increasingly unhappy over the playlist as it grew shorter and shorter. He was spending less time with the show and more time preoccupied with other business interests. When I visited him in the studios, he would frequently be on the telephone while his engineer tended the program.

• "Morning Train (9 to 5)" / *Sheena Easton* • "Endless Love" /

The night ratings were still number one, but now WNBC mounted a major campaign against Morrow. They hired Wolfman Jack and began sending out press releases saying that Wolfman was after Morrow's audience. I had heard Wolfman's show and knew it would never be a threat. I was more concerned about the growing FM challenges to our nighttime audience. Nevertheless, the press bit, and NBC's press department even suckered *Cosmopolitan* and *Oui* into doing feature stories on the supposed battle between the two jocks. They also delivered a tombstone to the entrance of the ABC building inscribed "Cousin Brucie's Days Are Numbered" and sent miniature copies of the tombstone to all the major advertising agencies in town. It was an old publicity technique. If your station has low ratings, you attack the station that is number one, and their notoriety will rub off on you.

My concern was that if Bruce didn't deliver, WABC would lose the nighttime ratings—and it wouldn't be to NBC. I had to get him back on the track. I waited until the end of a ratings cycle and reopened his contract, telling Bruce the terms woiuld be restructured to a base plus bonuses tied to the ratings.

At that time Bruce was represented by Sid Bernstein. Ever since Sid had brought the Beatles to the United States and staged the Shea Stadium concerts, I called him the "Sol Hurok of the Teenage Set." Sid told me that Bruce would not negotiate. By reopening the contract I had given Bruce an opportunity to leave. He and Sid saw a chance for a quick killing. They negotiated a deal with NBC. Bruce would replace Wolfman Jack on radio and also do television specials.

Replacing a disc jockey is never an easy task at any station. Finding another legend like Bruce, whose very name was synonymous with WABC, was a challenge. The entire radio industry tried to eavesdrop, fascinated. Madison Avenue held its breath.

Bruce Morrow's departure sent a wave of apprehension through ABC Radio. President Hal Neal called me, and I reminded him that the station ratings hadn't suffered when Herb Oscar Anderson departed. This time, however, ratings were only one of the concerns. Many of the sponsors had signed on because they wanted their products identified with Morrow's unique personality. We needed another "name" teen-appeal DJ if WABC was to retain certain lucrative accounts. At the same time I had to get a jock who could generate tremendous excitement over the air.

In terms of talent, all other stations were to WABC what the farm clubs are to the major league teams in baseball. Over the years I had kept in touch with top-rated air personalities in every market. An entire bank of file cabinets bulged with résumés, tapes, cassettes, correspondence, and ratings books. The ratings books showed which DJs consistently outperformed their stations. If a station averaged a 12 share but one jock regularly pulled off a 15, it was obvious that he was a star.

By listening to the tapes that corresponded with the best ratings and playing them over and over again to rooms filled with typical listeners, representative of the age groups that comprised the evening audience, I was rapidly able to narrow my choices. Eventually I focused on a Philadelphia evening air personality, George Michael.

Locating a jock and signing him are two distinctly different processes. Most good talent is usually tied up by contract. But with George Michael, the timing, at least, was good. His current contract was running out. I invited him to come to New York and took him to lunch with WABC general manager George Williams.

Once we got George Michael into the old-time saloon trappings of the Cattleman West restaurant, we fed him the steak special and offered him the job at a handsome salary. To our surprise he turned it down.

"I've done my jocking," he told us. "It's a kid's game. I'm about to sign to do the color for the Baltimore Orioles." Unbeknownst to us, George Michael's lifelong goal was to be a top sportscaster, and his dream was about to be fulfilled.

We returned to WABC without George Michael. I immediately called ABC television, found out that they were looking for a sportscaster for the late-night "Channel 7 Eyewitness News," arranged an audition for Michael and got him back into New York the next day. After talking to him further, I also worked out a clause permitting him to do weekend hockey broadcasts. Michael got the television job. As a closer, George Williams reminded him that he could sit in on picking the music. George Michael was a close friend of Elton John, Priscilla Presley, and many rock luminaries. And in the end, the Baltimore Orioles had to make do without George Michael. He was coming to WABC.

It wasn't the same show that Bruce did, but it was a great one. My two problems were Michael's tendency to slip in hockey and baseball scores between the records and the need to periodically patch studio walls when Michael, a stickler for precision, hurled cartridges and entire cartridge racks around the room when engineers missed cues.

At 11 P.M. we had to appeal to an older, more sophisticated listener. For most of my years at WABC, Chuck Leonard filled that bill. Chuck may have been our first black DJ, but over the air WABC was always color blind. Chuck was cool; Chuck was sophisticated; Chuck was grown up. The teens who stayed tuned after Bruce were beginning to make the transition to the twenties, and Chuck provided sex appeal.

In the sixties, morning man Harry Harrison was an anachronism, but perfect for our wake-up audience. Harry, his wife, and kids embodied fifties togetherness. They even wore matching clothes. The entire family would walk into the station in the same outfits. He sounded like everyone's favorite solid citizen, perfect for morning information.

Harry was a very private person, a consummate professional whose life had to be governed by the demands of his unique time schedule. He had to be up at 4:30 A.M. and asleep by 9:30 P.M. If he deviated, his show suffered. Working the morning show breeds a special personality. Most morning men have the capacity to be adaptable. As a result they are among the most stable of radio performers. They seem to stay in the same job longer and their marriages are usually happy and lasting.

There were other voices over the years covering weekends and vacation relief. Names like Jim Nettleton, Frank Kingston Smith, Steve O'Brien, Jim Perry, Johnnie Donovan, and others came and went during my years at WABC. Each jock was good, but it was the particular combination of the jocks and the sound of WABC that made them superstars.

CHAPTER 21

The Super Promotions

As WABC moved on through the seventies, the very size of the audience began to present a formidable problem when it came to planning station promotions. Ongoing audience promoting had become even more of a necessity as ratings systems grew more sophisticated. Gone were the simple home interviews conducted by Pulse Inc. Now Arbitron, a subsidiary of Control Data Corporation, conducted sweeps of all the important radio markets by distributing home diaries. The rating books based on those diaries contained incredible amounts of data on who was listening to each station every hour. Audiences were chopped up and described by every possible age, sex, and daypart combination; newer studies were beginning to dissect them by life style. All this information was fed into computers and translated into marketing information. Gone also were the days when glib salesmen could wine, dine, and sometimes even seduce the mostly female agency time buyers into committing huge chunks of money to radio time. Now salespeople of both sexes came with calculators, ready to sell on the basis of sophisticated data.

Getting listeners to remember our name and call letters to ensure the credit in the rating diaries had become more critical than at any time in the past. With FM now proliferating, New York had forty-five stations in the central area and another dozen and a half in the suburbs. That meant that upwards of sixty signals were clamoring for recognition.

If you stopped typical listeners on the street and asked them to name all the radio stations they could think of, most people would be hard pressed to come up with seven out of the sixty, and could only cite two or three that they actually tuned in. To help me promote WABC to millions of listeners, I enlisted the aid of a clever logistics expert, promotion man Pat Pantonini, who had previously worked for Mike Douglas.

Because WABC's signal reached sixteen million potential listeners, I would spend hours thinking of how to reach and motivate millions of people at once. The $25,000 Button was one of those ideas. We offered prizes including checks for $25,000 to people spotted wearing a button with the WABC call letters on it. Rewards of that magnitude would be enough of an inducement for people to pin on the buttons, giving us millions of walking billboards. Pantonini handled the details and eventually made up fourteen million buttons. The job was farmed out to every button factory in the country and took months. The coiled wire in each button had to be inserted by hand. No machine could do it. The cost of that many buttons would have wiped out our entire promotion budget for the year, but in an ingenious ploy, the promotion cost us nothing. We sold the buttons to McDonalds. To get a free button, a listener had to visit one of the fast food chain's branches, sprinkled by the hundreds across the WABC listening area. The McDonalds marketing people knew that once those millions of people walked up to the counters to pick up the free $25,000 button, they wouldn't walk away without buying a burger or at least a soft drink. The public snapped up the buttons and gobbled up Big Macs.

Pantonini used bonded college students to spot the button wearers. I'll never forget the first time $25,000 was given away. A spotter called in from Newark, New Jersey. He was elated. "She's black," he told us over the phone, "and pregnant!"

Manager George Williams, sensing a publicity coup, called all the newspapers in New York and New Jersey and announced that he was going to award the prize money in his office. Williams, a former marine who prided himself on being a good father and husband and attended church every Sunday, personally handed the check to the winner.

"Your husband must really be excited," he said into the microphone as photographers snapped away and TV cameras recorded the event for "Channel 7 Eyewitness News."

"Husband! I ain't got no husband," she protested. "I ain't married."

George Williams's smile disappeared.

Band • "Physical" / *Olivia Newton-John* • "Waiting for a Girl Like

"But you're going to get married now," he said.

"Hell, no!" she replied, stuffing the check into her pocketbook.

The $25,000 button was good for the ratings. The only miscalculation we made was on air freight costs. Who thinks of weight when it comes to something as small as a button? We should have allocated an extra $25,000 check just for the shipping. Fourteen million buttons weigh a lot when they're made out of steel.

Because it was so successful, the button contest was repeated once more. This time it was heard all the way to Moscow. The United States and the Soviet Union were conducting their joint Apollo–Soyuz space mission, and the broadcast line between the two countries had to be kept open around the clock. An engineer had a bright idea and fed WABC radio over the line when it wasn't being used for official broadcasts. In no time at all, bootleg tapes of WABC were on the black market in Moscow, selling for more than a hundred dollars. We made up some of the $25,000 buttons in Russian and sent them over, but we never did figure out how to do our button spotting in front of the Kremlin.

At another mass audience promotion, this one in 1975, we ran a concert to mark the conclusion of a March of Dimes Walkathon. Although we didn't book "name" acts to perform, John Lennon and Harry Nilsson agreed to speak and Alice Cooper was a surprise visitor. Over one hundred thousand people filled Central Park's Sheep Meadow. Lennon had not been seen at a public event in three years. He thought that his battles with U.S. Immigration officials, who were trying to get him deported, would be helped if he got involved with "good deed" groups like the March of Dimes. He agreed to speak if we could get him there, but as our limousine pulled into the area it was obvious that we could not get closer than five hundred feet from the stage. We would have to make it through the crowd the rest of the way on foot. Then the audience spotted the car and we were surrounded by fans. We got out of the car just as the roof started to cave in under the weight of the many fans who climbed all over it. A flying wedge of police pushed us to the stage.

"This is why I gave up performing in public," Lennon said.

The last of the great promotions I saw launched at WABC was called "The Big Ticket." It made the fullest possible use of data processing and of ABC's mainframe computers in Hackensack.

You" / *Foreigner* • "I Love Rock and Roll" / *Joan Jett and the*

The idea was simple enough. On a certain Sunday, every major newspaper in the area would include a four-color cardboard supplementary insert. It would contain numbered tickets and would show fantastic prizes, ranging from automobiles to fabulous vacations to color television sets and appliances of every type. If your ticket number was announced over the radio, you would win a gigantic prize. If only the first three digits of your number were called, you would still win a prize, albeit a smaller one, admission to a movie perhaps. All you had to do when you heard your number was to call WABC and claim your prize. To verify your claim we would ask you to read back the winning number from your ticket and also a second or verification code number that was on the ticket and unique to it. Our computer operators would punch up the verifying number on a screen and if your winning number accompanied it, we knew we had a legitimate winner.

Tens of millions of tickets were dropped on the marketplace at the same moment. We gave away prizes for three months. The ratings jumped two entire share points. "The Big Ticket," under other names, was seized on by stations everywhere. In Chicago, a station mailed tickets to listeners instead of including it in the Sunday papers. Houston, Detroit, Boston, and other markets saw ratings leap when the tickets went out before a rating period.

While the super promotions had the same goals as earlier contests, I realized that they were also a culmination. By wedding computer power to showmanship, we had reached a new peak in the art of creating and sustaining mass radio audiences.

One day while I was at my desk listening to Big Ticket winners phoning in for their prizes, I visualized those millions of people with individually coded tickets in their hands and their wallets. Then another image pushed the picture aside. I remembered the two hundred dog owners, twenty years earlier, lined up along Central Park West at WINS Columbus Circle studios with their "pooped pooches," trying to win a trip to Florida. It had been my first attempt to draw attention to a station, to get people to listen and to talk about it. From 200 contestants to 20 million. Our team at WABC had climbed more than a new peak. This was our Everest.

I turned up the volume and listened as the sound of the next record filled the room.

Blackhearts • "Hurts So Good" / *John Cougar* • "Don't Stop

Epilogue

I left WABC in March 1977, with the station still number one in the ratings, having been promoted to vice president of programming of ABC's radio division. Radio station WABC passed into other hands. For the first time in fifteen years, I was no longer picking the music or calling the shots.

In October of 1978, WABC dropped almost two share points in a single rating book and lost its standing as the market leader to a new FM station, WKTU, that had come on the air during the summer with a format based on the then new disco craze.

After the audience loss, WABC's disc jockey lineup and music policies were modified. Additional changes were made over the next four years under a succession of program directors. The ratings continued to decline in a market situation that saw music audiences turning increasingly to FM for their radio entertainment. By the winter of 1983, WABC was down to a 3.8 share in the New York ratings. In May of that year, Musicradio WABC changed formats and became Talkradio WABC. Some of its new programming came from a satellite-distributed talk network on which I had just completed development work for ABC.

The impact of Musicradio WABC cannot be summed up in a corporation's profit-and-loss statements. To the listener, radio is a personal medium. During the dozen years of its heyday, WABC, its music, and its air personalities became an intimate part of the lives of tens of millions of people who lived in the Northeastern United States. Mornings without Herb Oscar Anderson or Harry Harrison, afternoons without Ron Lundy or Big Dan Ingram, evenigs without Cousin Brucie were unthinkable to WABC listeners. Those voices, each so unusually amiable and delivered with the warmer-than-life resonance of the WABC sound, were friend, family, and counselor all in one. The songs they played were so popular that they became the national hit music for America—hundreds of tunes that everybody knew and could hum. Their appeal crossed every demographic barrier. Whatever their ages,

Believin'" / *Journey* • "Rosanna" / *Toto* • "Every Little Thing She

whatever they did for a living, whoever they were, they responded to the same rhythm. Whether they lived in Woodstock or Asbury Park, New London or Coney Island, WABC was their station. Whatever their ethnic background, the WABC disc jockeys were buddies who reflected their thoughts and feelings, cheered them up, and never let them down.

Ruben Rodriguez, for many years Neil Bogart's national promotion manager at Casablanca Records and later promotion head at Island Records, grew up with WABC. He summed the station up this way:

"When I was a kid, WABC was my best friend. Cousin Brucie was like my real cousin. Anything worth hearing was on WABC. That's where it all happened. That's where the excitement was. There was always something new going on. That's where the Beatles were. All the best music was on WABC. The variety of the WABC music was what was so great. It appealed to everybody. I'm Hispanic. I lived in a black neighborhood and went to a school where most of the kids were Jewish. We all listened to WABC. The Spanish kids learned English listening to WABC. WABC was everybody's station."

An entire generation lived their lives with WABC—its jingles, its music, and even its sponsors imprinted forever in their memories. The people who listened to WABC still remember Palisades Amusement Park's commercial "Come On Over" and Dennison Clothiers, Route 22, Union, New Jersey, where "Money Talks, Nobody Walks." No other generation of radio listeners was ever part of a group in which so many of one's friends, family, neighbors, and co-workers so intensely shared the same listening experience.

The growth of FM, and the resulting "population explosion" of radio stations, triggered a wave of specialization in radio. Individual station audiences grew smaller as broadcast economics forced old stations as well as new ones to target their audience appeal and narrow their programming offerings in order to survive. By programming only for adults, or teens, or over-54s, or a black/Hispanic urban mix, stations that were no longer able to deliver listeners in massive quantities again had something specific to offer to the advertiser.

The segmentation of radio programming and audiences also greatly reduced the number of national hit songs that had formed

Does" / *The Police* • "Who Can It Be Now" / *Men at Work* •

the broad base of the music business, and may have contributed to that industry's decline in the late seventies and early eighties.

Will mass-appeal stations like WABC again dominate the airwaves? Radio is constantly changing. Its programming always reflects the predominant values of the time. America is a pluralistic society, made up of individuals who share certain common experiences. In recent years, important sociological changes polarized groups and gave us the so-called Me generation. Now we seem to be moving once again into a cycle that emphasizes those aspects of life that unify rather than divide us. During such times, radio formats based on the popularity of widely enjoyed hit songs may again find a broad spectrum of support among listeners.

Americans are again starting to enjoy stations with playlists and presentation techniques reminiscent of those that characterized WABC. The formats go by many names, and the personality DJs are not always there (it takes years for a new crop of air stars to develop), but the sound proclaims the reality. What started in the middle of the twentieth century as Top Forty radio is undergoing a resurgence.

During 1982, significant numbers of FM stations began instituting contemporary hit music formats. By 1983, stations by the dozens had changed their music and their call letters. However they spelled it, the message was the same—tune to us for the hits. In 1984, statellite networks began sending 24-hour format versions of Top Forty programming to stations all over the country, and a weekly countdown show featuring Dan Ingram went into national syndication, competing with Casey Kasem's American Top Forty, which could already be heard in almost every city.

This rebirth has been helped by the gathering of most of the music radio listeners on a single spectrum—FM—and by the refinement of rating measurement techniques to include more blacks, teens, and young adults. It is also being aided, paradoxically, by the growth of music video, whose high production costs (a single music video can easily run up a six-figure outlay) require producers to focus on individual songs rather than on entire albums. The increasingly successful MTV music television cable channel owes some of its popularity to the use of WABC-like promotions and repetitive playlists. In the future, stereo-enhanced AM may also play a role.

Few broadcasters believe that any station will again achieve the decade-long dominance that WABC enjoyed. But nobody predicted it the first time. It has been called a marathon run. How apt. Like the successful completion of a marathon by a runner, it took the most careful planning, an unwavering commitment, the ability to draw inspiration from the public, and the determination to reach a goal in spite of the most difficult obstacles.

Public taste is only one of the factors that will shape tomorrow's radio. It was technology that brought the fidelity of FM and the lifelike quality of stereo to radio. It is technology that is making it possible for sophisticated personal receivers to provide stock quotes, personal paging, and individualized two-way broadcasting via cellular radio. We are already seeing rock concerts sent by satellite from one continent to another. From there it is only one step to worldwide radio programs that will enable people everywhere to listen to the pop rock hits that began in America and became everybody's music. Radio is full of surprises. Stay tuned.

THE SONGS THAT GOT THE RATINGS

The lists of songs that follow represent the actual rankings, year by year, on radio stations where I worked. As such, the standings differ somewhat from national playlists. Some decided regional preferences can be detected.

In most cases the lists reflect the results of my own research techniques for determining the *shared* music preferences of several demographic groups.

A few songs may appear two years in a row because they started to become popular late in the year in which they were released. Other songs are listed in the year following their release, because that is when they achieved their playlist importance on the radio station. Where there were competing versions of the same song and only one version is shown, it is because that was the version that was on the playlist.

1953

"Song from *Moulin Rouge*"	*Percy Faith*
"Vaya con Dios"	*Les Paul and Mary Ford*
"Doggie in the Window"	*Patti Page*
"I'm Walking Behind You"	*Eddie Fisher*
"You, You, You"	*The Ames Brothers*
"Till I Waltz Again With You"	*Teresa Brewer*
"April in Portugal"	*Les Baxter*
"Don't Let the Stars Get in Your Eyes"	*Perry Como*
"I Believe"	*Frankie Laine*
"Ebb Tide"	*Frank Chacksfield*
"Pretend"	*Nat "King" Cole*
"Eh Cumpari"	*Julius LaRosa*

"Rags to Riches"	*Tony Bennett*
"Your Cheatin' Heart"	*Joni James*
"C'Est Si Bon"	*Eartha Kitt*

1954

"Little Things Mean a Lot"	*Kitty Kallen*
"Wanted"	*Perry Como*
"Hey, There"	*Rosemary Clooney*
"Sh-Boom"	*The Crew-Cuts*
"Oh, My Papa"	*Eddie Fisher*
"Three Coins in the Fountain"	*The Four Aces*
"Secret Love"	*Doris Day*
"Hernando's Hideaway"	*Archie Bleyer*
"Young at Heart"	*Frank Sinatra*
"This Ole House"	*Rosemary Clooney*
"Cross Over the Bridge"	*Patti Page*
"That's Amore"	*Dean Martin*
"Happy Wanderer"	*Frank Weir*
"Stranger in Paradise"	*Tony Bennett*
"If I Give My Heart to You"	*Doris Day*

1955

"Cherry Pink and Apple Blossom White"	*Perez Prado*
"Rock Around the Clock"	*Bill Haley and his Comets*
"Yellow Rose of Texas"	*Mitch Miller*
"Autumn Leaves"	*Roger Williams*
"Unchained Melody"	*Les Baxter*
"Ballad of Davy Crockett"	*Bill Hayes*
"Love Is a Many-Splendored Thing"	*The Four Aces*
"Sincerely"	*The McGuire Sisters*
"Ain't That a Shame"	*Pat Boone*
"Dance With Me, Henry"	*Georgia Gibbs*
"Melody of Love"	*Billy Vaughn*
"Sixteen Tons"	*Tennessee Ernie Ford*
"Learnin' the Blues"	*Frank Sinatra*
"Hearts of Stone"	*The Fontane Sisters*
"Tweedle Dee"	*Georgia Gibbs*
"Moments to Remember"	*The Four Lads*
"Mr. Sandman"	*The Chordettes*
"A Blossom Fell"	*Nat "King" Cole*
"Ballad of Davy Crockett"	*Fess Parker*

1956

"Heartbreak Hotel"	*Elvis Presley*
"Don't Be Cruel"	*Elvis Presley*
"Lisbon Antigua"	*Nelson Riddle*
"My Prayer"	*The Platters*
"The Wayward Wind"	*Gogi Grant*
"Hound Dog"	*Elvis Presley*
"The Poor People of Paris"	*Les Baxter*
"Whatever Will Be, Will Be"	*Doris Day*
"Memories Are Made of This"	*Dean Martin*
"Rock and Roll Waltz"	*Kay Starr*
"Moonglow (Theme from *Picnic*)"	*Morris Stoloff*
"The Great Pretender"	*The Platters*
"I Almost Lost My Mind"	*Pat Boone*
"I Want You, I Need You, I Love You"	*Elvis Presley*
"Love Me Tender"	*Elvis Presley*
"Hot Diggity"	*Perry Como*
"Canadian Sunset"	*Hugo Winterhalter and Eddie Heywood*
"Blue Suede Shoes"	*Carl Perkins*
"The Green Door"	*Jim Lowe*
"Sixteen Tons"	*Tennessee Ernie Ford*

1957

"All Shook Up"	*Elvis Presley*
"Love Letters in the Sand"	*Pat Boone*
"Little Darlin'"	*The Diamonds*
"Young Love"	*Tab Hunter*
"So Rare"	*Jimmy Dorsey*
"Singing the Blues"	*Guy Mitchell*
"Too Much"	*Elvis Presley*
"Round and Round"	*Perry Como*
"Bye Bye Love"	*The Everly Brothers*
"Tammy"	*Debbie Reynolds*
"Party Doll"	*Buddy Knox*
"Banana Boat (Day-O)"	*Harry Belafonte*
"Jailhouse Rock"	*Elvis Presley*
"A White Sport Coat (and a Pink Carnation)"	*Marty Robbins*
"Come Go with Me"	*The Del-Vikings*
"Wake Up, Little Susie"	*The Everly Brothers*
"You Send Me"	*Sam Cooke*
"Searchin'"	*The Coasters*
"School Day"	*Chuck Berry*

"Diana"	*Paul Anka*
"That'll Be the Day"	*The Crickets*
"Chances Are"	*Johnny Mathis*

1958

"Volare"	*Domenico Modugno*
"All I Have to Do Is Dream"	*The Everly Brothers*
"Don't"	*Elvis Presley*
"Witch Doctor"	*David Seville*
"Patricia"	*Perez Prado*
"Catch a Falling Star"	*Perry Como*
"Tequila"	*The Champs*
"It's All in the Game"	*Tommy Edwards*
"Return to Me"	*Dean Martin*
"The Purple People Eater"	*Sheb Wooley*
"Get a Job"	*The Silhouettes*
"Little Star"	*The Elegants*
"Twilight Time"	*The Platters*
"He's Got the Whole World (in His Hands)"	*Laurie London*
"At the Hop"	*Danny and the Juniors*
"Yakety Yak"	*The Coasters*
"Sugartime"	*The McGuire Sisters*
"Tom Dooley"	*The Kingston Trio*
"Sweet Little Sixteen"	*Chuck Berry*
"Topsy II"	*Cozy Cole*
"Book of Love"	*The Monotones*
"Tears on My Pillow"	*Little Anthony and the Imperials*
"Short Shorts"	*The Royal Teens*
"Great Balls of Fire"	*Jerry Lee Lewis*
"Splish Splash"	*Bobby Darin*

1959

"The Battle of New Orleans"	*Johnny Horton*
"Mack the Knife"	*Bobby Darin*
"Personality"	*Lloyd Price*
"Venus"	*Frankie Avalon*
"Lonely Boy"	*Paul Anka*
"Dream Lover"	*Bobby Darin*
"The Three Bells"	*The Browns*
"Come Softly to Me"	*The Fleetwoods*
"Kansas City"	*Wilbert Harrison*
"Mr. Blue"	*The Fleetwoods*
"Sleep Walk"	*Santo and Johnny*
"Put Your Head on My Shoulder"	*Paul Anka*

1959 cont'd

"Stagger Lee"	*Lloyd Price*
"Donna"	*Ritchie Valens*
"Pink Shoe Laces"	*Dodie Stevens*
"Charlie Brown"	*The Coasters*
"The Happy Organ"	*Dave "Baby" Cortez*
"I'm Gonna Get Married"	*Lloyd Price*
"Sorry (I Ran All the Way Home)"	*The Impalas*
"Teenager in Love"	*Dion and the Belmonts*
"16 Candles"	*The Crests*
"There Goes My Baby"	*The Drifters*
"Red River Rock"	*Johnny and the Hurricanes*
"Waterloo"	*Stonewall Jackson*
"Kookie, Kookie (Lend Me Your Comb)"	*Edward Byrnes and Connie Stevens*

1960

"The Theme from *A Summer Place*"	*Percy Faith*
"The Twist"	*Chubby Checker*
"I'm Sorry"	*Brenda Lee*
"Alley-Oop"	*Dante and the Evergreens*
"Cathy's Clown"	*The Everly Brothers*
"Everybody's Somebody's Fool"	*Connie Francis*
"Itsy Bitsy Teenie Weenie Yellow Polkadot Bikini"	*Brian Hyland*
"Good Timin'"	*Jimmy Jones*
"Save the Last Dance for Me"	*The Drifters*
"Running Bear"	*Johnny Preston*
"Only the Lonely"	*Roy Orbison*
"Greenfields"	*The Brothers Four*
"Wild One"	*Bobby Rydell*
"He'll Have to Go"	*Jim Reeves*
"Are You Lonesome Tonight?"	*Elvis Presley*
"Sink the Bismarck"	*Johnny Horton*
"Walk—Don't Run"	*The Ventures*
"Stuck on You"	*Elvis Presley*
"Teen Angel"	*Mark Dinning*
"Handy Man"	*Jimmy Jones*
"A Thousand Stars"	*Kathy Young and The Innocents*
"Finger Poppin' Time"	*Hank Ballard and The Midnighters*
"I Want to Be Wanted"	*Brenda Lee*
"Chain Gang"	*Sam Cooke*
"Sweet Nothin's"	*Brenda Lee*
"Mr. Custer"	*Larry Verne*

"My Heart Has a Mind of Its Own"	*Connie Francis*
"Poetry in Motion"	*Johnny Tillotson*
"Puppy Love"	*Paul Anka*

1961

"Runaround Sue"	*Dion*
"Quarter to Three"	*Gary "U.S." Bonds*
"Please Mr. Postman"	*The Marvelettes*
"Runaway"	*Del Shannon*
"Blue Moon"	*The Marcels*
"Bristol Stomp"	*The Dovells*
"Travelin' Man"/"Hello, Mary Lou"	*Ricky Nelson*
"Mother-in-Law"	*Ernie K-Doe*
"There's a Moon Out Tonight"	*The Capris*
"Tossin and Turnin'"	*Bobby Lewis*
"Pony Time"	*Chubby Checker*
"Take Good Care of My Baby"	*Bobby Vee*
"Will You Love Me Tomorrow"	*The Shirelles*
"Big Bad John"	*Jimmy Dean*
"Michael"	*The Highwaymen*
"Daddy's Home"	*Shep and the Limelites*
"A Hundred Pounds of Clay"	*Gene McDaniels*
"Barbara-Ann"	*The Regents*
"My True Story"	*The Jive Five*
"Pretty Little Angel Eyes"	*Curtis Lee*
"Shop Around"	*The Miracles*
"The Lion Sleeps Tonight"	*The Tokens*
"Calcutta"	*Lawrence Welk*
"Heart and Soul"	*The Cleftones*
"Spanish Harlem"	*Ben E. King*
"Hats Off to Larry"	*Del Shannon*
"Exodus"	*Ferrante and Teicher*
"Angel Baby"	*Rosie and the Originals*
"Crying"	*Roy Orbison*
"Dedicated to the One I Love"	*The Shirelles*

1962

"Mashed Potato Time"	*Dee Dee Sharp*
"Duke of Earl"	*Gene Chandler*
"I Can't Stop Loving You"	*Ray Charles*
"Big Girls Don't Cry"	*The Four Seasons*
"Sherry"	*The Four Seasons*
"The Loco-Motion"	*Little Eva*

1962 cont'd

"Roses Are Red"	*Bobby Vinton*
"Twist and Shout"	*The Isley Brothers*
"Hey! Baby"	*Bruce Channel*
"Do You Love Me"	*The Contours*
"Soldier Boy"	*The Shirelles*
"The Twist"	*Chubby Checker*
"The Stripper"	*David Rose*
"Wah Watusi"	*The Orlons*
"He's a Rebel"	*The Crystals*
"Monster Mash"	*Bobby (Boris) Pickett*
"Johnny Angel"	*Shelly Fabares*
"Midnight in Moscow"	*Kenny Ball*
"Playboy"	*The Marvelettes*
"Green Onions"	*Booker T. and the MGs*
"Bobby's Girl"	*Marcie Blane*
"Stranger on the Shore"	*Mr. Acker Bilk*
"Palisades Park"	*Freddy Cannon*
"All Alone Am I"	*Brenda Lee*
"She Cried"	*Jay and the Americans*
"Don't Hang Up"	*The Orlons*
"Breaking Up Is Hard to Do"	*Neil Sedaka*
"Peppermint Twist"	*Joey Dee and the Starlighters*
"Sheila"	*Tommy Roe*
"Ramblin' Rose"	*Nat "King" Cole*
"Slow Twistin'"	*Chubby Checker and Dee Dee Sharp*
"The Wanderer"	*Dion*
"Sealed with a Kiss"	*Brian Hyland*
"Return to Sender"	*Elvis Presley*
"Surfin' Safari"	*The Beach Boys*

1963

"Be My Baby"	*The Ronettes*
"I Will Follow Him"	*Peggy March*
"He's So Fine"	*The Chiffons*
"Easier Said Than Done"	*The Essex*
"Our Day Will Come"	*Ruby and the Romantics*
"My Boyfriend's Back"	*The Angels*
"So Much in Love"	*The Tymes*
"Hey Paula"	*Paul and Paula*
"Fingertips—Part 2"	*Little Stevie Wonder*
"Sugar Shack"	*Jimmy Gilmore and the Fireballs*
"If You Wanna Be Happy"	*Jimmy Soul*
"Dominique"	*The Singing Nun*
"Blue Velvet"	*Bobby Vinton*
"Go Away Little Girl"	*Steve Lawrence*

"I'm Leaving It Up to You"	*Dale and Grace*
"Washington Square"	*The Village Stompers*
"Walk Like a Man"	*The Four Seasons*
"It's My Party"	*Lesley Gore*
"Walk Right In"	*The Rooftop Singers*
"Deep Purple"	*Nino Tempo and April Stevens*
"Candy Girl"	*The Four Seasons*
"You Can't Sit Down"	*The Dovells*
"It's All Right"	*The Impressions*
"Surf City"	*Jan and Dean*
"Donna the Prima Donna"	*Dion*
"Denise"	*Randy and the Rainbows*
"She's a Fool"	*Lesley Gore*
"Heat Wave"	*Martha and the Vandellas*
"Louie Louie"	*The Kingsmen*
"Da Doo Ron Ron"	*The Crystals*
"Rhythm of the Rain"	*The Cascades*
"Tell Him"	*The Exciters*
"Blowin' in the Wind"	*Peter, Paul and Mary*
"Surfin' U.S.A."	*The Beach Boys*
"Up on the Roof"	*The Drifters*
"Sukiyaki"	*Kyu Sakamoto*
"Then He Kissed Me"	*The Crystals*
"El Watusi"	*Ray Barretto*
"Puff the Magic Dragon"	*Peter, Paul and Mary*
"Wipe Out"	*The Surfaris*

1964

"Hello, Dolly!"	*Louis Armstrong*
"I Want to Hold Your Hand"	*The Beatles*
"She Loves You"	*The Beatles*
"Where Did Our Love Go"	*The Supremes*
"Chapel of Love"	*The Dixie Cups*
"Oh, Pretty Woman"	*Roy Orbison*
"Rag Doll"	*The Four Seasons*
"A Hard Day's Night"	*The Beatles*
"Everybody Loves Somebody"	*Dean Martin*
"Do Wah Diddy Diddy"	*Manfred Mann*
"I Get Around"	*The Beach Boys*
"A World Without Love"	*Peter and Gordon*
"Do You Want to Know a Secret"	*The Beatles*
"The House of the Rising Sun"	*The Animals*
"Dawn"	*The Four Seasons*
"She's Not There"	*The Zombies*
"Baby Love"	*The Supremes*
"Under the Boardwalk"	*The Drifters*
"Dancing in the Street"	*Martha and the Vandellas*

1964 cont'd

"Twist and Shout"	*The Beatles*
"My Guy"	*Mary Wells*
"Leader of the Pack"	*The Shangri-Las*
"Can't Buy Me Love"	*The Beatles*
"Remember (Walkin' in the Sand)"	*The Shangri-Las*
"Java"	*Al Hirt*
"Love Me Do"	*The Beatles*
"Please Please Me"	*The Beatles*
"Last Kiss"	*J. Frank Wilson and the Cavaliers*
"You Don't Own Me"	*Lesley Gore*
"Time Is on My Side"	*The Rolling Stones*
"My Boy Lollipop"	*Little Millie Small*
"Love Me with All of Your Heart"	*The Ray Charles Singers*
"Forget Him"	*Bobby Rydell*
"There! I've Said It Again"	*Bobby Vinton*
"Shoop Shoop Song (It's in His Kiss)"	*Betty Everett*
"A Summer Song"	*Chad and Jeremy*
"Ronnie"	*The Four Seasons*
"Because"	*The Dave Clark Five*
"Louie Louie"	*The Kingsmen*
"People"	*Barbra Streisand*

1965

"(I Can't Get No) Satisfaction"	*The Rolling Stones*
"Help!"	*The Beatles*
"I Can't Help Myself"	*The Four Tops*
"Downtown"	*Petula Clark*
"1-2-3"	*Len Barry*
"Lover's Concerto"	*The Toys*
"Let's Hang On"	*The Four Seasons*
"I Got You Babe"	*Sonny and Cher*
"Come See About Me"	*The Supremes*
"Stop! in the Name of Love"	*The Supremes*
"You've Lost That Lovin' Feeling"	*The Righteous Brothers*
"Wooly Bully"	*Sam the Sham and The Pharaohs*
"Love Potion No. 9"	*The Searchers*
"I Hear a Symphony"	*The Supremes*
"Help Me, Rhonda"	*The Beach Boys*
"I Feel Fine"	*The Beatles*
"Mrs. Brown You've Got a Lovely Daughter"	*Herman's Hermits*
"This Diamond Ring"	*Gary Lewis and the Playboys*

"The Name Game"	*Shirley Ellis*
"Hang On Sloopy"	*The McCoys*
"Mr. Tambourine Man"	*The Byrds*
"Yesterday"	*The Beatles*
"Get Off of My Cloud"	*The Rolling Stones*
"Eight Days a Week"	*The Beatles*
"Ticket to Ride"	*The Beatles*
"I'm Henry VIII, I Am"	*Herman's Hermits*
"Eve of Destruction"	*Barry McGuire*
"I'm Telling You Now"	*Freddie and the Dreamers*
"Mr. Lonely"	*Bobby Vinton*
"Cara, Mia"	*Jay and the Americans*
"Taste of Honey"	*Herb Alpert and the Tijuana Brass*
"Go Now!"	*The Moody Blues*
"Unchained Melody"	*The Righteous Brothers*
"Like a Rolling Stone"	*Bob Dylan*
"Game of Love"	*Wayne Fontana and the Mindbenders*
"Goldfinger"	*Shirley Bassey*
"The 'In' Crowd"	*The Ramsey Lewis Trio*
"What's New Pussycat"	*Tom Jones*
"Back in My Arms Again"	*The Supremes*
"My Girl"	*The Temptations*
"King of the Road"	*Roger Miller*

1966

"The Ballad of the Green Berets"	*S/Sgt. Barry Sadler*
"You Can't Hurry Love"	*The Supremes*
"Strangers in the Night"	*Frank Sinatra*
"Good Lovin'"	*The Young Rascals*
"Reach Out, I'll Be There"	*The Four Tops*
"Last Train to Clarksville"	*The Monkees*
"Cherish"	*The Association*
"We Can Work It Out"	*The Beatles*
"Turn! Turn! Turn!"	*The Byrds*
"Monday, Monday"	*The Mamas and the Papas*
"(You're My) Soul and Inspiration"	*The Righteous Brothers*
"The Sounds of Silence"	*Simon and Garfunkel*
"California Dreamin'"	*The Mamas and the Papas*
"Summer in the City"	*The Lovin' Spoonful*
"Taste of Honey"	*Herb Alpert and the Tijuana Brass*
"Born Free"	*Roger Williams*
"Lightnin' Strikes"	*Lou Christie*
"Paint It, Black"	*The Rolling Stones*
"Red Rubber Ball"	*The Cyrkle*
"96 Tears"	*? and and the Mysterians*

1966 cont'd

"You Keep Me Hangin' On"	*The Supremes*
"19th Nervous Breakdown"	*The Rolling Stones*
"These Boots Are Made for Walkin'"	*Nancy Sinatra*
"Winchester Cathedral"	*The New Vaudeville Band*
"Wild Thing"	*The Troggs*
"A Groovy Kind of Love"	*The Mindbenders*
"Lil' Red Riding Hood"	*Sam the Sham and the Pharaohs*
"Walk Away Renee"	*The Left Banke*
"Sloop John B"	*The Beach Boys*
"Nowhere Man"	*The Beatles*
"Well Respected Man"	*The Kinks*
"Sunny"	*Bobby Hebb*
"Let's Hang On"	*The Four Seasons*
"Good Vibrations"	*The Beach Boys*
"Sunshine Superman"	*Donovan*
"Paperback Writer"	*The Beatles*
"I Hear a Symphony"	*The Supremes*
"Yellow Submarine"	*The Beatles*
"Uptight (Everything's Alright)"	*Stevie Wonder*
"Rainy Day Women #12 & 35"	*Bob Dylan*

1967

"To Sir with Love"	*Lulu*
"Light My Fire"	*The Doors*
"Can't Take My Eyes Off of You"	*Frankie Valli*
"Happy Together"	*The Turtles*
"Groovin'"	*The Young Rascals*
"The Letter"	*The Box Tops*
"Windy"	*The Association*
"Georgy Girl"	*The Seekers*
"Little Bit o' Soul"	*The Music Explosion*
"Respect"	*Aretha Franklin*
"Ode to Billie Joe"	*Bobbie Gentry*
"I'm a Believer"	*The Monkees*
"Somethin' Stupid"	*Nancy and Frank Sinatra*
"Apples, Peaches, Pumpkin Pie"	*Jay and the Techniques*
"Expressway to Your Heart"	*The Soul Survivors*
"All You Need Is Love"	*The Beatles*
"How Can I Be Sure"	*The Young Rascals*
"I Think We're Alone Now"	*Tommy James and the Shondells*
"The Happening"	*Diana Ross and the Supremes*
"Penny Lane"	*The Beatles*
"I've Been Lonely Too Long"	*The Young Rascals*
"Ruby Tuesday"	*The Rolling Stones*

"Kind of a Drag"	*The Buckinghams*
"Jimmy Mack"	*Martha and the Vandellas*
"Reflections"	*Diana Ross and the Supremes*
"Love Is Here and Now You're Gone"	*Diana Ross and the Supremes*
"I Got Rhythm"	*The Happenings*
"Little Bit Me, A Little Bit You"	*The Monkees*
"Never My Love"	*The Association*
"This Is My Song"	*Petula Clark*
"I Was Made to Love Her"	*Stevie Wonder*
"Snoopy vs. the Red Baron"	*The Royal Guardsmen*
"Gimme Some Lovin'"	*The Spencer Davis Group*
"Pleasant Valley Sunday"	*The Monkees*
"A Whiter Shade of Pale"	*Procol Harum*
"She'd Rather Be With Me"	*The Turtles*
"Soul Man"	*Sam and Dave*
"Dedicated to the One I Love"	*The Mamas and the Papas*
"It Must Be Him"	*Vikki Carr*
"There's A Kind of Hush (All Over the World)"	*Herman's Hermits*

1968

"Hey Jude"	*The Beatles*
"Young Girl"	*Gary Puckett and the Union Gap*
"People Got to Be Free"	*The Rascals*
"Mrs. Robinson"	*Simon and Garfunkel*
"Love Is Blue"	*Paul Mauriat*
"Beautiful Morning"	*The Rascals*
"Those Were the Days"	*Mary Hopkin*
"MacArthur Park"	*Richard Harris*
"This Guy's in Love With You"	*Herb Alpert*
"Simon Says"	*The 1910 Fruitgum Co.*
"Honey"	*Bobby Goldsboro*
"Cry Like A Baby"	*The Box Tops*
"Born to Be Wild"	*Steppenwolf*
"Love Child"	*Diana Ross and the Supremes*
"Tighten Up"	*Archie Bell and the Drells*
"Stoned Soul Picnic"	*The Fifth Dimension*
"Green Tambourine"	*The Lemon Pipers*
"Judy in Disguise (with Glasses)"	*John Fred and his Playboy Band*
"Lady Willpower"	*Gary Puckett and the Union Gap*
"Harper Valley P.T.A."	*Jeannie C. Riley*
"Lady Madonna"	*The Beatles*
"Hello I Love You"	*The Doors*
"Turn Around, Look At Me"	*The Vogues*
"Woman, Woman"	*The Union Gap*
"Jumpin' Jack Flash"	*The Rolling Stones*

1968 cont'd

"Little Green Apples"	*O. C. Smith*
"Midnight Confessions"	*The Grass Roots*
"Mony Mony"	*Tommy James and the Shondells*
"Bend Me, Shape Me"	*The American Breed*
"Reach Out of the Darkness"	*Friend and Lover*
"(Sittin' on) the Dock of the Bay"	*Otis Redding*
"Spooky"	*The Classics IV*
"Sunshine of Your Love"	*Cream*
"Yummy Yummy Yummy"	*The Ohio Express*
"Angel of the Morning"	*Merrilee Rush*
"Theme from Valley of the Dolls"	*Dionne Warwick*
"Magic Carpet Ride"	*Steppenwolf*
"I've Gotta Get a Message to You"	*The Bee Gees*
"I Heard It Through the Grapevine"	*Gladys Knight and the Pips*
"Dance to the Music"	*Sly and the Family Stone*

1969

"Aquarius/Let the Sunshine In"	*The Fifth Dimension*
"Sugar, Sugar"	*The Archies*
"Honky Tonk Women"	*The Rolling Stones*
"Get Back"	*The Beatles*
"Crimson and Clover"	*Tommy James and the Shondells*
"Dizzy"	*Tommy Roe*
"Jean"	*Oliver*
"Build Me Up, Buttercup"	*The Foundations*
"Touch Me"	*The Doors*
"Hair"	*The Cowsills*
"Sweet Caroline"	*Neil Diamond*
"Crystal Blue Persuasion"	*Tommy James and the Shondells*
"Everyday People"	*Sly and the Family Stone*
"Good Morning Starshine"	*Oliver*
"In the Year 2525"	*Zager and Evans*
"I Can't Get Next to You"	*The Temptations*
"Love Theme from Romeo and Juliet"	*Henry Mancini*
"Proud Mary"	*Creedence Clearwater Revival*
"Spinning Wheel"	*Blood, Sweat and Tears*
"One"	*Three Dog Night*
"Love (Can Make You Happy)"	*Mercy*
"Traces"	*The Classics IV*
"You've Made Me So Very Happy"	*Blood, Sweat and Tears*
"This Magic Moment"	*Jay and the Americans*
"Worst That Could Happen"	*The Brooklyn Bridge*

"I Heard It Through the Grapevine"	*Marvin Gaye*
"It's Your Thing"	*The Isley Brothers*
"A Boy Named Sue"	*Johnny Cash*
"Wedding Bell Blues"	*The Fifth Dimension*
"Get Together"	*The Youngbloods*
"Easy to Be Hard"	*Three Dog Night*
"Little Woman"	*Bobby Sherman*
"I'm Gonna Make You Love Me"	*Diana Ross and the Supremes*
"These Eyes"	*The Guess Who*
"Baby, It's You"	*Smith*
"I'll Never Fall in Love Again"	*Tom Jones*
"My Cheri Amour"	*Stevie Wonder*
"Hooked on a Feeling"	*B. J. Thomas*
"Smile a Little Smile For Me"	*The Flying Machine*
"Baby, I Love You"	*Andy Kim*

1970

"Raindrops Keep Fallin' on My Head"	*B. J. Thomas*
"Let It Be"	*The Beatles*
"Band of Gold"	*Freda Payne*
"I'll Be There"	*The Jackson 5*
"(They Long to Be) Close to You"	*The Carpenters*
"The Love You Save"	*The Jackson 5*
"Bridge Over Troubled Water"	*Simon and Garfunkel*
"Ball of Confusion"	*The Temptations*
"Signed, Sealed, Delivered, I'm Yours"	*Stevie Wonder*
"War"	*Edwin Starr*
"Make It With You"	*Bread*
"Ain't No Mountain High Enough"	*Diana Ross*
"I Want You Back"	*The Jackson 5*
"ABC"	*The Jackson 5*
"Spirit in the Sky"	*Norman Greenbaum*
"We've Only Just Begun"	*The Carpenters*
"Venus"	*Shocking Blue*
"Cracklin' Rosie"	*Neil Diamond*
"Which Way You Goin' Billy?"	*The Poppy Family*
"Candida"	*Tony Orlando and Dawn*
"Thank You (Falettinme Be Mice Elf Agin)"	*Sly and the Family Stone*
"Hey There Lonely Girl"	*Eddie Holman*
"Patches"	*Clarence Carter*
"Leaving on a Jet Plane"	*Peter, Paul and Mary*
"American Woman"	*The Guess Who*

1970 cont'd

"Instant Karma!"	*John Lennon*
"Cecelia"	*Simon and Garfunkel*
"Indiana Wants Me"	*R. Dean Taylor*
"The Rapper"	*The Jaggerz*
"Mama Told Me (Not to Come)"	*Three Dog Night*
"Someday We'll Be Together"	*Diana Ross and the Supremes*
"Turn Back the Hands of Time"	*Tyrone Davis*
"In the Summertime"	*Mungo Jerry*
"Reflections of My Life"	*Marmalade*
"Hitchin' a Ride"	*Vanity Fare*
"Love Grows (Where My Rosemary Goes)"	*Edison Lighthouse*
"O-o-h Child"	*The Five Stairsteps*
"The Long and Winding Road"	*The Beatles*
"Whole Lotta Love"	*Led Zeppelin*

1971

"Joy to the World"	*Three Dog Night*
"One Bad Apple"	*The Osmonds*
"Maggie May"	*Rod Stewart*
"It's Too Late"	*Carole King*
"Knock Three Times"	*Dawn*
"Indian Reservation"	*The Raiders*
"Theme from *Shaft*"	*Isaac Hayes*
"Want Ads"	*Honey Cone*
"What's Going On"	*Marvin Gaye*
"Just My Imagination"	*The Temptations*
"Never Can Say Goodbye"	*The Jackson 5*
"Rose Garden"	*Lynn Anderson*
"Jesus Christ Superstar"	*Murray Head*
"Gypsys, Tramps and Thieves"	*Cher*
"Mr. Big Stuff"	*Jean Knight*
"Superstar"	*The Carpenters*
"Go Away Little Girl"	*Donny Osmond*
"Uncle Albert/Admiral Halsey"	*Paul McCartney*
"Treat Her Like a Lady"	*Cornelius Brothers and Sister Rose*
"Spanish Harlem"	*Aretha Franklin*
"Have You Seen Her"	*The Chi-Lites*
"One Less Bell to Answer"	*The Fifth Dimension*
"How Can You Mend a Broken Heart"	*The Bee Gees*
"Put Your Hand in the Hand"	*Ocean*
"I Feel the Earth Move"	*Carole King*
"Don't Pull Your Love"	*Hamilton, Joe Frank and Reynolds*
"My Sweet Lord"	*George Harrison*

"Doesn't Somebody Want to Be Wanted"	*The Partridge Family*
"Rainy Days and Mondays"	*The Carpenters*
"Family Affair"	*Sly and the Family Stone*
"Proud Mary"	*Ike and Tina Turner*
"Stick-Up"	*Honey Cone*
"Lonely Days"	*The Bee Gees*
"For All We Know"	*The Carpenters*
"Brown Sugar"	*The Rolling Stones*
"Imagine"	*John Lennon*
"The Night They Drove Old Dixie Down"	*Joan Baez*
"Take Me Home, Country Roads"	*John Denver*
"Me and Bobby McGee"	*Janis Joplin*
"Mr. Bojangles"	*The Nitty Gritty Dirt Band*

1972

"Alone Again (Naturally)"	*Gilbert O'Sullivan*
"American Pie"	*Don McLean*
"Candy Man"	*Sammy Davis, Jr.*
"Lean on Me"	*Bill Withers*
"Without You"	*Nilsson*
"Let's Stay Together"	*Al Green*
"First Time Ever I Saw Your Face"	*Roberta Flack*
"Horse With No Name"	*America*
"Brandy"	*Looking Glass*
"I'll Take You There"	*The Staple Singers*
"Rockin' Robin"	*Michael Jackson*
"Nights in White Satin"	*The Moody Blues*
"I Can See Clearly Now"	*Johnny Nash*
"Nice to Be With You"	*Gallery*
"Oh Girl"	*The Chi-Lites*
"Black and White"	*Three Dog Night*
"Daddy Don't You Walk So Fast"	*Wayne Newton*
"Outa-Space"	*Billy Preston*
"The Lion Sleeps Tonight"	*Robert John*
"(If Loving You Is Wrong) I Don't Want to Be Right"	*Luther Ingram*
"Baby Don't Get Hooked on Me"	*Mac Davis*
"Precious and Few"	*Climax*
"Ben"	*Michael Jackson*
"Everybody Plays the Fool"	*The Main Ingredient*
"I'll Be Around"	*The Spinners*
"Brand New Key"	*Melanie*
"Back Stabbers"	*The O'Jays*

1972 cont'd

"Too Late to Turn Back Now"	*Cornelius Brothers and Sister Rose*
"If You Don't Know Me By Now"	*Harold Melvin and the Blue Notes*
"Heart of Gold"	*Neil Young*
"Betcha By Golly, Wow"	*The Stylistics*
"I Gotcha"	*Joe Tex*
"Saturday in the Park"	*Chicago*
"Hurting Each Other"	*The Carpenters*
"Puppy Love"	*Donny Osmond*
"Papa Was a Rollin' Stone"	*The Temptations*
"I Am Woman"	*Helen Reddy*
"Day after Day"	*Badfinger*
"Clean Up Woman"	*Betty Wright*
"I'm Still in Love With You"	*Al Green*

1973

"Killing Me Softly with His Song"	*Roberta Flack*
"Tie a Yellow Ribbon 'Round the Ole Oak Tree"	*Tony Orlando and Dawn*
"Crocodile Rock"	*Elton John*
"My Love"	*Paul McCartney and Wings*
"Let's Get It On"	*Marvin Gaye*
"Brother Louie"	*Stories*
"You're So Vain"	*Carly Simon*
"Playground in My Mind"	*Clint Holmes*
"Touch Me in the Morning"	*Diana Ross*
"Angie"	*The Rolling Stones*
"The Night the Lights Went Out in Georgia"	*Vicki Lawrence*
"Half-Breed"	*Cher*
"Heartbeat—It's a Lovebeat"	*The DeFranco Family*
"Frankenstein"	*The Edgar Winter Group*
"Love Train"	*The O'Jays*
"Say, Has Anybody Seen My Sweet Gypsy Rose"	*Tony Orlando and Dawn*
"Neither One of Us"	*Gladys Knight and the Pips*
"Bad, Bad Leroy Brown"	*Jim Croce*
"Daniel"	*Elton John*
"Could It Be I'm Falling in Love"	*The Spinners*
"Photograph"	*Ringo Starr*
"Sing"	*The Carpenters*
"Midnight Train to Georgia"	*Gladys Knight and the Pips*
"Oh, Babe, What Would You Say"	*Hurricane Smith*
"Superstition"	*Stevie Wonder*
"Delta Dawn"	*Helen Reddy*

"Live and Let Die" — *Wings*
"Shambala" — *Three Dog Night*
"Dueling Banjos" — *Deliverance*
"The Morning After" — *Maureen McGovern*
"Last Song" — *Edward Bear*
"Top of the World" — *The Carpenters*
"Pillow Talk" — *Sylvia*
"Ain't No Woman" — *The Four Tops*
"Kodachrome" — *Paul Simon*
"Give Me Love (Give Me Peace on Earth)" — *George Harrison*
"You Are the Sunshine of My Life" — *Stevie Wonder*
"Stuck in the Middle With You" — *Stealers Wheel*
"Ramblin' Man" — *The Allman Brothers Band*
"Loves Me like a Rock" — *Paul Simon*

1974

"Rock the Boat" — *The Hues Corporation*
"Can't Get Enough of Your Love Babe" — *Barry White*
"Rock Your Baby" — *George McRae*
"Seasons in the Sun" — *Terry Jacks*
"You Make Me Feel Brand New" — *The Stylistics*
"Boogie Down" — *Eddie Kendricks*
"The Night Chicago Died" — *Paper Lace*
"Dancing Machine" — *The Jackson 5*
"The Streak" — *Ray Stevens*
"You're Sixteen" — *Ringo Starr*
"Annie's Song" — *John Denver*
"The Way We Were" — *Barbra Streisand*
"I Shot the Sheriff" — *Eric Clapton*
"I Honestly Love You" — *Olivia Newton-John*
"TSOP" — *MFSB*
"(You're) Having My Baby" — *Paul Anka and Odia Coates*
"Then Came You" — *Dionne Warwick and the Spinners*
"Billy Don't Be a Hero" — *Bo Donaldson and the Heywoods*
"Bennie and the Jets" — *Elton John*
"Hooked on a Feeling" — *Blue Swede*
"The Entertainer" — *Marvin Hamlisch*
"Do It ('Til Your Satisfied)" — *B.T. Express*
"Sunshine on My Shoulders" — *John Denver*
"Love's Theme" — *The Love Unlimited Orchestra*
"The Locomotion" — *Grand Funk Railroad*
"Band on the Run" — *Paul McCartney and Wings*
"Feel Like Makin' Love" — *Roberta Flack*

1974 cont'd

"Nothing from Nothing"	*Billy Preston*
"Smokin' in the Boys' Room"	*Brownsville Station*
"The Joker"	*The Steve Miller Band*
"Sundown"	*Gordon Lightfoot*
"Time in a Bottle"	*Jim Croce*
"My Melody of Love"	*Bobby Vinton*
"You Haven't Done Nothing"	*Stevie Wonder*
"You Ain't Seen Nothing Yet"	*Bachman Turner Overdrive*
"Don't Let the Sun Go Down on Me"	*Elton John*
"Rock Me Gently"	*Andy Kim*
"Mockingbird"	*Carly Simon and James Taylor*
"Whatever Gets You Thru the Night"	*John Lennon*
"The Air That I Breathe"	*The Hollies*

1975

"The Hustle"	*Van McCoy*
"Love Will Keep Us Together"	*The Captain and Tennille*
"Philadelphia Freedom"	*Elton John*
"Swearin' to God"	*Frankie Valli*
"Lady Marmalade"	*Labelle*
"Lovin' You"	*Minnie Riperton*
"My Eyes Adored You"	*Frankie Valli*
"Get Down Tonight"	*K.C. and the Sunshine Band*
"Fly, Robin, Fly"	*Silver Convention*
"Jive Talkin'"	*The Bee Gees*
"Have You Never Been Mellow"	*Olivia Newton-John*
"Bad Luck"	*Harold Melvin and the Blue Notes*
"Mandy"	*Barry Manilow*
"Rhinestone Cowboy"	*Glen Campbell*
"Love Won't Let Me Wait"	*Major Harris*
"Mr. Jaws"	*Dickie Goodman*
"Pick Up the Pieces"	*The Average White Band*
"Laughter in the Rain"	*Neil Sedaka*
"Fire"	*The Ohio Players*
"Feelings"	*Morris Albert*
"Someone Saved My Life Tonight"	*Elton John*
"Magic"	*Pilot*
"Listen to What the Man Said"	*Wings*
"Ease on Down the Road"	*Consumer Rapport*
"One of These Nights"	*The Eagles*
"Bad Blood"	*Neil Sedaka*
"Before the Next Teardrop Falls"	*Freddy Fender*

"Games People Play"	*The Spinners*
"Fame"	*David Bowie*
"Fallin' in Love"	*Hamilton, Joe Frank and Reynolds*
"Doctor's Orders"	*Carol Douglas*
"No No Song"	*Ringo Starr*
"It Only Takes a Minute"	*Tavares*
"Dance With Me"	*Orleans*
"Who Loves You"	*The Four Seasons*
"Walking in Rhythm"	*The Blackbyrds*
"Lucy in the Sky With Diamonds"	*Elton John*
"That's the Way (I Like It)"	*K.C. and the Sunshine Band*
"You're No Good"	*Linda Ronstadt*
"He Don't Love You (Like I Love You)"	*Tony Orlando and Dawn*

1976

"Kiss and Say Goodbye"	*The Manhattans*
"A Fifth of Beethoven"	*Walter Murphy and the Big Apple Band*
"You'll Never Find Another Love Like Mine"	*Lou Rawls*
"Love Hangover"	*Diana Ross*
"Silly Love Songs"	*Wings*
"Disco Duck"	*Rick Dees and His Cast of Idiots*
"Disco Lady"	*Johnnie Taylor*
"I Write the Songs"	*Barry Manilow*
"Don't Go Breaking My Heart"	*Elton John and Kiki Dee*
"December, 1963 (Oh, What a Night)"	*The Four Seasons*
"Shake Your Booty"	*K.C. and the Sunshine Band*
"Play That Funky Music"	*Wild Cherry*
"Welcome Back"	*John Sebastian*
"If You Leave Me Now"	*Chicago*
"Right Back Where We Started From"	*Maxine Nightingale*
"You Should Be Dancing"	*The Bee Gees*
"Get Up and Boogie"	*Silver Convention*
"Love Machine"	*The Miracles*
"Lowdown"	*Boz Scaggs*
"Misty Blue"	*Dorothy Moore*
"Theme from S.W.A.T."	*Rhythm Heritage*
"Turn the Beat Around"	*Vickie Sue Robinson*
"Fifty Ways to Leave Your Lover"	*Paul Simon*
"Afternoon Delight"	*The Starland Vocal Band*
"Love Rollercoaster"	*The Ohio Players*
"All By Myself"	*Eric Carmen*
"Bohemian Rhapsody"	*Queen*

1976 cont'd

"Convoy"	*C. W. McCall*
"Heaven Must Be Missing an Angel"	*Tavares*
"Boogie Fever"	*The Sylvers*
"I Love Music"	*The O'Jays*
"Lonely Night (Angel Face)"	*The Captain and Tennille*
"More, More, More"	*The Andrea True Connection*
"Dream Weaver"	*Gary Wright*
"Sweet Thing"	*Rufus*
"Let 'Em In"	*Wings*
"I'd Really Love to See You Tonight"	*England Dan and John Ford Coley*
"The Rubberband Man"	*The Spinners*
"Walk Away From Love"	*David Ruffin*

1977

"I Just Want to Be Your Everything"	*Andy Gibb*
"You Light Up My Life"	*Debby Boone*
"*Star Wars* Theme"	*Meco*
"Best of My Love"	*The Emotions*
"When I Need You"	*Leo Sayer*
"Torn Between Two Lovers"	*Mary MacGregor*
"Evergreen (Theme from *A Star Is Born*)"	*Barbra Streisand*
"Boogie Nights"	*Heatwave*
"Car Wash"	*Rose Royce*
"(Your Love Has Lifted Me) Higher and Higher"	*Rita Coolidge*
"Nobody Does It Better"	*Carly Simon*
"Rich Girl"	*Hall and Oates*
"Undercover Angel"	*Alan O'Day*
"Gonna Fly Now (Theme from *Rocky*)"	*Bill Conti*
"Got to Give It Up"	*Marvin Gaye*
"Dreams"	*Fleetwood Mac*
"Dancing Queen"	*Abba*
"I'm in You"	*Peter Frampton*
"You Make Me Feel like Dancing"	*Leo Sayer*
"Float On"	*The Floaters*
"I Like Dreamin'"	*Kenny Nolan*
"Hotel California"	*The Eagles*
"Whodunit"	*Tavares*
"Southern Nights"	*Glen Campbell*

"Keep It Comin' Love"	*K.C. and the Sunshine Band*
"Sir Duke"	*Stevie Wonder*
"The Things We Do for Love"	*10cc*
"New Kid in Town"	*The Eagles*
"I Wish"	*Stevie Wonder*
"Blinded by the Light"	*Manfred Mann's Earth Band*
"Don't Give Up on Us"	*David Soul*
"You Don't Have to Be a Star (to Be in My Show)"	*Marilyn McCoo and Billy Davis, Jr.*
"Enjoy Yourself"	*The Jacksons*
"I'm Your Boogie Man"	*K.C. and the Sunshine Band*
"I've Got Love on My Mind"	*Natalie Cole*
"Hot Line"	*The Sylvers*
"Don't Leave Me This Way"	*Thelma Houston*
"Da Doo Ron Ron"	*Shaun Cassidy*
"Don't It Make My Brown Eyes Blue"	*Crystal Gale*
"Angel in Your Arms"	*Hot*

1978

"Boogie Oogie Oogie"	*A Taste of Honey*
"Stayin' Alive"	*The Bee Gees*
"Night Fever"	*The Bee Gees*
"Shadow Dancing"	*Andy Gibb*
"MacArthur Park"	*Donna Summer*
"Three Times a Lady"	*The Commodores*
"You Needed Me"	*Anne Murray*
"Last Dance"	*Donna Summer*
"Just the Way You Are"	*Billy Joel*
"Grease"	*Frankie Valli*
"You're the One That I Want"	*John Travolta and Olivia Newton-John*
"Can't Smile Without You"	*Barry Manilow*
"Miss You"	*The Rolling Stones*
"Baby Come Back"	*Player*
"Emotion"	*Samantha Sang*
"Too Much, Too Little, Too Late"	*Johnny Mathis and Deniece Williams*
"How Deep Is Your Love"	*The Bee Gees*
"Hot Child in the City"	*Nick Gilder*
"Baker Street"	*Gerry Rafferty*
"The Closer I Get to You"	*Roberta Flack and Donny Hathaway*
"(Love Is) Thicker Than Water"	*Andy Gibb*
"Sometimes When We Touch"	*Dan Hill*
"Reminiscing"	*Little River Band*
"With a Little Luck"	*Wings*
"Dance With Me"	*Peter Brown*
"We Are the Champions"	*Queen*
"If I Can't Have You"	*Yvonne Elliman*

1978 cont'd

"Feels So Good"	*Chuck Mangione*
"Summer Nights"	*John Travolta and Olivia Newton-John*
"Copacabana (At the Copa)"	*Barry Manilow*
"Use ta Be My Girl"	*The O'Jays*
"Dance, Dance, Dance (Yowsah, Yowsah, Yowsah)"	*Chic*
"Hopelessly Devoted to You"	*Olivia Newton-John*
"Le Freak"	*Chic*
"It's a Heartache"	*Bonnie Tyler*
"Lay Down Sally"	*Eric Clapton*
"You Don't Bring Me Flowers"	*Barbra Streisand and Neil Diamond*
"Hot Blooded"	*Foreigner*
"Dust in the Wind"	*Kansas*

1979

"I Will Survive"	*Gloria Gaynor*
"Bad Girls"	*Donna Summer*
"Ring My Bell"	*Anita Ward*
"Hot Stuff"	*Donna Summer*
"Reunited"	*Peaches and Herb*
"My Sharona"	*The Knack*
"Rise"	*Herb Alpert*
"Y.M.C.A."	*The Village People*
"Da Ya Think I'm Sexy?"	*Rod Stewart*
"Good Times"	*Chic*
"Le Freak"	*Chic*
"Sad Eyes"	*Robert John*
"Knock on Wood"	*Amii Stewart*
"No More Tears/Enough Is Enough"	*Barbra Streisand and Donna Summer*
"Pop Muzik"	*M*
"Ain't No Stoppin' Us Now"	*McFadden and Whitehead*
"I'll Never Love This Way Again"	*Dionne Warwick*
"Still"	*The Commodores*
"Tragedy"	*The Bee Gees*
"Too Much Heaven"	*The Bee Gees*
"Don't Stop 'til You Get Enough"	*Michael Jackson*
"Heart of Glass"	*Blondie*
"Babe"	*Styx*
"Dim All the Lights"	*Donna Summer*
"Heaven Knows"	*Donna Summer*
"She Believes in Me"	*Kenny Rogers*
"In the Navy"	*The Village People*
"The Main Event"	*Barbra Streisand*
"The Logical Song"	*Supertramp*

"The Devil Went Down to Georgia"	*The Charlie Daniels Band*
"Ladies Night"	*Kool and the Gang*
"What A Fool Believes"	*The Doobie Brothers*
"We Are Family"	*Sister Sledge*
"When You're in Love With a Beautiful Woman"	*Dr. Hook*
"Rock With You"	*Michael Jackson*
"My Life"	*Billy Joel*
"Shake Your Body (Down to the Ground)"	*The Jacksons*
"Shake Your Groove Thing"	*Peaches and Herb*

1980

"Another One Bites the Dust"	*Queen*
"Call Me"	*Blondie*
"Funky Town"	*Lipps, Inc.*
"Another Brick in the Wall (Part II)"	*Pink Floyd*
"Upside Down"	*Diana Ross*
"Working My Way Back to You"	*The Spinners*
"It's Still Rock and Roll to Me"	*Billy Joel*
"Woman in Love"	*Barbra Streisand*
"Rock With You"	*Michael Jackson*
"Do That to Me One More Time"	*Captain and Tennille*
"Fame"	*Irene Cara*
"Take Your Time (Do It Right)"	*The S.O.S. Band*
"Sexy Eyes"	*Dr. Hook*
"Coming Up"	*Paul McCartney*
"All Out of Love"	*Air Supply*
"Magic"	*Olivia Newton-John*
"Crazy Little Thing Called Love"	*Queen*
"Lady"	*Kenny Rogers*
"Stomp"	*The Brothers Johnson*
"On the Radio"	*Donna Summer*
"Coward of the County"	*Kenny Rogers*
"Give Me the Night"	*George Benson*
"Shining Star"	*The Manhattans*
"One in a Million You"	*Larry Graham*
"Special Lady"	*Ray, Goodman and Brown*
"Ride Like the Wind"	*Christopher Cross*
"Escape (the Piña Colada Song)"	*Rupert Holmes*
"He's So Shy"	*The Pointer Sisters*
"Lost in Love"	*Air Supply*
"Never Knew Love Like This Before"	*Stephanie Mills*
"The Wanderer"	*Donna Summer*

1980 cont'd

"With You I'm Born Again"	*Billy Preston and Syreeta*
"The Rose"	*Bette Midler*
"Too Hot"	*Kool and the Gang*
"Emotional Rescue"	*The Rolling Stones*
"And the Beat Goes On"	*The Whispers*
"Sailing"	*Christopher Cross*
"Master Blaster"	*Stevie Wonder*
"Whip It"	*Devo*
"I Pledge My Love"	*Peaches and Herb*

1981

"Bette Davis Eyes"	*Kim Carnes*
"Morning Train (9 To 5)"	*Sheena Easton*
"Endless Love"	*Diana Ross and Lionel Richie*
"Celebration"	*Kool and the Gang*
"Theme from 'The Greatest American Hero' (Believe It or Not)"	*Joey Scarbury*
"For Your Eyes Only"	*Sheena Easton*
"The Tide Is High"	*Blondie*
"Private Eyes"	*Hall and Oates*
"Arthur's Theme (Best That You Can Do)"	*Christopher Cross*
"Slowhand"	*The Pointer Sisters*
"Love on a Two-Way Street"	*Stacy Lattisaw*
"Rapture"	*Blondie*
"Just the Two of Us"	*Grover Washington, Jr.*
"Sukiyaki"	*A Taste of Honey*
"(Just Like) Starting Over"	*John Lennon*
"Medley: Intro Venus/Sugar Sugar/No Reply"	*Stars on 45*
"She's A Bad Mama Jama (She's Built, She's Stacked)"	*Carl Carlton*
"9 to 5"	*Dolly Parton*
"Keep on Loving You"	*REO Speedwagon*
"Queen of Hearts"	*Juice Newton*
"The One That You Love"	*Air Supply*
"Lady (You Bring Me Up)"	*The Commodores*
"Physical"	*Olivia Newton-John*
"Why Do Fools Fall in Love"	*Diana Ross*
"Guilty"	*Barbra Streisand and Barry Gibb*
"Love on the Rocks"	*Neil Diamond*
"Lady"	*Kenny Rogers*
"Kiss on My List"	*Hall and Oates*
"Being With You"	*Smokey Robinson*

"Hearts"	*Marty Balin*
"I Don't Need You"	*Kenny Rogers*
"A Woman Needs Love (Just Like You Do)"	*Raydio*
"Never Too Much"	*Luther Vandross*
"Angel of the Morning"	*Juice Newton*
"We're in This Love Together"	*Al Jarreau*
"Shaddap You Face"	*Joe Dolce*
"All Those Years Ago"	*George Harrison*
"Jessie's Girl"	*Rick Springfield*

1982

"Centerfold"	*J. Geils Band*
"Physical"	*Olivia Newton-John*
"Waiting For a Girl Like You"	*Foreigner*
"I Can't Go for That"	*Hall and Oates*
"Ebony and Ivory"	*Paul McCartney and Stevie Wonder*
"Harden My Heart"	*Quarterflash*
"Let's Groove"	*Earth, Wind and Fire*
"Leather and Lace"	*Stevie Nicks*
"I Love Rock and Roll"	*Joan Jett and the Blackhearts*
"Hurts So Good"	*John Cougar*
"Turn Your Love Around"	*George Benson*
"Eye of the Tiger"	*Survivor*
"Truly"	*Lionel Ritchie*
"Hold Me"	*Fleetwood Mac*
"Shakĕ It Up"	*The Cars*
"Young Turks"	*Rod Stewart*
"The Sweetest Thing"	*Juice Newton*
"Hooked on Classics"	*Royal Philharmonic Orchestra*
"Jack and Diane"	*John Cougar*
"Don't Talk to Strangers"	*Rick Springfield*
"Don't Stop Believin'"	*Journey*
"Abracadabra"	*Steve Miller Band*
"Comin' In and Out of Your Life"	*Barbra Streisand*
"Why Do Fools Fall in Love"	*Diana Ross*
"Trouble"	*Lindsey Buckingham*
"Open Arms"	*Journey*
"Hard To Say I'm Sorry"	*Chicago*
"Up Where We Belong"	*Joe Cocker and Jennifer Warnes*
"We Got the Beat"	*The Go-Go's*
"Freeze-Frame"	*J. Geils Band*
"Oh No"	*Commodores*
"Heart Attack"	*Olivia Newton-John*
"The Girl Is Mine"	*Paul McCartney & Michael Jackson*
"Rosanna"	*Toto*

1982 cont'd

"That Girl"	*Stevie Wonder*
"Theme from *Chariots of Fire*"	*Vangelis*
"Make a Move On Me"	*Olivia Newton-John*
"Every Little Thing She Does Is Magic"	*The Police*
"Who Can It Be Now"	*Men At Work*
"Eye in the Sky"	*Alan Parsons Project*

INDEX